Partnerships in Maths:
Parents and Schools
The IMPACT Project

Partnerships in Maths:
Parents and Schools
The IMPACT Project

Edited by

Ruth Merttens and Jeff Vass

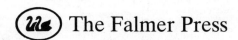 The Falmer Press

(A member of the Taylor & Francis Group)
London • Washington, DC

UK   The Falmer Press, 4 John St, London WC1N 2ET
USA   The Falmer Press, Taylor & Francis Inc., 1900 Frost Road, Suite 101, Bristol, PA 19007

First published 1993

A catalogue record of this publication is available from the British Library

ISBN 0 75070 154 4 cased
ISBN 0 75070 155 2 paperback

Library of Congress Cataloging-in-Publication Data are available on request

Jacket design by Caroline Archer

Typeset in 10/12pt Times by
Graphicraft Typesetters Ltd., Hong Kong

Printed in Great Britain by Burgess Science Press, Basingstoke on paper which has a specified pH value on final paper manufacture of not less than 7.5 and is therefore 'acid free'.

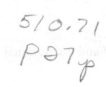

5/0.71
P27p

Contents

Contents

Introduction

The subject at the heart of this book is that of parental involvement in maths. The IMPACT Project is the largest such initiative in Europe and through IMPACT many thousands of children and parents share regular maths activities together, the results of which are brought back into class to inform the following week's work. The project was started in north London in 1985 and it has since expanded to include the thirty-four Local Education Authorities who are, at the time of writing, members of the IMPACT National Network. There are IMPACT schools across England, Wales, and Scotland, as well as a smattering in other countries, including the USA. It is literally impossible to keep up with the spread of this way of working collaboratively with parents.

This book aims at a kaleidoscopic approach. Rather than focusing on one or more examples of parental involvement in maths, or providing endless redescriptions of IMPACT in practice, we have elected to publish a variety of different and diverse perspectives on the work in this area over the last five years. We have looked at IMPACT from the point of view of the 'insiders', those who may be said to have started it, those who are currently involved, including advisors, parents, teachers and children. We have stepped back and encouraged those 'outside' to look in and write about what they see. We have asked many people whose work bears directly or indirectly on the work of IMPACT — therapists, educational psychologists, researchers and academics — to share their thoughts. The result is indeed a kaleidoscope; each twist of the wrist, no matter how slight, reveals a different pattern.

We, the editors, feel that the notion 'parental involvement' is far too artificially unified — we all use the same term and mean different things by it. This book is a set of statements by people occupying very diverse roles in relation to the world of education. The reader will be aware, however, that any contributor's statement is not only addressed to a specific problem, but is also grounded by the role s/he occupies. Furthermore any role is oriented toward the particular polemics *within* the field of which it is part. As both

1

Vass and Merttens argue in this volume, parental involvement 'disturbs' the inward looking proclivities of people occupying particular roles in education. Any such disturbance may not necessarily make for some 'better' way of life — that is, 'better' by some particular criterion. It does make us stop and think at a time when much of our mental energy is focused on finding ways to implement policies we feel we have had little hand in concocting and which keep us busy in all kinds of details.

There is no issue in education more urgent than that concerning the relationships between parents, teachers and children. We are living at a time when issues such as parental involvement in the education process are key issues not only in education but also in the development of our sense of what our 'kind of society' is turning into. In other words, one of the ways we are all currently experiencing fundamental changes within our culture is through the pattern of relationships that exist between homes and schools. Brighouse (this volume) for example, asks us to consider the transformation to our lives that is incurred by thinking of teachers as producers and parents as consumers. Hughes (also this volume) and his colleagues encourage us to examine the explicit assumptions behind current legislation and to ask ourselves if these notions match what specific parents actually reveal of their own wishes and demands when questioned. Andrew Brown takes up the notion of 'parents' and quarrels with the idea that it is unified category about which we can sensibly make any generalized statements.

'Parental Involvement' as a term may have a comfy ring to it. Too often, it is a flag which we all salute whenever and wherever it is hoisted. As Hamilton and Dyne, as well as Border and Merttens, argue, however, the involvement of parents can disturb the comfortable and established routines of those doing a particular job or occupying a specific role within the educational process. It may also force a critical awareness of hitherto unquestioned routines or tacit assumptions, the unreflective habits of those involved in the processes of schooling. Particularly within a curriculum areas such as maths, the participation of parents can generate a number of potentially uncomfortable or even explosive situations. When it comes to individual participants in specific circumstances and particular contexts, IMPACT and projects like it may cast doubt where once there was certainty, cause comment or even cacophony where there was silence, and bring conflict in place of cosiness. If this disruption were all, teachers and parents alike could be forgiven for desiring nothing more than to give these initiatives the widest possible berth. However, with comment often comes constructive dialogue, and out of an apparent cacophony we can create a rhythm and even a melody. Silence can, after all, indicate conspiracy rather than consent. As Gary Thomas (this volume) puts it, quoting Shaw: 'All professions are conspiracies against the laity'. Conflict, peacefully resolved, leads to the development of a genuine understanding, and certainty in anything, but especially in education, always has to be regarded with the utmost suspicion! Our experience is that out of struggle — and sometimes conflict — comes conversation between those occupying very different roles, and the joint negotiation of shared outcomes and mutually agreed practices.

This discussion brings us to the IMPACT project which has been described as being at the heart of the book. The project itself is not a unified or unitary object. IMPACT is one of many attempts to involve parents in their children's formal education. In this aspect, it has a great deal in common with the shared reading initiatives such as PACT upon which it is obviously based. It is also an attempt to give homework, and to make a virtue out of a necessity in not only *recognizing* that children will talk about their homework and get help with it where they can, but in *requiring* that they do so. Under another heading, IMPACT is an initiative in mathematics in-service training, and in yet another guise it is a form of peer tutoring. It is both a research project and a major intervention initiative. Many of the contributors to the book have their own ideas and present their own accounts of what, for them, IMPACT is all about. The two directors of the project and editors of this book recognize the diverse and varied nature of the events and encounters they have themselves experienced over the last six years setting up and running IMPACT.

However, we nevertheless find ourselves able to speak of IMPACT as if it were an identifiable whole, *as if we all know what we are talking about.* We can point to 'IMPACT' practice and 'IMPACT' processes. The work of the many teachers, parents, children and support staff has been the subject not only of recognition and, in some cases, acclaim, but also of critical evaluation and analysis. In discussing the work of IMPACT then, we too often behave as if we can describe one aspect, one perspective, and like a butterfly pinned to the page, then subject it to our gaze. This book represents an attempt to counter the static and finalized nature of such accounts through its acceptance that IMPACT is always changing, a 'becoming' rather than a 'become', a 'happening' rather than a 'has happened'. Attempts to describe IMPACT can be seen as spasmodic and somewhat haphazard attempts to capture a moving target. Each image generated represents no more than one moment, one perspective, within a particular set of commonalities and assumptions.

We have attempted to aid the reader by dividing the book into parts. These parts are selections of papers loosely grouped around the focus of a particular perspective on parental involvement. Thus we have a section with chapters by those most closely involved in the day to day running of IMPACT, that is, parents and class-teachers. Another part contains the chapters of those offering support to these parents and teachers, or in a managerial role: the advisers, support teachers and inspectors. The chapters of those who have carried out research in this — or related areas — are grouped in another part, and the final part consists of writing by those concerned to reflect upon the statements made and the practices developed in the course of initiatives such as IMPACT, and who are attempting to locate the work within a wider theoretical framework. The first chapter is the personal history of IMPACT provided by one of the directors of the project.

Introduction

To facilitate the usefulness of the book as a text for those with a particular perspective — student, teacher, parent, governor, academic, inspector or education officer — we have provided a brief description at the start of each paper which will enable readers to make their own selections in terms of reading priorities.

Our aim then is to compile a set of diverse statements. The loudest message of this array of texts is perhaps simply there *are* diverse perspectives and that all address their situations diversely however much it appears we are grouped around some common 'theme'. We hope that this material gives people insights into what engages others across the margins that divide us on questions that have more perennial importance than the transient glamour afforded them by fear surrounding unpredictable changes to the organization of schools and their relationships with their communities.

Ruth Merttens and **Jeff Vass**
Directors of IMPACT

Part I

Starting IMPACT

Chapter 1

IMPACT: Pride, Prejudice and Pedagogy: One Director's Personal Story

Ruth Merttens

Ruth Merttens describes how the IMPACT Project started and gives a personal account of the changes in practices and assumptions which she charted in her field notes kept throughout the first four years of IMPACT. IMPACT *in situ* is illustrated with reference to detailed case notes. The theoretical framework within which her descriptions are embedded is outlined. She then goes on to discuss the 'knots' or 'points of conflict' in the weave of IMPACT which, for her, problematize some of the more commonly held assumptions about the purpose and effectiveness of IMPACT.

In a sense this chapter has to represent a piece of biography. I am widely credited with having started IMPACT, and with being one of its main apostles. Certainly, working on, or for, IMPACT has occupied every available ounce of energy, moment of time and inch of space in my life. However, this devotion does not prevent my reflecting constantly upon the project, and being able to distance myself on occasion from the interactive aspect of my work in order to pursue the reflective, and research, side of IMPACT. There is the inevitable and, I believe, creative, cross-fertilization of the reflection with the actions involved in instigating change. These practices are not, except momentarily and financially, separable parts of the job.

This chapter is written in such a way as to maximize the intrusiveness of the 'I'. The reasons for attempting this are first of all to accentuate the impression of a personal story told. Aristotle reminds us that, 'Fiction is truer and more universal than history'. Second, I want to underline the lack of any pretended objectivity or scientificity which can be the hallmark of writing in education or the social sciences. Third, I hope that it will enable me to make visible the process of writing itself, to emphasize the graphic quality of language, so that the means by which the story is related instead of being transparent, becomes opaque and thereby problematized.

7

This is a personal and reflective history. It presents my observationally derived understanding of IMPACT practices *in situ*. I shall pose a few questions from a position explicitly situated within the day to day routines of running IMPACT and I shall try to make a number of grounded and quite context-specific points. The validity of their extrapolation to any other context would remain in doubt.

One final and stylistic point: it is very hard to convey in writing a 'sense' of IMPACT and the issues it has raised. This is because the concern I feel about IMPACT and what it is, or is not, is not primarily an intellectual concern; it is an experienced worry, a matter of feelings and of conscience. I have always found it relatively unproblematic to communicate by *speaking* about IMPACT. However, the speaking world, as has been pointed out by others before (Ong, 1958, Olson, 1977, Halliday, 1980, Baker and Freebody, 1989), is a 'happening' world, a world which is created and negotiated as the conversation proceeds. The written world, to a much greater extent, has already happened. There seems less room for negotiation, for suggestion and response and more of a tendency towards an 'expert' or authoritarian reading. In an effort to combat this I have attempted to render the written text both suggestive and perplexing.

Once Upon a Time . . .

It certainly was not the 'me' of nowadays who, as legend, and at least some versions of recent history (Merttens and Vass, 1990b) suggest, sat on the heath near my home and contemplated the setting up of IMPACT. In those days I could have been described as being not unlike the Paul Newman character in the film *Butch Cassidy and the Sundance Kid*, who says, 'Boy! I got vision and the rest of the world wears bi-focals!' Well, IMPACT was certainly a vision. It was a vision which meant that the next five years of my life I would work, not at the centre of the schooling process, but at the boundaries. I have always been drawn to the margins, and IMPACT was to keep me fascinated by the rationales and justifications, the assumptions and beliefs, the 'common senses', which made the centre the hub, and the edges marginal.

In those sitting-on-the-heath days of early IMPACT, I shared my vision with Dorothy Hamilton (1984) of 'PACT' (1) fame. She and I used to air certain worries which were appearing like cracks in the new plaster of the imposing Cockcroft (1982) edifice. Questions which seemed to us to be important were, it appeared, disallowed by those in the higher regions of the maths educational world. This we found strangely disquieting; and the discomfort which the very strength of the Cockcroft orthodoxy caused us was to prove a fertile breeding ground in which were germinated many of the developments on IMPACT. Questions which bothered Dorothy and me at that time included:

Is not a serious gap developing between the maths curriculum and its related pedagogy, and what parents expect maths to look like in schools? Does this matter?

Should rote-learning and skills practice be so heavily discouraged when we observe, with parents, that many children do give every appearance of doing well at these things, and that, although they are sometimes working a little ahead of themselves, 'relational under-standing' (Skemp, 1964) almost always follows the initial practice?

Is it possible that the emphasis on practical maths and investiga-tional tasks actually disadvantages certain children? Might we be un-wittingly engaging in discriminatory practices rather than combating them?

Are not some children bored by investigations and practical activi-ties? Is this any better for them than the previous curriculum was for those bored by pages of sums?

It might be imagined that after five years on IMPACT, which is after all a major research as well as intervention project, answers to these questions and others like them would have been found. Of course, IMPACT has gen-erated answers. But I am now as dissatisfied with the answers as I was then with the situation which produced the questions in the first place. IMPACT *has* been a voyage of discovery but, I suspect like any such voyage, it has caused those on board to encounter more storms than calm.

> The last and lingering troubadour to whom the bird has sung.
> That once went singing southward when all the world was young;
> In that enormous silence, tiny and unafraid,
> Comes up along a winding road the noise of the crusade...
> *Lapanto* (John Masefield).

Sometimes IMPACT has felt like an 'enormous silence', while times at other it has resembled a positive cacophony. Only at rare moments have I had the sense of a symphony or opera. Of course, we have made it almost a point of principle that there is not step-by-step prodecure or set of procedures which determine 'good IMPACT practice' or by which IMPACT can be defined (Merttens and Vass, 1989; 1990b). It presents no difficulty for us on IMPACT that each school, or each area, or even each classroom, has a different flavour. Different features of IMPACT may be emphasized in different regions or areas, and this results in a marked variety of IMPACT practice.

So IMPACT is not easy to describe. It is not a whole, a unified or unitary object. It does not name a particular set of practices, an educational philosophy, or approach to teaching or learning, or even an identifiable group of people no matter how large. To be sure, there are IMPACT schools; we can point to IMPACT teachers or IMPACT parents. We can even call upon the odd IMPACT child or two! Some of the above, however, would not describe themselves as 'IMPACT'. Yet others would not be described as IMPACT at all by some IMPACTers!

IMPACT is amorphous, fragmented and dispersed. What it is depends, as the cowboys say, upon who's asking. For some it describes a set of experiences, for others it may be a methodology. For some it represents a particular type of approach, for a few it is a materials-based scheme, and so on. The descriptive list could be long if not infinite. Amidst this confusion of criteria, this plethora of descriptors, this human chaos, IMPACT does retain an identity as a community. It may be scattered, but it is still a real and living community. It has its hangers-on and its central characters, its marginals and its safe seats, its grey areas and its better-lit zones.

What sort of a community? Sociologically and philosophically speaking, the community cannot be said to embrace any particular set of assumptions or system of beliefs. There are not even any specific identifiable shared attitudes to classroom practice or to home intervention. IMPACT includes very formal schools, and schools who could be regarded as progressive in their ethos and approach. There are village schools, urban schools, small schools, large schools, private schools, church schools and state schools. The community is widely scattered, not merely geographically, though IMPACT now exists in Germany, Canada, Australia, Ireland, and in many other places as well, but also professionally and spiritually. This scattering does not in any way negate the strong sense of 'communitas' which exists on IMPACT. There are identifiable insider-practices, codes, rhetorics, forms of knowledge and behavioural strategies.

The second thing I have come to believe about IMPACT is that it fundamentally concerns 'otherness'. It is worth exploring this idea. We are attempting to instigate change: changes in the ways in which teachers and parents interact, changes in the relationship parents have with the school, changes in the classroom practice to take account of the shared activities at home. In this sense, IMPACT concerns what *is not*, rather than what *is*. We do not, as a matter of routine practice, comment on existing conditions, much less do we attempt an analysis. (It is, however, true that such an analysis must form a part of the construction of the theoretical explication of IMPACT in practice). In creating the conditions in which change is possible — even probable — we imagine possible worlds rather than dissecting lived experience; we envisage possibilities rather than detailing actualities. Any intervention project like IMPACT must, in the Sartrean sense, concern itself with 'that which is not' rather than with 'that which is'.

IMPACT also implies the constant consideration of 'otherness'. In the training sessions with teachers, it is often parents who are predicated as 'the other'. When talking with parents, it is usually children, or sometimes teachers or psychologists, who are thus positioned. In almost any given situation on IMPACT, a multiplicity of possible positions for 'the other' will be constructed.

Because IMPACT involves working always at the margins of what is constructed as professional discourse, the constitution and reconstitution of particular subject positions is a constant feature. These positions are the subject of repeated explication and negotiation on the project. This not only enables the transformation in and through practice of these professionally defining roles; it unfortunately also allows the development of a particular space for discriminatory practices. Through the construction of boundaries, with the concomitant notions of insiderness and outsiderness, particular forms of 'otherness' are construed and created. The use of generalization and universalizing descriptions assist in the formation and maintenance of stereotypical positionings. Thus statements of the type, 'Parents like that won't/can't help their children with maths . . .' both create a position and simultaneously force its occupation upon those who might otherwise cause disruption.

IMPACT then, involves mechanisms which eventually come to be transcribed in the process of schooling. Such mechanisms are effective but they also have an effectiveness beyond the scope of either the predictions or the justifications produced by those involved. The ways in which certain groups or individuals can come to occupy the role of 'other' mean that IMPACT can be particularly vulnerable to the development of new forms of discriminatory practices. By such means can others be positioned so as to render them impotent. Through relegation to the 'outside', potentially disruptive elements become safe.

There is an important sense in which these dangers are not confined to IMPACT, but are merely made more visible, or highlighted by the IMPACT processes. In this way, IMPACT acts rather like one of those mouth-wash dyes which are designed to display plaque. Discriminatory practices exist at all levels in education, and even those most committed to their eradication in one area are always open to the (self) accusation of failure in another. Once a dye has shown us the extent of the contamination, it becomes a matter of conscious decision whether and how to address it. This is a subject to which I shall return later on in the chapter.

Once Upon a Time There Was a School . . .

Before continuing to address the issues on IMPACT which perplex and trouble me now, it is important to share an image of IMPACT in practice. Since IMPACT cannot be characterized as a set of routines or procedures, it is impractical to attempt a description of a theoretical IMPACT scenario. Furthermore, such a description would inevitably fail to communicate a sense of IMPACT *in situ*, of everyday experience, the ups and downs, the minor hurdles, the small triumphs, and so on. These contingencies, minor and context-dependent as they may be, are crucial for the formation and transformation of specific IMPACT mechanisms in any particular situation. The specifics which are developed in response to contingencies characterize 'IMPACT in practice'. Unless the description centres around the particularities of a given situation, then the attempt to prioritize experience, and to take account of the ways in which immediate reflection can inform action, is of little practical value.

However, in the story of a *particular* IMPACT school, no matter how carefully I attempt to transmit an accurate representation of events, there will be a problem inasmuch as there will inevitably be more than one 'reading' of their personal history of IMPACT. The headteacher will have one reading, IMPACT teachers another, non-IMPACT teachers another, and so on. The logical end product is a multiplicity of readings in a futile attempt to represent the plurality of shared experience.

I have decided to circumvent this difficulty by presenting three 'petites histoires'. The will consist of three separate conflations of IMPACT-school experiences in which I participated as an active member of the IMPACT team. In each of the three, the aims, reasoning, rhetoric, behaviour patterns, justifications and subsequent accounts of IMPACT are remarkably dissimilar. It is therefore the extent to which they are different which makes them, as 'histoires', interesting and illuminating.

The three case studies described should not be read as consisting of three individual and actual schools. Neither can any of the descriptions as given, be mapped in a linear fashion on to any particular sequence of circumstances experienced by myself on IMPACT. But taken as 'histoires' they present as nearly as I can make it, an account of IMPACT *in situ*.

Histoire: Primrose School

Il était une fois . . .

Primrose school has seven teachers and a headteacher. Each teacher has a year group of thirty children. The children in the school come from a wide variety of different backgrounds, in terms of social class and of ethnic origin. Many different — and conflicting — assumptions about education exist within the school community. Some of the children have English as their second language.

The school could be described as a fairly informal school, where most of the children's work is topic-based. However, they do use a commercial maths scheme, and there are some fairly rigid timetabling structures which exist across the whole school, such as reading after lunch and maths or language work first thing in the morning. The school has a headteacher who is keen on IMPACT and who agrees to support any staff who would like to give it a go. There are two very keen staff — one a probationer, Linda, the other, Sara, a young and confident teacher in her third year of teaching.

Linda feels ill-at-ease in her first year of teaching. She feels particularly vulnerable in maths and she believes that IMPACT will give her some extra and individual support in this area. She has a vague feeling that to involve the parents would be 'a good thing' and certainly has no wish to keep them at a distance.

The other teacher, Sara, embraces the idea of IMPACT with great enthusiasm. She talks about her own parents and what a support they were to her and her sisters, and she describes how she has instigated a 'PACT'-type shared reading initiative with diaries in which she and the parents write. She is certain that this programme has made a big difference to the childrens' progress in reading and also to their attitude to books.

Both teachers elect to send activities home on a weekly basis. I am in the school for approximately two half-days a week, and participate in all the planning sessions as well as teaching on occasion in each class and helping to organize the follow-up work. We often work together and share ideas, and it is common for the other staff to participate in these discussions.

IMPACT gets a good response in both classes. Sara regularly gets twenty-six or twenty-seven of the children sharing the activity at home. Even the 'non-responders' will on occasion bring something in, especially if it happens to be an activity with which the child does not need much help. The parents are extremely enthusiastic, to the point of suggesting activities, helping to mount displays and coming in to play maths games or do maths tasks with the children in class.

Linda gets fewer responses, but still averages around 60–70 per cent and sometimes higher. She is very pleased with the way that the IMPACT activity sets up the subsequent week's maths in class, and she finds the help with planning invaluable. Some parents are critical of the type of activities sent home. They would like to see more formal mathematical recording, and feel that some of the activities are 'too easy'. They are worried that their children are not acquiring the 'proper' mathematical skills such as multiplication and division.

After a year, it is decided at a staff meeting that all the staff will have a go at sending out regular maths activities from September onwards. This decision is reached at least in part because of Sara's enthusiastic lobbying. Another important factor is the amount of help offered by IMPACT in the shape of my time and expertise. However, all the staff do agree to give it a whirl.

The following year sees IMPACT activities being sent to all the children in the school with varying degrees of 'success'. The three most enthusiastic teachers get extremely good responses in terms of the numbers of children taking part. The others get fewer, but the response rate is haphazard and reflects a large number of contingent factors as well as more stable characteristics. A great deal of support is still offered and accepted from IMPACT and I continue to spend a great deal of time in the school. I assist with planning the IMPACT activities, designing sheets, and take care of some of the reproduction of the actual activities. I occasionally work with small groups engaged on follow-up activities in class, and I attend parent meetings.

After eighteen months, the school has a new headteacher. She is reticent about her commitment to IMPACT and although she does nothing to impede its progress, neither does she offer particular assistance or support. The practice on IMPACT then was to withdraw external support after two years, and in fact this school was left very much on its own after the initial two years.

Teachers are left to run IMPACT or not as they choose. The head-teacher does not positively discourage them from sending activities but she makes it plain as the year wears on that she has grave reservations about this form of parental involvement. She feels that parents should not be encouraged to 'teach' their children since they have had no training and therefore are more likely to do harm than good. Furthermore, IMPACT and curriculum involvement schemes like it, allow, even encourage, parents to have an input into the curriculum. This, she feels, is a bad move on the teachers' part.

For this headteacher, the issues are clear-cut. Teachers are professionals. By both commitment (greatly stressed — a valued quality) and training, they are the best people to decide what and how to teach. They must make it their business to understand how the children learn and are the only ones in a position to make judgments as to what children should do next. It would be stupid to employ an electrician and then instruct him or her on the best way to wire the house. Similarly it is stupid (and insulting) for parents to try to tell teachers what or how they should be teaching.

Two further points are raised during the series of staff meetings held during the subsequent year. Some parents do not appear to take part in IMPACT and it is felt that this places those children at a disadvantage. Although there was not evidence of which I was aware to support the idea, it is assumed that the parents who do not take part are working-class, and that therefore IMPACT will further disadvantage working-class children. It is also believed that working-class parents will be unlikely to be able to give the same quality of help as the more educated middle-class parents and therefore this could increase the disadvantage to certain children.

The second point concerns the headteacher's expressed view that school provides a haven for many children to which they can escape and in which they are able to develop their interests and learn without pressure or violence. It is felt that for children such as these, and all the teachers agree that they know who these children are, schemes which demand more of a link between school and home are simply counter-productive. Children are able to 'be themselves' and 'relax' at school and they should not be required to jeopardize this freedom by involving the parents in school-type events.

Over the following two years, IMPACT flounders somewhat at Primrose School. Sara leaves the school, and moves on. Linda continues, although now more isolated on the staff, to send activities home, and receives a moderately good response, depending upon the activity. One other teacher continues with IMPACT and the rest slowly, more or less by default, abandon it.

Histoire 2: Dandelion School

Il était une fois . . .

The school has many children of very young parents. Most of the pupils are white and very few have English as their second language. The school is in a fairly poor area on a large estate.

The school has a nursery and two classes for each year group throughout the rest of the school. The classes are large, over thirty-five children, and the school is not particularly well resourced. The staff is very stable, many of the teachers having been there for more than ten years, and some for the whole of their teaching career. The pedagogy is fairly formal with a fair amount of 'chalk and talk', especially in the juniors. The teachers use a commercial scheme for language and maths work, and stick fairly rigidly to a reading scheme. The school gives the impression of being down-to-earth, if not very exciting. However, the school comes out well on the LEA's formal test results and all the children entering the juniors can read.

The headteacher who has been in the school for many years decides to join IMPACT. Her decision is most likely influenced by two factors. First, IMPACT seems to promise some support in an area in which she feels the school is weak, namely, mathematics. Second, she has the political acumen to realize that parents are likely to gain a great deal more power and influence over the next few years (NB: this is before ERA or even GERBIL), and she feels that it would be a good thing to get ahead of the game and involve the parents more in what the children are doing.

The headteacher makes no pretence of being a democrat and the school is run on strictly authoritarian lines. She decrees that three teachers will take part to start with, and having informed them of her decision, she sweetens the pill by allowing them support in terms of time out of the classroom to prepare and plan their IMPACT, and secretarial support with the duplication of the sheets. The teachers seem to be very pleased with this deal, since they clearly feel that help with planning and delivering their maths curriculum is not to be sneezed at. I agree to support the teachers by coming into school to plan the IMPACT and their maths in general. They will also receive weekly help from the local IMPACT support teacher.

Both the headteacher and the teachers are very anxious to know how IMPACT 'should' be done. They do not seem interested in discussion as to the most comfortable or suitable way of doing things in their school. They simply wish to know what is needed so that they can get on with it with the least possible fuss. IMPACT is duly launched with the 'correct' number of parent meetings and the teachers send their weekly activity and dutifully follow it up in class according to the plan agreed.

15

It is quickly realized that both the IMPACT support teacher and I are interested in the number of responses, and this becomes, for the teachers, an index of how well IMPACT is going. Two out of the three teachers regularly receive 100 per cent of their activities back completed, and the other teacher gets 80–90 per cent. The children in her class are older, which is generally agreed to make a difference. On one occasion, when I am in the school, I witness an assembly at which two of the children in the school are given a special prize of one pound each for remembering to bring back their IMPACT on a Monday every week for a whole year. In several classes, there are star-charts for IMPACT activity returns, but there are also star-charts for a number of other things, including reading a whole book.

The teachers do not manifest great enthusiasm for IMPACT, although it would be fair to say that they do not manifest great enthusiasm for anything to do with education or schooling. However, they send activities regularly and they take care to pay attention to what the children have done at home. There is definitely a sense that what the children and parents do at home is valued, and also that it is an important aspect of the childrens' maths — hence the star-charts.

Parents' comments on the weekly response sheets are not recorded and scant attention is paid to them unless someone says something very much out of the ordinary. The teachers mainly send much the sort of activity that the parents expect — quite a few number games and skills-practice activities, interspersed with more practical tasks which are nevertheless, clearly mathematical.

Two years on, monitoring meetings in the school reveal that things have changed very little. With the gradual withdrawing of both central IMPACT support and local advisory teacher time, the teachers are relying more heavily upon the written packs of IMPACT materials and their own past practice from previous years as a model. The secretarial support for the duplication of the activity sheets is still being supplied so that this burden does not fall on the teachers, and the headteacher clearly sees this as a worthwhile use of scarce secretarial time.

The responses to the activities is very good, averaging out at over 90 per cent in the school, with pockets of the school (especially the nursery) regularly getting every child taking part. Very little fuss is made about IMPACT either by the parents or by the children or teachers. New routines, such as IMPACT parent meetings have simply been incorporated into regular school procedures. No one seems to take much notice of the change that has been implemented. It is rather as if IMPACT has always existed at Dandylion school.

Histoire 3: Cowslip School

Il était une fois . . .

The school is in a fairly affluent area and quite a few of the children in the neighbourhood go to private schools. A percentage leave Cowslip school and move into the private sector at age 11. However, those that attend the school come from a variety of backgrounds and there is a genuine social mix within the school. The majority of the children are white, and there are no bilingual children.

The school is divided into three classes: infants, lower juniors and upper juniors. There are two teachers in the infants, and four teachers for the whole of the juniors. The two infant teachers and the four junior teachers work together, teaching as teams and planning jointly. Topics are chosen by each team which last half a term, and most of the children's work is integrated with the topic. This planning applies predominantly to language and science, but less so to maths where the children do follow a standard maths scheme in the juniors. The pedagogy is overtly and explicitly child-centred, and the teachers aim to encourage and direct rather than coerce the children, who have more than the usual amount of freedom in deciding what tasks to do each day.

The headteacher decided, in consultation with the staff, to join IMPACT because she believes it will help to change parents' attitudes to maths. The fact that the pedagogy of the school differs from the expectations of many of the parents means that the teachers feel under almost constant pressure to justify their way of working. IMPACT, they hope, will assist in the process of educating the parents as to how children really learn maths and the value of practical activities, investigational tasks and topic work.

The teachers welcome me into their joint planning sessions and adopt suggestions as to possible IMPACT sheets with enthusiasm. They admit that as far as they are concerned, a major reason for being a part of IMPACT is the assistance with planning the maths curriculum alongside the topic, which they all say they find hard to do. A considerable amount of guilt is clearly felt over any reliance upon the commercial maths scheme. However, several of the teachers 'confess' in private that the children's progress in maths, especially in terms of their acquisition of purely formal skills, worries them a great deal.

In the infants, IMPACT fits well with the teachers' way of working and it goes very well. All the children respond and the parents seem fairly keen and prepared to at least give it a go. In the juniors, for the first half-term the responses are quite good, and then they rapidly start tailing off until only a fairly small percentage of children are actually doing IMPACT. The teachers feel that the parents do not see the point of what they are doing and that they are no longer bothering with the IMPACT task, seeing it as peripheral only.

Over the next year, the teachers and I consider various organizational strategies to try to improve the way IMPACT runs in the school. In the infants, after a honeymoon period and then a brief dropping off, the responses have settled down and the majority of the parents do share each week's activity with their child. The parents are moderately positive about the activities and do see the point of most of the tasks.

In the juniors the picture is very different. One teacher says that if they send an activity that the children want to do, then the parents don't see the point of it and refuse to do it, so very few come back. If they send a more number-based activity, however, then the children don't want to do it, and so not many come back. Another teacher says that she thinks that the children and the parents have decided that IMPACT is a waste of time, and they have 'dropped out'.

After two years, the staff and various IMPACT support staff meet to discuss why IMPACT has failed to get off the ground in the junior part of the school. Various hypotheses are put forward. I am impressed by the difference between what the teachers will say in private and what is said in public discussion with the headteacher and other staff present. One idea, strongly supported by the headteacher, is that this school, unlike others, does not put any pressure on the children or the parents to share the activities, and therefore most of them actually don't give it a very high priority. In other schools, perhaps with a less child-centred pedagogy, more pressure is put on children and parents and therefore the response rates are higher.

In this school, unusually for IMPACT, not only do relatively few of the junior parents respond by sharing the maths activities on a regular basis, neither do they come into school for the IMPACT meetings. It is almost as if they have opted out of the whole event. Nevertheless, the teachers persevere, and are keen to continue. They feel that the IMPACT materials are a help in planning the maths curriculum through a topic-based approach and they like the way some skills practice activities are integrated with data-handling and investigational work. As far as the maths education aspect of IMPACT goes, it is regarded as a success. It is only the parental involvement part which is problematic. The headteacher expresses their disappointment, 'We really hoped that it would help us to change the parents' attitudes to maths.'

Broad Brush-Stroke Outline of Results . . .

Nowadays I am often asked to give the results of IMPACT, rather as if it were a football match or an examination! Clearly there are major objections to any simplistic categorization in terms of success or failure, or even in measureable terms at all. IMPACT is obviously an 'effective' project, but the use of this criteria has itself become part of a political agenda with which, on IMPACT, we do not feel entirely comfortable (see Ball, 1990).

However, it is possible, using a very large brush and few rather than many colours, to paint a picture of some of what we have learned over the last five years on IMPACT. Perhaps the best way to record and convey all that we now believe, know, speculate, about IMPACT would be to design and sew a tapestry. Somehow in the different weaves of designs, we might be able to come close to communicating all that we want to convey. This is a rather longer project than a chapter in a book, and so for the present, words must suffice.

The maths activities which the children actually share at home with their parents are either designed by the teachers or selected from a bank of pre-existing IMPACT ideas. They can be divided into two categories:

1 Those which, by and large, the parents perceive as 'maths'.
2 Those which are more focused towards a topic or a less familiar mathematical area and which the parents do not recognise as 'maths'.

These are obviously not hard and fast categories. What is recognized as 'maths' is not static or universal, and varies widely from school to school and even from parent to parent. There are certainly several factors which play a part in determining what specific parents do or do not perceive as 'maths'. In field notes taken during the first two years of IMPACT, I have recorded observations concerning parental attitudes to maths. With reference to any specific class of children, I was interested in what the attitudes of the parents to maths seemed to be at the start of IMPACT and how, if at all, they changed over a period of sharing activities with their children at home. This is a highly complicated area which is written up elsewhere in this book (see Border and Merttens, this volume) but certainly the school in general and the children's work in particular can change the image that the parent has of what counts as maths. However, for the purposes of the general picture we are trying to paint, these categories, rough and ready, and fuzzy at the edges as they may be, will be useful.

Most schools and teachers send a mixture of activities, consciously choosing some which will fall into category 1 and which will be clearly recognized as 'maths', and others which are in category 2 and which fit into the topic work on which the class is engaged.

Some teachers send only activities in category 1, for one or more of the following reasons:

— These activities reflect their maths curriculum in that they do not expect to integrate the maths with topic or project work;
— They have decided to reserve the topic-based maths for the classroom and to send home activities which the parents will feel positive about sharing;
— The topic for that term is one which fits into a traditional mathematical area, e.g. 'Time'.

Some teachers send only activities in category 2. There are far fewer teachers of this type and I have questioned them individually as to why they choose to work this way. Without exception the responses make reference to the fact that the teacher believes that maths 'should' come out of the topic work or out of 'real life'. The appeal is to a version of what is popularly believed to be good practice in maths education. Indeed, the consensus is so strong that teachers do not feel it to be necessary to articulate why this belief is the case. They simply appeal to the current orthodoxy; Well, the maths *should* come out of the topic or things that the children are *naturally* doing, rather than being a separate subject . . . (My emphasis).

Overall the response rate (in terms of the numbers of parents and children actually doing the activities at home) does seem to be affected by the category from which the activity is selected, although the relationship is not a simple one.

For those teachers who do only or mainly activities in the first category, the responses are generally good and there is relatively little parental criticism or complaint. The nature of the comments will depend upon such matters as the level and suitability of the activity, the familiarity of the methods of calculation, and the clarity and readability of the instructions.

For those teachers who do a mixture of activities from categories 1 and 2, the response can be good, although perhaps more variable, as there may be more of a tendency to 'opt out' of those activities the parents are not sure about. However, many parents will feel that IMPACT is basically worthwhile and will do all the activities, even though they are not too clear about the point of those in category 2. The comments will reflect this uncertainty: 'We couldn't see the point of this week's activity . . .' Furthermore, these activities may be singled out as the point of criticism when it comes to the follow-up parents' meetings, but basically, the parents as a group are likely to take the view that:

— many of the activities are clearly maths and clearly useful,
— those that appear strange or unfamiliar *might* be useful, and the teacher seems to be doing a good job and so s/he probably has a good reason for doing them. Most parents *want* to trust the teacher. They want to believe that the teaching is effective, and in fact the majority actually do think that this is the case (Hughes, 1992, Chapter 12).

If there are too many activities which seem to the parents to be of uncertain value, they feel that they have a real opportunity, both through the comment sheets and the follow-up parent meetings, to complain and get things changed. Parents who feel they *can* influence the school, *do* share the activities and *do* comment critically.

For those teachers who do only or mainly activities in the second category, a gap can develop between what the parents perceive as 'maths' and therefore, by implication, *not* a waste of time, and what the teacher sees as important. This difference can have a direct effect upon the response rate since parents may drop out of IMPACT, and simply cease doing the activities. It would be wrong to conclude that these parents do not want to help their children, that they are apathetic, or indeed, that they are not doing maths at home. Many parents *are* sharing maths tasks at home with their children, and are even teaching maths explicitly to their children. They simply are not telling the school about it, or doing the IMPACT activities. They have decided first that the activities are a waste of time and the children are learning nothing from them. (They may of course be quite wrong about this, certainly from the perspective of current educational orthodoxies, but this is of no consequence). Second, they feel that nothing they say is going to influence the school's pedagogy or curriculum.

Of course, this situation is not necessarily or uniformly the case with this type of approach. Some teachers, and schools, can 'carry' the parents with them through a mixture of charismatic teaching and excellent communication. Parents can see if the children are happy, enthusiastic and appear to be learning well. Those parents who have less than happy memories of their own schooling may be only too pleased that the experience of their children is that much more positive. Sometimes parents have witnessed an older child suffering through an excessive reliance upon formal methods of skills practice, and are keen for the younger children to get chances they feel were denied by those methods. It remains true that the quality of the work of certain teachers will 'convince' the parents of the validity of their approach.

How Is IMPACT?

The answer to the question, 'How is IMPACT going?' may be, 'Fine', or it may be, 'Terrible', but in either case, any analysis of the practices involved will require the explication of the detailed techniques, behavioural patterns, rhetorics, and the 'common sense' notions embodied in these practices. Through the process of keeping detailed and constant notes on every aspect of the individual schools in which I was working, I became increasingly aware of the complexity of every situation and of the particularities of each IMPACT context which made it hard, if not impossible, to extrapolate within a more generalized theoretical description.

This heightened awareness led to a growing dissatisfaction with the traditional vocabulary and the language available for the writing up and evaluation of educational projects such as IMPACT. Such descriptions tend to employ notions of 'success' and 'failure'. They are couched in terms of pre-defined objectives with their concomitant requirements of quantification and measurement. Furthermore, an 'objective' style adopted, and its use of the passive rather than the active voice and its de-personalization of events, increases the tendency to read such descriptions as universal rather than specific, and, as others have pointed out (Shotter, 1989), masks the relationship between the participants and the writing or evaluation process itself. The consciousness of the specificity of IMPACT practices within a situation and the discontinuities between situations, has led some of us to attempt alternative evaluative and analytic explanations of IMPACT. Such explanations will aim to preserve the sense of a field of complex relations and interactive processes in which the contingent specificities will always preclude universal descriptors or predictions.

We have therefore developed a *modus operandi* in terms of everyday feedback to teachers, parents, advisers and others involved in the project. We have to address specific queries and problems as they arise. It is obviously necessary to share the fruits of experiences elsewhere, and to discuss any sustained reflection upon that experience. It is possible, however, simultaneously to posit a critique of the generalizability of IMPACT experiences, and to register a degree of uncertainty as to the possibility of 'transferring' strategies, procedures or routines. It is helpful to develop as much understanding as possible of the contingent factors involved.

What is being suggested here is that we exercise a degree of caution as to the extent to which any 'results' or findings are taken as universal, and read as if they can be somehow extracted from the complex web of social relations and interactions. However, we must, as a matter of routine practice on IMPACT, attempt to capture the unfolding character of the practices involved, and we are required to present adequate general and theoretical formulations of IMPACT in process.

Points of Conflict for Teachers and Myself

From very early on, knots or holes were appearing as points of conflict in the textual weave of IMPACT. These snags have sometimes threatened to unravel the whole, and it has been occasionally tempting, in a sort of deconstructive urge, to pull at the threads which would encourage the unravelling process. These snags, or breaks in the weave, can be summarized under three headings:

1 The vexed question of 'pressure' and the connected issue of the response rate,
2 The design and content of parent comment sheets or response forms,
3 The positivist stance on maths as 'part of a given reality'.

'Pressure' and Response Rates

One of the questions which we and others used to ask the teachers when IMPACT was first getting going concerned how many children had actually brought back their IMPACT. As I recall, and as I noted it at the time, this enquiry was not at all motivated by a desire to produce statistics, or persuasive evidence, but was a manifestion of our concern as to how many children might be being 'left out'. I used to suggest to various teachers that they kept a note of which children had shared the IMPACT activity at home each week so that we could make alternative arrangements for those who were seemingly never participating at home. This led to the development of a whole range of strategies by which IMPACT activities came to be shared with other non-teaching adults in the school; witness the occasion when I saw a caretaker lying flat out on the playground with his feet up against the wall, being measured with spoons by a group of earnest 5-year-olds!

However, this general enquiry had the unintended effect of focusing attention, in the early and formative stages of IMPACT, upon the percentages of parents and children who responded in any one class. The effect was to prove remarkable. The 'response rate' was immediately identified as an easy and ready-to-hand means of comparison between teachers, between classes and between schools. As such it produced two responses; first, the production of a systematic analysis attempting to isolate the causes for inter-teacher and inter-school differences. The analysis involved the isolation and identification of the various causal or possibly causal factors. The second response was the manufacture and explication of accounts by the participating teachers which could act as possible explanations of difference, and would help to forestall criticism. These accounts were varyingly described, and polarized, as accurate representations of the facts on the one hand, and rationalizations having no basis in reality, on the other.

The analysis of differences on the part of the central IMPACT project was assimilated into a much wider and more holistic approach to the evaluation of IMPACT. By agreement, the response rates became something which were recorded when mentioned by the participating teacher or parents and which could form part of a general discussion about IMPACT and its progress in the classroom or school. A policy decision agreed to deliberately avoid the temptation to use response rates as a means of comparison or evaluation of schools or teachers. However, the fact that response rates of 100 per cent did happen in more than a few classrooms and schools was a feature of the information given out in initial INSET. The purpose of making this aspect explicit at this point connects directly to the desire to question the assumptions concerning the type of parents who will or will not respond.

A major part of the accounts produced by teachers and others in attempting to explain differences in the numbers of parents reponding rest upon what have become 'common-sense' expectations of parents in particular social classes. The work of Bernstein and others in the 1970s (Bernstein, 1971, 1973), and Tizard and Hughes in the 1980s (Tizard and Hughes, 1984), has been misappropriated into popular teacher culture to generate an apparently theoretically-grounded and shared understanding that working-class parents will not support their children's learning in the same effective ways or to the same degree as middle-class parents. This theory lends quasi-academic credibility to popular prejudices. Such an understanding fails completely to take into account the existing complexity of current social class relations, in which it makes no sociological sense to speak of 'working-class' and 'middle-class' as if they were still unified and stable categories. In this particular aspect of educational discourse, teachers are operating with an almost nineteenth-century notion of social class, and without any regard for the complex and often transient interrelations between the subcultures, groups and ethnic communities which make up modern society in Britain.

Clearly, the assumption that certain types of parent *will not* respond to an initiative like IMPACT removes the onus of responsibility from the teacher and places it firmly on the parent. The implication that the teacher does all s/he can to involve the parents but the parent is too lazy/ignorant/ busy/apathetic/ uncaring etc. to respond, neatly renders the teacher's practice safe from possible criticism. To a certain degree, IMPACT is concerned with undermining some of these defences, and to make the common-sense under-standings on which they rest appear problematic and possibly discrimin-atory. In the initial INSET sessions, we point out that there is no evidence from five years of IMPACT that the social class or ethnic origin of the communities within the catchment area of the school has any bearing upon the number of parents who will respond on a regular basis by sharing activi-ties with their children.

A second and more subtle explanation offered by teachers and schools for the fact that particularly low numbers of parents appear to be sharing the IMPACT activities with their children, concern the issue of 'pressure'. Typi-cal features of those who advance this type of account include describing their curriculum as 'child-centred', having started with reasonably good responses to IMPACT which have subsequently diminished, and perceiv-ing the school/classroom as approximating to what current educational orthodoxy would describe as 'good primary practice'. Such teachers usually perceive themselves as 'enablers' rather than 'instructors' and, in Walker-dine's terms, adopt a pedagogical position in which 'knowledge [is] defined in terms of experience and activity — that is, concepts to be acquired and not facts to be remembered' (Walkerdine, 1984).

The issue of putting 'undue pressure' on children and/or parents has appeared to be inextricably linked to this type of approach. It is argued that IMPACT activities should be voluntary and that some schools/teachers achieve the results (i.e. response rates) that they do because they put *undue* pressure on the children or the parents. This tactic obviously serves the function outlined above as a diversion, distracting attention from possible shortfalls in the particular activities or strategies used in that classroom. However, when we start to unpick this particular piece of the IMPACT text, a fascinating series of threads are made visible.

In any classroom a hierarchy of tasks is established. There are those tasks which the children know they will have to do, those which, if they post-pone them or prevaricate for long enough, will get forgotten about, and those which are entirely optional. This hierarchy may bear only a tangential relation to the official label which the task bears; for example, some 'optional' tasks are recognized by the children to be not a matter of choice at all, and other, so-called 'compulsory' tasks are ignored or side-stepped by the children as a matter of routine. The idea that in any classroom situation there are not compulsory tasks is either a piece of collusion between the children and the teachers, or it is a myth expounded by the teacher and denied in private by the children. The hierarchy referred to is well understood by the children in the class.

Furthermore, it is possible to 'map' this hierarchy almost directly on to the hierarchy of the perceived 'importance' or educational value of the tasks. Children think of those tasks which they are not allowed to wriggle out of as being, to a greater or lesser extent, the most important educationally speaking. Thus, no matter how much a teacher may overtly stress the importance of water-play, if s/he allows the children a choice as to whether to play in the water-tray or not, it will be perceived as less important than, say, reading, which the children know they *have* to do.

The question of interest then becomes, not 'Is IMPACT compulsory?', or even, 'Should IMPACT be compulsory?', but rather 'Where does IMPACT come in this hierarchy?'. Some teachers place the IMPACT activity on a par with, say, reading or doing a piece of classroom maths. Others will treat it more like playing in the water tray. Without wanting to imply any value judgment as to *which* tasks should be *where* on the hierarchy — this is a matter to which the current educational orthodoxies and those whose jobs depend upon their exposition speak — it is certainly the case that the number of children completing a task is, to a large extent, dependent upon the place in the hierarchy accorded to that task. Thus, it could be argued that the extent to which the teachers 'put pressure' on children and parents to complete the task, far from having negative connotations, is precisely a measure of the importance which the shared parental work has in the eyes of the teacher. If what goes on at home is really of very little or no value, then obviously the task is placed low in the hierarchy. If it is perceived as of real importance, then children and parents are expected to do the task, in much the same way, as, say, a piece of maths in the classroom may be expected to be completed.

It is not the case that I will advise teachers that IMPACT should — or should not — be placed high in the hierarchy, or that children and parents should be *expected* to complete the task. All that is being said is that if the IMPACT activity is regarded as entirely optional, in the same way that playing with Lego might be optional, then the number of responses is likely to be fewer, and teachers ought expect that this will be the case.

The Design and Content of Parent Comment Sheets

At the start of IMPACT I realized, talking to Dorothy about the shared reading projects, that some mechanism was required whereby the parents could report back how the IMPACT activity had gone at home. A whole series of strategies were then in use on PACT, from cards on which smiley/sad-faced stickers were stuck, to diaries in which teachers, parents and children wrote comments. I therefore designed a sheet which had four questions on it, and on which the parents were required to tick boxes revealing the most appropriate answer. The original questions were those which I had noted as the substance of the conversations at the parents' meetings held to date. They concerned how the activity had gone, whether it had been too hard or too easy, how long it had taken and whether the parent thought the child had got much out of it.

Later on, it struck me that the actual discussion which took place around the design and drafting of suitable comment sheets was immensely valuable in that it almost always caused the revelation and explication of some of the 'common-sense' assumptions normally invisible because they were unquestionable. Rather than leaving the production of the comment sheets in each LEA to the support staff involved on IMPACT, and thereby limiting the discussion to two or three people, I decided to organize inservice training sessions early in the IMPACT induction programme of which the explicit purpose was to design and draft a comment sheet suitable for all the schools taking part in IMPACT in that area. The requirement that there should be a common format ensured that both discussion and negotiation occured.

It is certainly worth mentioning that I have never before witnessed the displays of emotion — anger, anxiety, fear and distress — that I have seen and recorded in the discussion between groups of teachers during these sessions. INSET often requires teachers to assimilate new information, or to consider new ways of teaching or even seeing a subject to be taught. But it does not normally require that they unpick the very weave of the fabric of teaching, that they question what may have been hitherto unvoiced and tacit beliefs. In order to set about this, I realized that it was important, through previous in-service sessions with the same group of teachers, to pave the way for the creation and development of support structures within each group, and the formation and reformation of subgroups within which a feeling of companionship and safety could be generated. I found, empirically, that it helped if these subgroups were cross-school rather than in-school. Perhaps it is easier to take risks with those with whom a daily working relationship does not have to be maintained?

The questions which aroused the most heated and prolonged debate were:

— should parents be asked if the activity was too hard or too easy? Was not this an assessment question and one which only trained teachers could attempt to answer?
— should parents be asked if the child learned a lot?
— should parents be asked if the child needed more practice in that subject?

Each of these questions explicitly raises the issue of where the professional boundaries are to be located and in what specific practices, sequences of behaviour, and codes they are made manifest. Are parents professionals or not? Are they insiders or outsiders? Are teachers in danger of 'losing' their professionalism? Should 'insider practices' be shared? Can they be shared? All these, and other, questions were discussed, often explicitly, sometimes by implication, in the course of the negotiation which had to take place to decide which were appropriate questions to put to parents about a piece of the curriculum which the parent — not the teacher — supervises with the child. Some teachers, pragmatically recognizing the political imperatives of the times, suggested that it was, as President Johnson is reputed to have said of J. Edgar Hoover, better to have parents inside the tent pissing out, than outside the tent pissing in. Others felt that if the margins as to what counts as professional behaviour are allowed to become fuzzy or blurred, then the whole edifice of teaching as a profession is endangered at a time when there are political reasons for wanting to strengthen it.

Certainly, these sessions succeeded in raising to the level of conscious discussion the generally accepted ideas which in part constitute the 'givens' of current educational discourse. It is the process of rendering visible what is normally hidden or camouflaged which seems to be important if the terms of the dominant discourse are to change. In the processes by which discourses, as sites of the conjunctions of knowledge and power, can come to be reconstituted, we can see how the discourse itself constitutes not only objects, but also subjectivity, and thus constrains what *can* be said and done, as well as providing the spaces within which action and talk can occur. Here, in the IMPACT tapestry, it is as if, on occasion, by pulling at thread around a particular knot or point of tension in the design, we can lay bare, albeit temporarily, the threads of the weave itself. Of course, this weave is itself part of another tapestry of which it forms the design rather than the canvas....

The Positivist Stance on Maths as Part of a Given Reality

Much of the argument and discussion with separate groups of both teachers and parents concerns what maths is. I used to record conversation after conversation in which teachers explained that parents, while very well-meaning, do not understand what maths *is*; that it is not *just* number work, or computation, or sums. Similarly, groups of parents, in playgroups, outside the school gates, and even in IMPACT meetings, would express their worries that the children were not getting to grips with 'proper' maths, the really difficult stuff, 'like we used to do', and that when they come to secondary school, they would be unable to do the maths required of them because they had not done enough 'real' maths in the primary school. Such parents may not be fully reassured by teachers' and advisers' assurances that maths has changed, and that children are no longer required to do the things we/you remember from school.

As well as enabling isolated discussion within each group, IMPACT provides a site in which, with the insulation removed, parents and teachers can attempt to negotiate a joint image of 'what maths is'. This point is when sparks tend to fly, but it can also be when creative moments generating a real partnership and shared understandings can occur. It sometimes appears, during these discussions, as if the argument concerns what particular topics are to go inside a large bag labelled 'maths'. On IMPACT, we are trying to move away from the view, implicit in many INSET sessions, that there is a 'right' answer to the question as to what belongs in the bag. To a large extent, the advent of a National Curriculum in maths has pre-empted this debate. The function of IMPACT at such moments is not to legitimize one view of maths. Indeed, I see no role for IMPACT as an adjudicator as to who has the 'correct' notion of what maths is. In this sense, those who adopt IMPACT because they believe that 'it will help to change the parents' attitudes to maths', or because they hope that IMPACT 'will educate the parents about what maths *really* consists of', may have been misled. However, those who hope that IMPACT will facilitate a shared understanding of maths, and a closer working relationship as to how children can best be taught, are maybe nearer the mark. This may involve as much of a change in teachers' perceptions of maths as it does in the parents'.

The view of maths as somehow existing 'out there' and waiting to be discovered, and to which some people, i.e. mathematicians, have a privileged access, is not one which can be endorsed within the theoretical framework of IMPACT. We learn from Foucault that all forms of knowledge are permeated by power relations, that power and knowledge directly imply one another (Foucault, 1980). We understand that knowledge cannot be regarded as neutral, pure or uncontaminated by political or pragmatic considerations. Any redefinition of maths or the maths curriculum will have immediate and automatic repercussions for those professionals or experts whose credibility and role depend upon the exclusivity of mathematical knowledge. In these ways the unknowing (e.g. parents *vis-à-vis* teachers or teachers *vis-à-vis* advisers) are disempowered simultaneously as maths remains the provenance of the few. It is unsurprising then that the idea that parents might possess mathematical knowledge, or may have unique and powerful means of helping children acquire certain mathematical skills, necessitates a redefinition of the maths curriculum or its related pegagogy in such a way as to delegitimize such knowledge and ensure that such ways of helping children continue to be defined as ineffective or even damaging to the child's 'natural' development.

Parental involvement, through projects such as IMPACT, depends for its very existence upon this contradiction. Such initiatives mean that teachers — and more especially advisers and inspectors — are caught in a double bind situation. They *have* to believe in involving the parents. The rhetoric of current educational politics places parental participation centrally in its accounts and justifications. From the 1960s onwards, with the Plowden Report (Plowden, 1967) and the William Tyndale enquiry (ILEA Report,

1969) in which the headmaster's remarks that 'Ultimately the teacher must decide how best to teach the children *regardless* of the parents' (my emphasis) were ruled untenable, the rhetoric of involving the parents has been of increasing importance in maintaining or achieving legitimation for educational practices. But simultaneously, the entire *raison dêtre* for professionals, experts, specialists in education is fundamentally threatened by genuine collaboration with parents. Advisers, inspectors, teachers, all have to believe that they (exclusively) possess the knowledge as to what maths really is, and how it should be taught. The contradiction revealed here by IMPACT resonates with the discoveries of others such as Illich (1971), Friere and Macedo (1987), Giroux (1987).

Conclusion

IMPACT is the largest project of its kind in Great Britain. There is no doubt that as a direct result of our intervention, thousands of parents do share school-designed maths activities at home with their children every week. The children are 'Bringing School Home' (5). Through the research and monitoring side of the project, we have found that:

— More parents than teachers imagine do explicitly 'teach' their children maths at home irrespective of IMPACT;
— IMPACT does provide a focus for 'Maths' conversations in the home;
— Parents and children have to negotiate an outcome. In the course of this negotiation, school methods may be discussed and strategies developed. The child and the parents generate shared images of outcomes. Parent assistance may take many forms.

IMPACT can be 'read' as a means of helping parents to be 'better' teachers of their children. Parent-craft classes, programmes such as 'Head-Start', and so on have contributed to a change in what constitutes being a parent in our society. Older, more amorphous, less-well articulated beliefs and the orthodoxies which underlie them, have been replaced by newer, more 'scientific', 'rationally' produced, theoretically-based rationalizations for particular patterns of behaviour and sequences of action. There is some evidence that parents now see the need to provide types of theoretical justification for their routines and practices (Urwin *et al.*, 1985).

Although IMPACT, like every other theoretically-framed action initiative in the social sciences, cannot avoid being implicated in the processes by which norms are established and 'good practice' defined, there are grounds for continuing to act in good faith and with some optimism. Parent support within IMPACT activities may, as stated above, take many forms. Some of these have already been the subject of considerable study, analysis and description.

Parents can provide 'scaffolding' (Wood, 1986) and assist their child by supplying moment-to-moment help in a contingent and finely tuned responsiveness to the particular and highly specific demands of the unfolding situation. Parents may act as 'tutees' (Topping, 1988, Goodlad and Hirst, 1989), and may allow a child to learn or to develop particular skills through acting as the tutor and instructing the adult partner, or they may actively instruct the child, and explicitly teach or explain a process. On occasion, parents can work almost independently of the child, becoming involved in the mathematical task on their own account. One postman in Barnet got so interested in a mathematical investigation set as an IMPACT activity that he provided the teacher with six and a half pages of closely written text in which he had worked it out and found a general solution! For the child, seeing the parent actively involved and immersed in a piece of mathematics provides a major incentive to do likewise. Children, on the whole, do not do as we say, they do as we do! All of these — and other — ways of assisting children through sharing the activity at home, are described in IMPACT papers elsewhere (Merttens and Vass, 1988, 1989, 1990a+b).

IMPACT pitches not so much into a discourse on parenting, and what consitutes good practice here, but rather into teacher discourse, and into the rationalizations and accounts which teachers provide for parents and the wider community. It requires that teachers move away from a deficit model of parenting, that they question prevailing assumptions about the necessary skills base for 'quality' support in the home. We have discovered no evidence on IMPACT that a particular 'type' of parent is less likely to be able to support their child's learning than any other. There are certainly different sorts of assistance, but they cannot be mapped in any simplistic fashion onto particular social classes or categories of parents, nor can their effectiveness be easily assessed or compared.

IMPACT calls the bluff of teachers and inspectors. Do they really want parental involvement? IMPACT to some extent undermines the collusion between teachers, parents and children, in which it appears that teachers listen to or consult parents, and that children generate solutions, whereas knowledge is 'possessed' by professionals and answers elicited by cues and suggestions. In certain situations, IMPACT can illuminate the detailed practices which regulate the locus of control between teacher and child and teacher and parent.

Given the effectiveness of IMPACT, inspectors, advisers and teachers have few options. They can avoid the problem by side-stepping. They can render parental involvement 'safe' by adopting a 'conversion' approach. This explicitly states that the aim is to change parental attitudes or to convert parents to 'our way' of thinking about maths and maths education. Many parental involvement initiatives overtly express these sentiments (Wolfendale, 1983, Bastiani, 1988).

However, on IMPACT we have come to prefer a more risky, isolated and less well-lit path. If IMPACT is to encourage more emancipatory pedagogies, we must first recognize how insider practices and expert forms of knowledge act to limit, disorganize and marginalize the everyday experiences and common-sense understandings of parents and children. There is now ample research which problematizes the notion of a simple 'transfer of skills' metaphor (Hughes, 1986, Lave, 1988). It is argued that any connection between 'the conscious attentive application of correct knowledge' and success in any one particular context has never been adequately established. Given that the relation of intentional pedagogy with everyday practice is complex and distorted (Bourdieu, 1977), and that even arithmetical practice is, in a serious sense, 'constructed *in situ*' (Lave, 1990), it becomes of crucial importance that, as teachers, we 'listen' to accounts of home or street maths. We have then, as Friere challenges, 'to develop pedagogical practices ... that bring teachers, parents and students together around new and more emancipatory visions of community' (Friere, 1987).

We, as educators, can become more conscious of the processes in schooling by which and through which social control is exercised. The construction of shared professional expertise is simultaneously the construction of ignorance and neglect in others (Kenway, 1990, Knight, Smith and Sachs, 1990). Discriminatory practices depend upon jointly held tacit understandings. We can make visible some of the specific technologies of social reproduction, and can then begin to formulate a notion of empowerment, linked to the attempt to expose and eradicate discriminatory practices where they occur. I have been surprised by the extent to which many of those involved with IMPACT over the last few years have come to admit vulnerability and culpability. We and others can strive to be both auto-critical and self-reflective. IMPACT has to create those spaces through which critical dialogue and revolutionary practice can emerge.

Earlier on, I described IMPACT as a community. This notion still seems to be central to the direction we want to take. Education has largely become separated from community. Knowledge is fragmented, splintered and thereby appropriated by different interest groups. In the West, separated from the daily context of community life, education has become recontextualized and divided into component parts; academic disciplines, courses, classes, and so on. Professional experts have come to exist, often separated from their communities in time, culture and training. We select teachers on the basis of academic qualifications and certification. Older, perhaps wiser, more gentle communities do not see education in this way. Teachers are selected on the basis of their standing within the community, their sincerity, and their willingness to learn from the children.

On IMPACT we struggle to continue, to hold together a community, diverse as it may be. We want to find common ground without creating boundaries or producing exclusive zones. We want to admire and encourage without generating definitions of excellence or mechanisms of comparison. It is only by an act of faith that we can proceed at all.

References

AULD, R. (1976) *William Tyndale Junior and Infants Schools Public Enquiry*, London, ILEA.

BAKER, C.D. and FREEBODY, P. (1989) *Children's First School Books*, Oxford, Blackwell.

BALL, S. (1990) Management as Moral Technology: A Luddite analysis in BALL, S. (Ed.) *Foucault and Education* London, Routledge & Kegan Paul.

BASTIANI, J. (1989) *Working with Parents: A Whole-School Approach*, Windsor, Berkshire, NFER-Nelson.

BERNSTEIN, B. (1971, 1973, 1975) *Class, Codes and Control*, Vols 1–3, London, Routledge & Kegan Paul.

BORDER, R. and MERTTENS, M. (1991) Parental Partnership: Comfort or Conflict? in MERTTENS, R. and VASS, J. (Eds) *Ruling the Margins*, London, Falmer Press.

BOURDIEU, P. (1977) *Outline of a Theory of Practice,* Cambridge, Cambridge University Press.

COCKCROFT, W.H. *et al.* (1982) *Mathematics Counts*, London, HMSO.

FOUCAULT, M. (1980) *Power/Knowledge*, Edited by C. Gordon, New York, Pantheon Press.

FRIERE, P. (1972) *Pedagogy of the Oppressed*, Harmondsworth, Middesex, Penguin.

FRIERE, P. and MACEDO, D. (1987) *Literacy: Reading the Word and the World*, London, Routledge & Kegan Paul.

GIROUX, H. (1987) 'Literacy and the Pedagogy of Political Empowerment', in FRIERE, P. and MACEDO, D. (Eds) *Literacy: Reading the Word and the World*, London, Routledge, Kegan and Paul.

GOODLAD, S. and HIRST, B. (1989) *Peer Tutoring: A Guide to Learning by Teaching*, London, Kogan Page.

GRIFFITHS, A. and HAMILTON, D. (1984) *Parent, Teacher, Child: Working Together in Children's Learning*, London, Methuen.

HALLIDAY, M.A.K. (1980) *Spoken and Written Language*, Geelong, Victoria, Deakin University Press.

HUGHES, M. (1986) *Children and Number: Difficulties in Learning Mathematics,* Oxford, Basil Blackwell.

ILLICH, I. (1971) *Deschooling Society*, Harmondsworth, Middlesex, Penguin Education.

KENWAY, J. (1990) 'Education and the Right's Discursive Politics', in BALL, S. (Ed) *Foucault and Education*, London, Routledge & Kegan Paul.

KNIGHT, J., SMITH, S. and SACHS, J. (1990) 'Deconstructing Hegemony: Multicultural Policy and a Populist Response', in BALL, S. (Ed.) *Foucault and Education*, London, Routledge, Kegan and Paul.

LAVE, J. (1990) *Cognition in Practice*, Cambridge, Cambridge University Press.

MASEFIELD, J. (1946) *'Poems', Revised Edition*, London, Heinemann.

McLEOD, F. (1990) *Parents and Schools*, London, Falmer Press.

MERTTENS, R. and VASS, J. (1988) *Parents in Schools*, Leamington Spa, Scholastic Press Ltd.

MERTTENS, R. and VASS, J. (1989) *How to Plan and Deliver the National Curriculum*, Oxford, Heinemann.

MERTTENS, R. and VASS, J. (1990a) *Bringing School Home: Children and Parents Learning Together*, London, Hodder & Stoughton.

MERTTENS, R. and VASS, J. (1990b) *Sharing Maths Cultures: Inventing Maths for Parents and Children and Teachers*, London, Falmer Press.

OLSON, D.R. (1977) From Utterance to Text: The bias of language in speech and writing, *Harvard Educational Review*, 47, pp. 257–81.

ONG, W.J. (1958/1983) *Ramus, Method and the Decay of Dialogue*, Cambridge, MA, Harvard University Press.

PLOWDEN, B. (1967) *Children and their Pnmary Schools*, London, HMSO.

SHOTTER, J. (1989) Social Accountability and the Social Construction of 'You' in SHOTTER, J. and GERGEN, K.S. (Eds) *Texts of Identity*, London, Sage Publications.

SKEMP, R.R. (1964) *Understanding Mathematics*, London, University of London Press.

TIZARD, B. and HUGHES, M. (1984) *Young Children Learning: Talking and Thinking at Home and at School*, London, Fontana.

TOPPING, K. (1988) *Peer Tutoring: A Handbook of Co-operative Learning*, London, Croom Helm.

URWIN, C. and STEEDMAN, C. and Walkerdine, W. (1985) *Language, Gender and Childhood*, London, Routledge & Kegan Paul.

VASS, J. and MERTTENS, R. (1987) The Cultural Mediation and Determination of Intuitive Knowledge and Cognitive Developments, in MJAAVATN, E. (Ed.) *Growing into a Modern World*, Trondheim, Norwegian Centre for Child Research, University of Trondheim Press.

WALKERDINE, V. (1984) Developmental Psychology and the Child Centred Pedagogy: The insertion of Piaget into early education, in HENRIQUE, J., HOLLIDAY, W., URWIN, C., VENN, C., WALKERDINE, V. (Eds) *Changing the Subject*, London, University Paperbacks, Methuen.

WOLFENDALE, S. (1983) *Parental Participation in Children's Development and Education*, London, Gordon & Breach.

WOOD, D. (1986) Aspects of Teaching and Learning, in RICHARDS, M. and LIGHT, P. (Eds) *Children of Social Worlds*, Cambridge, Polity Press.

Olson, D.R. (1977) From Utterance to Text: The bias of language in speech and writing, *Harvard Educational Review*, 47, pp. 257–81.

Ong, W. (1982) *Orality and Literacy and the Technology of Reading*. London: Methuen.

Ong, W. (1982) *Orality and Literacy: The Technologizing of the Word*. London: Methuen.

Richards, B. (1990) *Language and their Status*. Schools. London: HMSO.

Scribner, S. and Cole, M. (1981) *The Psychology of Literacy*. Cambridge, MA: Harvard University Press.

Sutton, C. (1981) *Communicating in the Classroom*. London: Hodder & Stoughton.

Tizard, B. and Hughes, M. (1984) *Young Children Learning: Talking and Thinking at Home and at School*. London: Fontana.

Torrance, N. (1985) *Peer Tutoring: A Handbook of Co-operative Learning*. London: Croom Helm.

Wood, D. (1988) *How Children Think and Learn*. Oxford: Basil Blackwell.

Wertsch, J.V. (1985) *Vygotsky and the Social Formation of Mind*. Cambridge, MA: Harvard University Press.

Wertsch, J.V. (1991) *Voices of the Mind*. Hemel Hempstead: Harvester Wheatsheaf.

Wood, D.J. (1988) *How Children Think and Learn*. Oxford: Basil Blackwell.

Part II

Doing IMPACT

Chapter 2

IMPACT and the Early Years Classroom

Chris Tye

Chris Tye was a teacher in one of the pilot schools on IMPACT. Here he describes how IMPACT was started and developed in this school. He details some of the discussions which took place, and the issues which were raised by the new ways of working. He argues that IMPACT fitted well with what he describes as an integrated approach to the curriculum, and also that the increased contact with and assistance from parents was formative in the school's curriculum development.

I was first introduced to IMAPCT as part of an in-service course by the London Borough of Barnet under the title 'Organization and Integration in the Infant School'. This course sought to offer of forum for ideas, discussion and eventual implementation of a wide-ranging early years education provision. The challenge was to analyze not only the role of the teacher, but the ways in which parents can participate as an integral part of their children's learning, sharing experiences and hopefully gaining an insight into what we, as educators, are trying to achieve.

INSET Provided by the IMPACT Team

Ruth Merttens described the early experiences of IMPACT as it affected pilot schools in the ILEA. She commented on the interest children had shown and the enthusiasm with which the majority of children embraced the activities they were sharing at home. She opened the debate on how teachers are reacting to wider issues of parental involvement, their own maths teaching and planning as part of the early years curriculum, and most importantly, how such a scheme can benefit and enrich the learning of the children in their charge.

IMPACT began in Barnet on an experimental basis in 1987 and it coincided with my appointment as maths coordinator at Dollis Infants School, a three-form entry infant school with attached nursery. The school had already initiated and was developing a home involvement with reading scheme (PACT), which had received a good response from children, parents and teachers. It seemed a natural progression to introduce IMPACT on an experimental basis, initially involving a reception, a middle year (year 1) and a top infant (year 2) class.

Staffroom Discussion

At staff meetings to discuss this introduction, many questions were raised on the educational, organizational and resource implications such a scheme would entail. How would IMPACT affect our view of maths teaching? Would it extend the children's experience? Did we feel that a majority of parents would participate? What about the children who may not receive a satisfactory level of support from home? What added pressures would teachers face in terms of planning and producing activities? Finally, what would the resource implications be in terms of folders to take home and the sheer volume of paper required?

We are now in our fourth year of IMPACT, the scheme having become an integral part of our cross-curricular approach from the nursery to year 2. We are constantly reviewing and developing early years provision to suit the needs of our particular school as well as the statutory requirements of the National Curriculum. As a result of developing the scheme it is possible to begin to evaluate the effect of IMPACT and to quantify the difference it has made to my view of educational practice regarding the children, the parents, the teaching of maths and the wider early years curriculum.

Making Maths Meaningful

Making maths interesting, exciting, meaningful and relevant is a constant challenge. For IMPACT to be a success it is vital to instil enthusiasm in the child and show the value that we, as teachers and parents, attach to their efforts. There is evidence that this behaviour has important implications across the range of abilities prevalent in the average classroom.

Children who consider themselves 'poor' at number can discover they have a flair for it, which seems to be particularly true in practical or 'environmental' maths situations, such as where a child is handling real money, sorting and counting the contents of a purse and sharing these amounts in different ways. This activity extends to looking at what a given amount will actually buy in the local shops. Such activities underline the relevance of addition, subtraction, multiplication and division. Games type activities also build up confidence and an awareness for handling numbers which may not be so apparent when a child is facing pages of sums or where reading ability is not necessarily commensurate with numeracy skills.

It is often interesting to see how a child approaches an activity and interprets what is expected. One money activity asked the children to find as many ways as they could to make 50p. The teacher expected much coin sorting and adding to the value of 50p; — child in true entrepreneurial style listed ways he thought he could make 50p — washing the car or tidying the bedroom — real situations leading to creative thought!

This enriched experience also benefits children who already show a sound mathematical approach by extending their understanding and manipulation of number. Following the theme of money, another activity asked the children to 'Plan a menu — a meal for two'. Through discussion the children listed all the things they thought they might need, with the proviso that they must not overspend their allotted budget (possibly training for coping with LMS?). This activity placed the children in a 'real life' situation, requiring a range of mathematical concepts such as estimating, sorting, adding, subtracting, multiplying, dividing and planning strategies. It often seems to be the case that children are better at arithmetic when they see the point of it, not when they are faced by columns of sums on a page. Conversely, children who are good at recording sums in this way may not have the conceptual understanding for which we may give them credit.

Sibling Involvement

My experience has been that nursery and infant children enjoy taking IMPACT activities home. Those with older brothers or sisters who do 'real' homework see IMPACT as having a similar kudos. Often younger siblings are involved with activities as well. IMPACT has proved to be a good vehicle for developing communication skills as well as mathematical concepts. The children, having listened to instructions at school, are encouraged to explain the activity they have brought home, to place events in a logical sequence and thus show a good working understanding of the concepts involved. Parents are encouraged to listen, to guide and prompt rather than to take a purely prescriptive role. Even if the child gets it 'wrong', it is valuable in the sense that we (teachers and parents) can assess where the child is and take appropriate measures. With the degree of opportunity to explore that the child is given, often the reverse will happen and the child will confound our expectations in their approaches to different activities.

A Contract with Parents

The value we place on the children's efforts and achievements cannot be overstated. IMPACT is really a contract between the teacher, the parent and the child. The teacher carefully plans, prepares and presents an activity which is given time and commitment by the parent and child and which then makes a positive contribution to subsequent class work. An important way to show the emphasis we place on this work is by effective display. IMPACT may place extra burdens on the teacher in some senses, but you are never left short of excellent display material!

I feel this point is important. Work shared on a more intimate basis, either one to one or in a small group, is generally more comprehensively discussed, more positively approached, better presented and eventually more deeply understood. In a class of thirty children, my constant concern is that there is never sufficient time to give the individual the attention they need to reach their potential, at whatever level they might be working. Children who are fortunate enough to receive a good level of support at home often make good contributions to subsequent class work and will enjoy working along-side and encouraging those who may not have completed an activity. The positive point here is that it is not necessarily the more able helping the less able.

One child who is not particularly good or confident in reading and writing had built a model lorry as part of a transport topic. His elder brother had helped him to put in an electrical circuit to switch on headlamps and a horn. This child had clearly absorbed a great deal as he showed and explained the workings of his model to the class. He went off to help a small group of children explore simple circuits and another child worked with him to make a scale drawing of his model, something he would have found difficult on his own. I have found that as children continue to develop work like this from an IMPACT activity, I can create more time to give to children who do not receive satisfactory support at home.

As a result of completing an activity the children are encouraged to fill in their own evaluation sheet, including their response as to whether they enjoyed an activity and what, if anything, they feel they might have learned as a result. Often these observations contradict the parents' view! Each reponse is valued as perceptions are often different, notably more so in the apparent mismatch which is sometimes evident in a teacher's assessment and a parent's view of the child's capability.

An IMPACT Activity Day

As far as the children are concerned, IMPACT is now a routine part of the school week and enthusiasm has largely been maintained. The important 'fun' aspect of maths has been extended by an IMPACT Activity Day, held in the school grounds during the summer term, involving children, parents and teachers.

The range of activities reflected the broad base of maths skills we try to implement. For example the bucket balance game asked two teams to fill their respective bucket with water using yoghurt pots, estimating how many they might need and how much time it might take. Another activity was to estimate the distance around the climbing frame, to measure the perimeter using wooden building bricks and then to see the distance with the bricks in a straight line. This distance could be translated into standard measures where appropriate. Number activities included a dressing up number line, where items of clothing were donned at different points, aiming and throwing bean bags with different number values into the bucket, and a stepping stones number game. With other games including logic, sorting and decision making, the children were posed a range of challenges in a stimulating way.

New Lines of Communication

Through our commitment to a shared reading programme (PACT), the value of involving parents with their children's education was already evident. The school always welcomes parental help in the classroom with day to day activities and, with the shared responsibility of IMPACT, this has enriched the rapport between child, home and school.

The implementation of IMPACT throughout the school has certainly improved lines of communication and has helped us as teachers become better communicators. Certainly there was initial disquiet about the amount of time we envisaged being taken up in parental consultations and extra time and effort was clearly required to successfully launch the scheme. As IMPACT has developed both teachers' and parents' mathematical concepts have increased as we question our whole approach to maths teaching. This is an integral part of keeping the wider curriculum under constant review, so we can now recognize this time as positively spent.

Communication between home and school has developed in a number of ways and at different levels. Clearly the initial meetings to explain the ethos and aims of IMPACT have been vital, as I know that some parents were unclear as to what we, as teachers, meant by 'maths'. The led to interesting and animated discussion at organized meetings, through the activity evaluation sheets and on a day to day basis as parents visit the classroom. Important lessons have been learned and I offer this example as an initially negative response which opened up a useful debate.

As part of a topic on 'Houses', I sent home an activity asking the children 'to design and build a house of the future'. We had been looking at three-dimensional shape and measurement and drawing simple plans at school and at home. This work was intended as an extended activity over a half-term holiday, so we could use the models to do some more measuring and map work activities.

An irate father returned the evaluation sheet with 'GARBAGE' emblazoned across it! Although I did not relish the meeting, I thought I ought to respond and open up a more positive dialogue. Clearly he did not see the activity as 'maths' and had taken the sheet away from the child without prior discussion. It was not the sort of maths he did at school and he needed to have the mathematical skills and content explained in a much clearer way.

As a result of this parental response, every IMPACT activity contains 'A note for parents' where the aims of the activity are listed and which offers extension activities for those children who need the challenge. At the beginning of each term a letter goes home informing the parents about the topic we are going to be doing and the maths activities related to it. As an interesting footnote, the father concerned independently produced a beautiful model of an under-sea dwelling with working components, which the children used as a stimulus for their own model making and which gave rise to a wealth of language work. Every IMPACT cloud has a silver lining.

The vast majority of parental and child responses have been positive and encouraging. With the National Curriculum, observations and records of each child's achievements are vital and we now keep dated examples of these comments as part of this continuous assessment. It has been my experience that parents value the fact that they work as an integral part of the child's education, where their ideas are given credence, and where both teacher and parent feel they have their finger on the pulse of the child's ongoing achievement. This attitude definitely makes the termly Parents' Evening more viable and constructive and makes the child's annual written profile more meaningful to all concerned.

Just as I believe that IMPACT has helped the teacher as communicator, I also feel that it has helped make the parents more confident in their approach to school and in conversation with their children. This remark is not intended to be patronising as many parents who have been into school recognize the skill of eliciting responses from children through discussion, questioning and prompting rather than by directing and metaphorically leading the child by the hand. Displays in the classroom become more meaningful as the parents play their part in the work. There is also evidence from parental remarks that IMPACT activities have led to a positive development in some children's play at home, especially in a more creative use of construction equipment. Many parents now realize that mathematical thinking is not just a case of adding up, taking away, etc., but using these skills and concepts in a range of situations.

IMPACT is Complementary to the Early Years Curriculum

I have always viewed IMPACT as both complementing and enriching the early years curriculm in it broadest sense. We follow a topic-based approach and organize the classrooms as workshops in an integrated day. IMPACT has slotted into this organization very well and we as a staff feel more proficient at implementing our curriculum as a result of better planning techniques. When IMPACT was introduced, we planned activities with Pat Brown, the advisory teacher, who was always a source of stimulating ideas. We have naturally progressed to planning topics with year group colleagues, where individual expertise can be best utilized and which gives the children a consistency of experience. By 'pooling' ideas and resources the implementation of a broad curriculum is more effective and more carefully structured.

IMPACT activities are planned and sent home as part of this cross-curricular approach. Thus a year 2 topic on Transport which has been recently undertaken will give an example of this ethos. One activity involved the children in collecting information about their family car, e.g. make, colour, number of doors, etc. This was then fed into the computer at school using the 'Our Facts' data handling programme. From this, different graphical representations of the findings were generated. Another activity involving numeracy skills was called 'Amazing Squares'. Here the children collected the numerals from car registration plates to complete a 3 × 3 grid. They found that the total of the rows of numbers matched the total of the columns of numbers. Findings were then checked on calculators. As a half-term activity the children built model lorries. The lorry was not to be more than thirty-five centimetres long (for ease of display as well as setting parameters), should have freely revolving wheels, and a tail gate which should open and close. The child then decided on the load the lorry carries, how heavy the load is and where the load comes form. Thus a series of IMPACT activities will embrace elements of science, CDT, language and other humanities as well as the mathematical skills we hope the children will acquire, and maths can be seen as 'across the curriculum'.

In order for IMPACT to become part of our enriched curriculum, resource implications became a major factor. The introduction of the scheme had been cushioned resource-wise as we received valuable support from our advisory teacher, who also provided us with a steady flow of paper, evaluation sheets and other necessary equipment such as dice. The IMPACT team visited the school on a number of occasions and provided some good discussion points through videos of children interacting during an IMPACT activity, extending to interviews with parents during our Activity Day. Their comments were used as a basis for discussion at the first of the annual IMPACT conferences where we met colleagues from Oxfordshire and Redbridge to share experiences, discuss concerns and in true teacher tradition, collect more ideas.

In terms of collecting resources, we now have a wealth of activity ideas accumulated over the three years of the scheme so far which have helped to structure and sequence maths work throughout the school. These ideas have fed into the children's everyday maths experience and through constant appraisal and assessment of activities we have refined our maths teaching to the extent of producing our own school-based maths teaching and assessment scheme.

Chris Tye

Altered Emphasis

Something which IMPACT has shown is the need for a greater emphasis on practical, open ended, structured play and investigational activities alongside the more formal aspects of recorded work. It seemed to us that reliance on one particular published maths scheme did not give the breadth and depth of experience which children need to develop in all areas of skill and application. As a result of in-service training, year group meetings and staff discussion, we assessed different schemes and extracted elements we believed would fit this range of skills and recording. From this we developed a cumulative set of assessment activities and recording the children will experience throughout their early years' education at Dollis, to give a consistency of experience and aid in our continuous assessment of each child's achievement. We are now linking these activities to the statutory requirements of the National Curriculum along with the IMPACT activities which will continue to play an important role in our overall approach. We feel that teachers, parents and, most importantly, the children will be more confident in their approach and flexibility to maths and will be better prepared for what is to come.

Chapter 3

Maths in My Home

Sue Hunter

Sue Hunter is a parent of three IMPACT children in a Humberside school. She describes how she copes with IMPACT at home with her three children. Detailing the ups and downs of life with IMPACT, Sue is careful to suggest which aspects she feels are generally felt by parents of her acquaintance, and those which are particular to her own personal situation. She also mentions some of the effects of IMPACT upon the relations between the teachers and the parents and upon the maths curriculum, as they appear from a parent's perspective.

In January 1989 IMPACT was introduced into the 6 and 7–year-old classes at Welholme School and extended to a third class (4+ years) at Easter. As luck would have it, my 6-year-old and younger twin daughters are in the classes involved.

Personally I consider IMPACT to be an excellent scheme whereby young children can gain a grounding, not just in arithmetic, but in mathematics. The lateral thinking required for this subject is quietly brought into play, encouraged and developed subconsciously in the child.

My 6-year-old has been involved with every conceivable aspect of time, from the basic clock face, through days, weeks, months, to timing through pendulum swings. She has learnt how to measure using her hands and feet, relative sizes and weights. Currently she is involved with money-patterns, different values, shapes and colour. Overall, there were some difficult concepts for a 6-year-old to understand but all learnt — thanks to IMPACT.

My twins who will be 5 in August, began IMPACT with the same enthusiasm as my 6-year-old. They have learnt shapes — two and three dimensional. I had taught all my children the basic shapes in an abstract way using pencil and paper, the only practical demonstration being with sort and shape toys. I had not extended their knowledge to everyday items. However, as each new shape was presented, I was bombarded with delighted recognition from my girls almost non-stop every day. I have watched one of my daughters deliberately nibble a round biscuit into a square, and then a triangle.

I may have commented on a clock face being round, or a brick being rectangular. I may also have introduced an egg-timer as a timing device. However, I doubt that I would have thought of demonstrating that cutting through a hollow cylinder can produce a rectangle or showing that pendulum swings can measure time. Once a train of thought is suggested, such as the cylinder cutting, it was automatic for me to expand this idea by showing that cutting a square can make rectangles and cutting a rectangle can make triangles. However, then comes the problem. Should you teach more than is asked or not? Are you going to confuse the child or anticipate the following week's activity? Occasionally, the instructions have been ambiguous.

Though generally not a problem, I have experienced some difficulty in finding sufficient time to do justice to all three of my children and I can sympathize with other mothers working outside the home particularly those with pre-school age children. However, older brothers, sisters, uncles, aunts or grandparents can become involved too and should be encouraged since any pressure put on the child to complete 'at the eleventh hour' can have adverse effects. My husband and 15-year-old daughter have each helped on only one occasion and I accept readily the role of 'helper'. However, some parents do not share my enthusiasm for IMPACT, considering it an added burden, and either do not participate or participate in a negative way — grudgingly or impatiently.

This problem has made me consider another aspect of IMPACT. At Welholme there is ample evidence of IMPACT in the classrooms and IMPACT (home) activities are displayed on the walls. However, the child whose work was not displayed, simply because it had not been done, could perceive this as one more failure on his/her part. When I queried this aspect to another teacher I was reassured to learn that these children are encouraged to complete the particular activity during school hours and, in fact, that one child asks to do it. Fortunately, the number of non-participative children at Welholme requiring this 'special attention' are few but the problem might not so easily be overcome in other schools where the number was greater.

My children are familiar with the concept of homework as my eldest daughter has had this task for as long as my younger daughters can remember. However, in other households, homework may be completely new and could either be accepted as a novelty or rejected as an infringement. Similarly, all my children are involved with IMPACT but other mothers have expressed their concern that only one child in the family is involved. This could lead to jealousy on the part of the non-involved child or resentment on the part of the involved child — Why should he/she get all the attention? Why have I got to do extra work? It's not fair!

At a follow-up meeting (after the teachers concerned had left in order that the parents might discuss freely their opinions), some mothers expressed discontent with the scheme. One considered it not her job, another felt that it was not worthwhile and another expressed her difficulty in actually understanding the work required. Yet another considered the child too young (age 5), feeling that the activities were beyond him. However, the majority of parents do not share these views and are very pleased with the effects that IMPACT is having on their children's ability.

The original assessment method where boxes were ticked denoting levels of learning, assistance, etc., has been discontinued at Welholme and replaced with a notebook system. I had misgivings about the quality of the former assessment method. My 6-year-old's perception of a good Mummy is one who 'helps a lot' and, since she puts me in this category, she always answered in this way when in fact I had offered only minimal assistance. Furthermore, an older child recognizing the relevence of the question, could answer falsely to hide the fact that he had been unable to grasp an idea. Also, on one occasion, I realized that my daughter was simply making a pattern of the ticks and not actually considering the questions at all.

The 'smiley/sad face' method where mouth shapes (curving up, straight, curving down) denote different levels of learning, enjoyment, etc., could also present misconceptions. A child wanting to please could answer 'a lot' (the smile) to the amount of learning when in fact the particular activity simply reinforced previously learnt knowledge. Moreover, would a child of this age who, because of previous knowedge, answer with 'not much' (the frown)? Frowning is 'frowned upon' so children are less likely to associate themselves with that face. Similarly, most young children believe that working hard is what good boys and girls do and could answer that the work was hard simply to appear 'good' to the helper. Encouraging children's participation in their own assessment can foster self-esteem and motivate the child to progress to the next activity, but I would also expect teachers to be aware of potential misconceptions and take them into account.

The notebook system of record keeping used at Welholme is, in my opinion, a better method; each page records the date, the activity, the helper and the comments. These comments can be either the child's or the helper's (or both), the teacher adding her/his comments prior to the following week's activity. Although some parents may be restricted by time to comment every week on every child, at least some sort of communication between parent and teacher can be established which encourages active involvement between parents and the school.

The notebook method can bring to light any problems that have arisen. An example is when I commented on the difficulty of precise timing (emptying a one litre container in one minute). I received the reply that the children had been instructed that 'about a minute' would do. I then realized my oversight of the initial instruction; that the child should take the lead — on this occasion I had simply read the instructions. Initially I felt that the ensuing frustration experienced by both my child and myself was my fault but, on reflection, feel that it is the fault of bad design and that this particular activity should be amended at source. Some of the instructions are a little too involved for a child to remember and pass on verbally, and in these circumstances it is hard for a parent to know what to do.

Another advantage of the notebook system is that if too many activities on the same theme are presented and the children are becoming bored with the topic, the teacher can be informed through the comments and move on to the next topic. Similarly, if great enjoyment or interest is being expressed in the comments, additional activities on the same theme can be presented.

One mother expressed her concern that so many of the shape activities revolved around the kitchen as she considered this a dangerous place and did not want to encourage her children to work/play in that room. However, from the teacher's viewpoint, an awareness of potential danger is an essential lesson to be learned and, in the main, probably already has been, but a 'safety note' could perhaps be added to forestall this concern. Personally, I found the kitchen activities no problem whatsoever as they were always introduced when cooking was not taking place and, for comfort only, removed to another room for completion.

My children enjoy all the activities, whether it is cutting, colouring, sticking, drawing, or whatever and the games are especially welcomed, being perceived as play rather than work even though, by virtue of their nature, learning does take place. They share their IMPACT activities, join in with each other and learn together. I believe that with a helper with the right attitude, most children who undertake IMPACT can only gain from it, in confidence, in ability, in knowledge and especially in enjoyment of mathematics.

Chapter 4

A Probationer's Year on IMPACT's Probationary Year

Kerry Carrie

Kerry Carrie was a probationary teacher in the first year of the IMPACT project. At that time, no resource bank of IMPACT materials existed and to a large extent, teachers were having to create not only a bank of suitable IMPACT activities for the children to take home, but also the actual strategies and procedures which make up what is now described as 'IMPACT practice'. She describes how she, and the other teachers in her school, set about implementing the IMPACT philosophy in practice, and illustrates her account with some of the pitfalls they encountered and the incidents which caused them to think again or adjust their patterns of behaviour. The paper illuminates several aspects of IMPACT through tracing their development and the ways in which new procedures and routines became part and parcel of everyday teaching or school life.

I finished my PGCE course at Bishop Grosseteste College, Lincoln in the summer of 1987. The training we received as far as maths was concerned was based around the implications of the Cockcroft Report (1982). We were encouraged to approach maths through a topic/theme and provide appropriate activities which very much involved children in their own learning. However, as the prospect of teaching 'for real' approached I was worried about some of the implications of this approach. Would I have enough practical ideas? How would I know I was covering everything? How would I be able to structure the work to ensure progression and match the level to different abilities? Maths was the area of the curriculum which worried me most at the end of my training. However, despite these feelings of insecurity, I wanted to establish good relationships with parents and was keen to find a job in a school where parental involvement was seen as important.

The level of parental involvement already established at Stonesfield C.P. School, Oxon, was one factor which attracted me to apply for a job there. Parents were actively involved in their children's learning. There was an open door policy, parents working alongside children in classrooms, curriculum workshops for parents, a well-established shared-reading project and a shared maths project to be started that September. I was happy to be accepted for the post and so began my probationary year at the same time as IMPACT was begun — Stonesfield being of the six Oxfordshire pilot schools.

Making a Start

After the initial euphoria of getting the job, worries did begin to creep in. They mainly concerned not knowing exactly what to expect and this was particularly true as far as IMPACT was concerned. The worries centred around the curriculum implications already outlined. Furthermore I really had no experience/preparation for the eventualities I might meet with such a high level of parental involvement. In short, as a probationer one feels anxious and vulnerable in this area, as an IMPACT probationer that vulnerability seemed heightened.

Two weeks into the term, I couldn't really see where I was going. I was battling with planning the maths in my room over the long-term instead of for a day or a week. As a teacher with a new class it takes a while to work out where children are with their learning; as a probationer you are also in the situation of not being totally sure what to expect them to be able to do, or where to go next from different stages. IMPACT was vaguely related to the maths happening in my room but I wasn't happy with the situation. We were doing a project on medieval times, and one of the IMPACT activities did reflect this topic in that we asked the children to complete a time line. However, the other two activites were number games and I did not feel that they really connected with the number work I was trying to cover in class. One involved digital roots and some quite complicated arithmetic and the other was a routine tables game but I felt that both of these were somewhat isolated maths activities. At this stage I felt I wanted IMPACT to be more integrated, to be part and parcel of my practice.

The saving grace was that other members of staff were in the same boat as far as their feelings about IMPACT were concerned. We really could not continue to spend the whole of Friday explaining a game and playing it as we did the first week, nor spend two hours on two evenings after school devising sheets with which we still weren't happy; nor could we afford the amount of photocopying we were doing as we continually changed sheets or abandoned them altogether. This situation had arisen from our over-zealousness. We wanted to get it right. We were committed to IMPACT, we wanted it to be the way forward, the way we were going to work and therefore we wanted very much for the initial sheets to be a success in terms of parental and child reaction. We were teaching in a village where parents can be very supportive but also very quick to criticize. We could see already the positive effects

IMPACT was going to have in our classroom. Children were beginning to ask about the next IMPACT, to talk confidently about the mathematical activities they had been doing with their parents who were already beginning to say things like 'I never thought of that being maths before'.

Support

I was fortunate that I spent my probationary year in a very supportive environment. I never felt 'alone'. This wasn't just because everybody else was beginning with IMPACT too but because I taught in a cooperative situation and the staff planned and worked together as a whole.

Through spending lots of time talking about IMPACT amongst ourselves, we realized that we couldn't keep going at the rate we had started off. We still felt it had been important to go through that process of getting it going, trying out a variety of ideas, opening up the dialogue and that our enthusiasm to get it 'right' had been understandable but we began to refocus our energies. We realized that we didn't have to explain absolutely everything in great detail to the children each time. Finding the correct language to explain an activity is still what I find most difficult, but designing the sheets did get easier as time went on. If the activities related to the work going on in the classroom the children quickly grasped the idea as they could see the relevance of the activity and indeed the response was greater. We therefore focused our energies on longer and more in-depth planning for maths, incorporating IMPACT. We planned on a half-termly basis, enabling us to link IMPACT with our pre-planned classroom maths to a much greater extent. The number work we were hoping to cover with various groups of children, the maths aspects of the topic we were doing and the IMPACT activities all became part of our overall plan. In this way we hoped to avoid the situation of sending an activity such as a number investigation, which had previously been unconnected to any of the childrens' other mathematical work. If we chose a number activity, whether game, puzzle or investigation, it would be because it fitted in with the number work already organized for that week.

Looking Back: The Effects of the Revised Strategy

The end of my probationary year came around amazingly quickly and I was feeling much more confident as my second IMPACT year approached. I certainly felt I had learned a lot in three terms and evaluated what IMPACT had meant in terms of children, parents and myself.

I felt the children had benefited from spending time working with their parents in a one-to-one situation, something we can so rarely provide as teachers. The maths they were involved in was more meaningful in that they could see how it related to what they were doing at home and vice versa. For example the children made pie-charts showing how they used their time throughout the day and compared it with a pie-chart of an 'imagined' medieval child's day. They calculated the differences and discussed reasons. The open-endedness of the activities encouraged them to develop a wide variety of strategies for solving problems and the way they talked about maths showed the benefits. Most importantly, IMPACT strengthened the relationship and dialogue between home and school. Working together was providing benefits all round and certainly gave me a broader picture of the children and insights into their homes. After an activity making a pendulum, one child's written comment certainly made me wonder: 'I swung it, it hit the cat who went berserk and pulled the skeleton off the wall!'

Sometimes one got the distinct impression we hadn't been too popular in some households that weekend. A pairs activity involving sorting socks into pairs, brought the parental response: 'Andrew couldn't do this activity as we didn't have enough clean socks. He was not happy'. An Archimedes displacement activity in the bath was returned by a child, who said: 'The hot water cost a b _____ fortune. Well, that's what my Dad said anyway'.

Evaluation Meeting for Parents

We had arranged an evaluation meeting for parents at the end of the year and the overall response was positive. There were comments about parents feeling pressurized to do yet something else, but that the pressure came predominantly from the children wanting to do the activities, as the voluntary aspect was always stressed. There were comments about sometimes not always being able to see where the maths was in an activity or not being able to see the point of the activity. We responded to this query directly by sending half-termly letters about the IMPACT which would be coming home and how it fitted into classroom work. We sometimes put a rationale on individual activities. There were comments about how this 'sort of maths' seemed so much more relevant in comparison to the maths they had learned at school; One mother said:

> My 6-year-old knows 2×6 is 12 which I knew at his age but I didn't know why. Robert told me that $5 + 5$ is 10 and another one on each is another two altogether so $10 + 2 = 12$.

Parents were, it seemed to us, seeing the benefits of children developing their own strategies.

In working with parents so closely the main thing I had learned and came to accept was that if we invite comments from parents we have to be prepared for, and accept, any response. In providing parents with an evaluation sheet one is obviously in a very vulnerable position. People will write down things which they might not necessarily say face to face. In my third week of teaching I had received the following comment:

> This activity merely served to highlight the poor standard of maths teaching my daughter has received. She didn't know how to even set down a divison calculation and asked me if it was the same as sharing. I am quite certain she is among your brightest pupils and at 8 years old she should be used to mathematical terminology and how to set about such calculations. I am appalled.

Such a comment is very hurtful, more so when one is so new to the profession and feeling vulnerable in terms of home/school dialogue anyway. Many people will recognize this situation. It is the same as the one 'difficult' parent at a parents' evening one remembers, not the other twenty-nine, who were happy. My headteacher was always very supportive in such situations. Even from this very early stage he encouraged me to ask parents in to discuss the matter. Face to face it was nowhere near as difficult a situation as I had imagined and the discussion was profitable.

At the end of the year negative comments from parents were still hurtful but I could now accept them and discuss them more confidently. I felt in a better position to justify the way I was working and more confident to talk about what we were doing. This was partly because of the year's teaching experience but also because I had established good relationships with the parents and therefore could be open and honest in discussions with them. In these days of increased accountability I see this contact as all the more important and am very glad I have been working closely with parents from the start of my career.

I still am continually adapting my planning strategies to cover all the areas I need to, to take into account different ability levels and to ensure continuity and progression. I don't suppose any of us can see the day when we think we've cracked it. However, at the end of my probationary year, I did feel I had developed (in terms of planning) since the beginning. Through involvement with IMPACT I had been able to structure a practically-based non-scheme approach beyond the six weeks of final teaching practice. With colleagues I now planned very much in the long-term; half-termly in detail but with an overview of the term and of the whole year. I also had a good resource base of activities and ideas on which to build over the next year.

Reference

COCKCROFT, W.H. *et al*, (1982) *Mathematics Counts*, London, HMSO.

Chapter 5

IMPACT: A Parent's Personal Perspective

Sylvia Harrison

Sylvia Harrison is the mother of four children, all of whom have been involved with IMPACT over the last five years. She writes about how IMPACT was presented to her as a parent, and the types of justification which were given. She remembers the doubts she had at the start, and then provides a review of the subsequent IMPACT practices and the ways in which some of her assumptions underwent a process of interrogation and analysis.

We were introduced to IMPACT with a meeting of staff, parents and the IMPACT team, arranged for two occasions to give every family a greater chance to be represented. The team was very warm and approachable and sold the scheme well: maths would no longer hold any fears (the very name had put panic into the heart of many of the parents); maths was fun; maths should have a relevance to life, to a child's experiences; children should be encouraged to look for and observe patterns, etc. Industry had found its young employees lacking in 'relevant' maths, and this problem ought to be examined; children learned best from an environment where home and school worked alongside (as in shared reading) and parents might learn something too.

A few concerns were voiced: some parents were still concerned as to their ability to cope; I felt that IMPACT should not be the only maths, that some more formal (even, dare I say, repetitive) tasks should be undertaken alongside for the sake of reinforcement of concepts and skills if nothing else. On the positive side I looked forward to seeing what my children were doing and sharing with them and encouraging them in their work. It would be good to have a legitimate excuse to go into school and discuss topics raised with the staff. I was excited by the possibilities of taking maths to the individual child's own level, not leaving them dissatisfied with the 'accepted level' in areas where they were obviously motivated and capable of going further.

54

So Three Years Down the Line, How Has It All Gone?

I have watched this programme particularly through the eyes of my four children. This in itself presents a problem; it is quite a logistical feat to fit in four lots of IMPACT over a busy weekend! Their attitude to it is markedly different: one, though generally positive and competent mathematically, resents any encroachment on his free time, especially as he regards it as unfair to call IMPACT a voluntary task when he knows he will be 'in trouble' at school if it is not done. Having said that, this same child once started, enjoys many of the activities. The fact that the children regard IMPACT as compulsory does pressurize parents to put time aside solely for their child, a very important side effect since it is all too easy to lose sight of the importance of shared activities in this fast-moving age. The time and commitment of the school staff has a sobering effect and further encourages me to find the time to tackle the tasks.

The activities themselves vary greatly, some being very recognizable as mathematics, others perhaps having more of a slant towards science (e.g. growing crystals) or even CDT (e.g. 'design something useful for an egg'). This last activity led one son (the child who objects to IMPACT) into a very explicit description of movement of contained liquids (a hydrologist in the making?) after I had suggested that I would like something to help me test which eggs I had hard boiled for the sandwiches. He then designed a pleasing model for the test.

Some activities take very little time, others a great deal, especially if 'optional extras' are taken up. Some appear less useful than others, but unless it is known what follow-up has occurred in the classroom it is impossible to judge the value of each task. Some tasks stand on their own and need little or no follow-up, others may lead to a week or more of further activities in school. One example here that I would like to give is that of the potatoes! My two girls, then in their reception year, were asked to bring to school the biggest, heaviest potato they could find and to draw two things, found in the home, each weighing less than their potato. This task was reasonably easy, leading to great fun weighing things at home; however the amount and complexity of work that followed at school was inspiring. Sorting, weighing, measuring circumferences, recognizing that size and weight of different objects were not necessarily directly related, even volume measurement by displacement were all undertaken and, of course, all this new-found information had to be recorded and communicated both in book form and verbally. Here access to the school was very important, otherwise parents would have been unaware of the immense amount of follow-up work. In this case too, the class explained and described all their work in an assembly for the whole school, open to parents (a regular occurrence at this school). It is a very useful tool, apart from the obvious advantages of good communication, for through having to describe new-found information a child reinforces and clarifies their own knowledge and understanding, and if handled well, grows in confidence.

There were activities that an able child could manage without parental help. I would sometimes arrive home late on a Friday to find my enthusiastic girls had already completed their work, usually correctly. This may have made me feel guilty, but it was very good in encouraging self-sufficiency and confidence in finishing a task unaided.

One of my initial concerns, as previously mentioned, was that not all maths could be properly assimilated this way. This remained a concern for some time. I appreciated that what was being done was very good but I felt some of the basic groundwork was being brushed over or ignored. Now however, I see more conventional maths undertaken as well as IMPACT; whether this was always there, or whether the need for it was acknowledged after an initial trial period I have never been entirely sure.

Certainly, as was mentioned as a positive possibility, the children have sometimes taken tasks further than required, and assimilated new concepts when they were ready for them by so doing. One child, now at secondary school, will still sometimes do his brother's IMPACT, taking it further, spending hours perhaps trying to find a pattern and an equation to cover all possibilities.

As a parent observing and being closely involved in their maths, I have found it fascinating to see how my four children tackle problems, or even simple computations, in a different way. Their procedures are all perfectly valid but they have worked them out to fit their understanding and individually preferred methods of approach (as long as these methods are checked to be valid) instead of being forced to use some strictly laid down series of operations which hold no meaning for them.

There were really very few problems as such in carrying out the IMPACT tasks as long as they were treated confidently. Usually the children had been told what to do which helped enormously in activities which were difficult to explain on paper. Some had to be modified for reasons of ability levels or time considerations, but this was regarded as perfectly acceptable. It was helpful when staff wrote a brief note about where they hoped the task would ultimately lead, or what concepts they were hoping to tackle for the next few weeks. This perhaps needs to be done fairly regularly to keep up the initial enthusiasm and impetus in the project.

Chapter 6

IMPACT — Does It Really Make a Difference? A Teacher's Personal View

Linda Calvert

Linda Calvert is a class teacher who, at the time of writing, had been working on IMPACT for just over a year. Here she describes how IMPACT was set up in her school. She details the school context, the attitudes of the teachers to the parents and how familiar and previously unquestioned assumptions were made explicit and interrogated. Her enthusiasm for IMPACT is explained by outlining what she feels the processes IMPACT incorporates have enabled her to achieve.

In 1988, in the reorganization of Hull schools (see Chapter 7 for further details) I moved to Griffin Primary School, Bilton Grange. From the start we seemed to be faced with the problems of either parental antipathy, or indifference and apathy. Parents were finding it hard to accept new staff, who in turn seemed burdened with all the stresses and strains of movement, change of direction and the proposed implementation of the National Curriculum. IMPACT appeared to hold an answer to crossing the 'seeming great divide' from parent to staff and also to provide another useful resource for overworked staff.

Ruth Merttens' enthusiasm was carried from her training course back to Griffin. Following her guidelines on 'Introducing IMPACT', we started the scheme with great optimism. A meeting for the parents of all the children involved in IMPACT was called and the response was amazing. At a lively meeting we realized that 'they' wanted to help: 'If our children will benefit, we'll give it a try.' The following night was Parents' Night and comments such as 'We've always wanted to help but didn't know how', 'We were frightened of showing them wrong', and 'I like to know what they're doing in maths', came across. IMPACT was already at work even though it hadn't quite started.

The response to the sheets was tremendous. The ingenuity and imagination shown by children and helpers has been stimulating. Parents seem much more confident in asking us for help if they have problems, not just problems related to the IMPACT sheets. They are often to be seen in the playground swapping sheets and discussing results. Confidence encourages critical assessment. The success of the scheme was revealed at the 'Friends of IMPACT' follow-up meeting. Over coffee and biscuits we asked what they liked and disliked about IMPACT. They found it very hard to find faults:

Sometimes too long, sometimes too quick.

Sometimes boring.

Not enough information to help parents.

But on the credit side:

Loved being involved.

Didn't seem like maths.

Child was the teacher, parents the learners.

Children much more motivated.

Learning was fun.

Whole family involved.

Better parent/teacher relations and better access to staff.

The barriers were falling. Perhaps the most exciting part was when they asked to be 'educated alongside their children'. They were 'frightened of being left behind'. They wanted to know about the mathematical reasons behind the sheets. The more they knew, they felt, the more they could positively affect their child's progress. Since that meeting IMPACT has gone from strength to strength. The two reception classes with their own unique problems, have joined in. Little-seen working mums and dads were just as willing to help, and contact has been established with many parents who were reluctant, through fear or diffidence perhaps, to come into the school building. They are very regular with their activity and assessment sheets. It's another way through.

The return sheets have given an amazing wealth of information about family life, which has given a greater understanding of the children, their attitudes and some of the problems. The most negative response yet has had a positive result: 'When are you going to stop sending home this IMPACT. We've better things to do with our time'.

This reaction made me rethink my attitude to the child involved. Perhaps he had only felt indifference at home. A positive approach has worked wonders. His brother helped him with the next sheets but slowly his mother has become interested and for the first time has begun the hear him read at home! What a difference it has made to him.

What started as a Home School Maths Scheme has now evolved into a cross-curricular scheme which is even more exciting. Sheets have gone home ranging from family trees, to growing and monitoring seeds, to the most spectacular (by popular request) designing and making musical instruments. For a little extra planning many of the National Curriculum Attainment Targets have been covered in greater depth and with real enjoyment.

A huge resource as been opened up to us and it's fun!

Part III

Supporting IMPACT

Chapter 7

IMPACT: A Humberside Perspective

Alwyn Morgan and Paul Tremere

Alwyn Morgan and Paul Tremere are currently responsible for coordinating IMPACT in Humberside. They have described how IMPACT was set up in Hull after the massive reorganization of schools in 1988. They detail the stages by which IMPACT was introduced into Hull schools, the problems which arose and how they were dealt with. An important aspect of the introduction of IMPACT here is the peculiarity of the context into which IMPACT was to be inserted. Following the reorganization, many schools in Hull had a 'half-time' teacher responsible for home/school liaison. Alwyn and Paul describe some of the work and the initiatives which were generated and how they have prospered since.

Our first encounter with IMPACT maths was at a one-day conference for parents and teachers in Oxfordshire, at which Ruth Merttens was a keynote speaker. We were immediately impressed by her concept of using maths at home as a means of reinforcing the ongoing work of the school. Consequently Ruth was invited to share her vision with some Humberside teachers. Quite coincidentally, this invitation was extended just as IMPACT maths was being launched semi-nationally. Naturally, our authority took the opportunity to buy into the project. This small investment, thanks to the willing commitment of all concerned, will not only have been worth every penny spent, but will demonstrate to Humberside teachers the potentially most exciting and productive means of working with parents to raise standards of education.

Widlake and Macleod (1984) have demonstrated graphically, how, through the medium of home/school reading schemes, that reading ages of children from multi-ethnic, disadvantaged city centre backgrounds can be put on a par with those pupils who come from more advantaged homes. If such a change can be brought about through the medium of reading, very exciting developments can be expected if we encourage such an approach on a cross-curricular basis, for both primary and secondary pupils alike. The

IMPACT maths initiative was therefore seen as a means to commence such a process.

Our initial aim was for teachers to appreciate the potential of parents as educators, reinforcing the work of the teacher, an aspect of home/school work which has not been fully appreciated or investigated to date. Additionally when such practice becomes well-established, enterprising teachers might see the potential to extend this way of working with parents into other curricular areas. This contact with parents also overcomes the age-old grouse from teachers, that for a variety of reasons (fear, employment, invisible barriers around schools and geographical locations) they were unable to involve parents in the work of the school. Home/school curricular projects enable potentially every school to enter into a working dialogue with all parents.

For one of the authors, the initial experience of parents as educators was personal, when as a pupil at both primary and secondary level, his father was always looking to support and encourage him. He always remembers his father asking anxiously why he couldn't bring a syllabus home. His attitude typified so many other parents who wish their children to succeed. The potential goodwill and commitment of parents simply was not being considered, appreciated or exploited.

We believe that the vast majority of parents, when their children first enter school, want them to succeed and achieve more than they did. Parents, as the initial and natural educators in the pre-school years, have done their best to help prepare children for school. The challenge facing nursery and reception class teachers is therefore to open the curriculum up and actively give parents the means to continue as educators and reinforce at home the ongoing work of the school.

Such collaborative action overcomes the sense of alienation or helplessness that many parents experience when their children first attend school. Without such action a tremendous amount of potential goodwill and support can subsequently be lost.

One of the authors, in his last authority (Clwyd, in north-east Wales), had the good fortune to become involved with two initiatives devised by teachers who were seeking a more effective working relationship with parents. The first came from the deputy head of an infants school, who one day out of sheer frustration over her pupils' TV culture, told her class to go home that evening, turn off the television for half an hour and make something from junk material. The following day, she was overwhelmed by the response and appreciated the potential of the exercise. For the following two years she devised numerous activities, reflecting all curricular areas for parents and children to do together. The following are a few examples:

1. produce a small model from junk material,
2. write a short story for the children to illustrate,
3. prepare a number board game for the child to play,

4   make an indoor garden on a tray,
5   produce a model from clay sent home with the child,
6   make something on the theme of Easter.

The second exercise involved top juniors from a small number of schools, who decided to research the 'Swinging Sixties' as a cross-curricular project. In this instance parents, friends and relatives were used as the major source of information. All parents, irrespective of background or ability could make some contribution in the field of music, sporting events, politics, fashion, employment, etc. The project focused on the local scene before exploring the national and international perspective of the 1960s.

This enlightening experience was later shared with forty-three newly created primary home/school liaison teachers, that were to commence their duties in Hull schools in September 1988. These teachers were given a 0.5 non-teaching allocation of time to support their work with parents. The creation of these posts came out of Humberside's decision to reorganise Hull schools — a massive exercise undertaken over a five-year period, costing a total of £28 million. The former three tier system of age 5–9 primary, 10–13 junior high and 14–18 senior high schools were being replaced by 5–11 primary and 11–16 high schools, feeding two sixth form colleges.

One major challenge encountered within reorganization was that of underachievement, which was reflected in a very small percentage of pupils looking to extend their studies into either sixth form, further or higher education. This attitude was particularly noticeable in some of the less advantaged areas of the city. The authority's response was two-fold, namely the appointment of home/school liaison and curriculum enrichment teachers for the schools in these areas. It was believed, in the case of the former, that if parents could become more actively involved in the education of their children, then educational standards could be raised.

Following a twenty-one day training course, the home/school liaison teachers took up their duties and quickly set about establishing strategies that would make schools more welcoming. Major success can only be measured in the long term (a generation or two) but nevertheless early indications look promising. Community rooms were established, pre-school activity mushroomed, supported by training courses for parents, daytime adult education opportunities developed and parents generally became more involved with the everyday life of schools. However, the great success story has been parent netball teams — sport was seen as an effective means of attracting parents into school. The response has been overwhelming; over thirty teams across the city are now playing and training on a weekly basis and have organized their own daytime league.

This initial 'spade work' with parents in Hull schools had been ongoing for approximately twelve months before the concept of IMPACT maths was brought to the attention of a number of maths coordinators. We were fortunate that these links and relationships were in the process of developing before parents were approached to become involved with the school curriculum. This initial preparatory work, which assisted in raising the mutual respect and confidence of teachers and parents for each other, has certainly contributed to the initial success of IMPACT maths. The curricular approach also assists in promoting a whole school approach to working with parents. No longer can it be seen as something simply encouraged by a home/school liaison teacher.

IMPACT–home/school maths differs from other aspects of parental participation in school-based activities in many ways, the most significant of which that sets it apart from other initiatives is the built-in facility for the participating parents to respond to the activities. This constant feedback gives, almost demands, a reaction to the curriculum and how it is delivered. Consequently parents are no longer passive and compliant towards the diet of learning that the school is feeding their children. They not only help to deliver that diet but also have some say in its constitution. If they do not like it or feel that it is inappropriate they are encouraged to say so. Furthermore the teachers are under an obligation to react to this parental influence. No longer can the class teacher deliver a didactic dogma leading towards a taught product; they have to listen to and heed the parental response. Those teachers who do not are undermining the very cornerstone of the foundations of IMPACT. Inviting comment and then ignoring the reply is not only ill-mannered but ill-judged and a recipe for failure.

Most schools employ a series of strategies to encourage parents to make an ongoing evaluation of IMPACT and its associated activities. The most formal and regular of these methods is the weekly parental response sheet which allows the teacher to gauge on a weekly basis how things are progressing. The replies are usually positive and much of this may be attributed to an halo effect — the parents wishing to give a favourable impression most of the time. Some however are painfully blunt, revealing a disturbingly damning indictment of parental attitudes towards school. One particular activity 'went well' took '5 minutes' and was understood, but the parent still replied:

I don't have time to mess about with this.

This comment led to positive follow-up by the teacher concerned. She re-examined her attitude towards the child concerned and began to wonder if he experienced indifference and apathy towards school at home due to parental attitudes. His brother was recruited to take an interest in the IMPACT activities and some were completed with his help. Eventually his mother noticed what was going on, and slowly responded by listening to him read at home for the first time — what a difference this attention made to the child's development and attitudes.

Personal contact is always a better alternative to written communication. Some schools facilitate it on a regular basis, reserving a specific time each week when teachers are available to discuss IMPACT. This is best done just before the end of afternoon school.

The half-termly formal (organized) parental meetings attract a varied response. Poor attendance is not necessarily an indication of apathy, rather, a reflection that all is well on the parental relationship front. Why come to an organized school meeting convened when there is already ample opportunity for effective home/school liaison? There is still an element of making the effort of coming to school only if something is amiss, and a formal exchange of views can be a threatening experience anyway!

At one such meeting a busy mum expressed a dread of Friday tea times. She was invariably preparing the family meal, and immersed in other household tasks when her children excitedly arrived home from school, demanding that an immediate start be made on their IMPACT activities. 'They are far too impatient and enthusiastic' she complained. 'IMPACT threatens to disrupt every Friday tea time!'

These strategies for increased parental contact have already affected the teachers' way of working, especially the casual, spontaneous meetings either before, after, or now more commonly, during school. The barriers are certainly being lowered and the crocodile-filled moat is being drained. The stepping stones are less slippery and the welcome more assured. Teachers who primarily experienced few positive parental approaches, now encounter many.

Parents are beginning to see the home as an extension of school and teachers are more aware of school relating to home, with learning taking place in both. Availability of access is increased. As one parent commented, school is seen in a much wider context: 'We appreciate what you are trying to do, and feel more confident of making further reinforcement at home'. Another was quick to show that the whole family was involved: 'We are all involved now — all the family; it's not just the children who come to school and the teachers that teach. We all talk about school now, everyone helps.'

There is certainly an influence felt back in the classroom. The teaching style and the teacher's delivery is becoming more flexible, with the children becoming more responsible for their own learning. The family's response affects the structure and nature of the activity. More importantly teachers' attitudes change in line with the parents, both beginning to share the responsibility for the presentation of appropriate learning experiences. It is useful to compare and contrast IMPACT with other parts of the curriculum that include parental participation. Non-IMPACT parental contact has been part of school life for many years, but has recently been brought more into focus as local initiatives have been developed to enhance home/school liaison.

Traditionally there has always been a small but often strong presence at school sporting events. The influence of parents on touchlines has often been a mixed blessing. A pupil from a car-owning family — with a parent willing to transport other team members — was always guaranteed a place in any sports team organized by one of the authors. Unfortunately he could some-times do without some of the basic vocal advice delivered from the sparsely populated 'terraces', especially when it was his turn to referee!

This parental interest was encouraged further when there was a need to raise money for the school fund, and parents were familiar sights organizing raffles or selling homemade cakes etc. Small cracks in the school's isolation appeared when some mothers came into class to help with knitting. This help was again extended into accompanying school excursions — as an extra pair of hands to help control the hordes as they descended on the chosen destin-ation. Most teachers have used parents in these ways in the past. However most of this involvement has short-term advantages, and suffers from severe limitations when any long-term development is sought. It involves only a small number of parents, who are often not working with their own children. The parents that contribute are from a restricted group because they need particular qualities before they can respond. First, they must be available at that particular time, which immediately excludes a large number. Then they must have some degree of motivation or enthusiasm, along with the personal qualities, patience, humour etc. and the right attitude to make them accept-able to the rest of the group. A degree of skill or knowledge in a specific area is also required — they must be able to knit, bake cakes, grow plants etc. When all these criteria are demanded, few parents fit the bill — if they do they are probably teachers anyway! Finally this super being is allowed into school to take a small group of children, none of which are likely to be their own.

It can be argued that this system does foster better home/school relations amongst those who participate, but in a very restricted way. The school may benefit materially from such contributions and some parents may gain an insight into what goes on in school. There are, however, still barriers to negotiate. The barriers may be of a different nature but they still exist — only a few parents are able to participate and contribute.

The parental contribution is still under the control of the teacher who decides what is to be done, when, and who does it. The activity takes place in finite chunks; it has a formal beginning and end. There is little scope for digression or individual development. It is essentially product-based rather than process-based. The child may have made a hedgehog, but does he/she know how to sew or can he/she make a tea cosy?

Are the learning experiences being shared, or is the parent an instructor, attempting to pass on skills and knowledge didactically? The parent may make a valuable contribution in enriching or broadening the curriculum for a few selected pupils but they are contributing anything to curriculum development?

IMPACT however achieves more than this limited situation. It involves far more parents (over 90 per cent uptake is a realistic norm) and the parents are involved with their own children. The facility to comment and report back is important, as it gives parents the opportunity to take an active part in the development of the curriculum. They are able to influence what goes on in school and the nature of the learning process. Parents like the opportunity to participate and share in their child's learning. This is often emphasized at parental meetings. One parent stated that the child becomes the teacher and that the parent takes on the role of learner. Others have agreed that with the whole family involved, talk about school has been encouraged and a greater understanding developed. There is acceptance of the school, with IMPACT becoming an integral part of their children's learning. Perhaps these spin-offs with a subsequent change of attitude, leading to better understanding and increased cooperation, are IMPACT's greatest achievements. The response sheets begin to give clues as to home/family life, to which the perceptive teacher can react, influencing the whole curriculum. Thus the parental involvement that was originally focused on the development of mathematical understanding begins to exert an influence on all aspects of schooling. This establishment of a true learning partnership is not achieved by other home/school initiatives, by so many, so quickly.

Parents become more confident and show an increased willingness to establish a meaningful contact with the school. Increased confidence leads to a more critical assessment of what is being offered and teachers must face up to this. The more that parents realize that they can influence and affect their children's progress, the more willing they are to participate. Consequently the commitment to IMPACT increases and the initiative goes from strength to strength.

Conclusion

Ideally, if IMPACT maths is to work to its maximum effect, it should be part of a wider approach to working with parents. An open school philosophy needs to be facilitated, where parents are welcomed and valued, and feel that they can talk freely and easily to the teachers. A wide ranging home/school activities programme should be encouraged to complement the home/school curriculum work. Thus parents are not seen solely as someone to help the child with a home activity and all other forms of contact with the school are limited. If a quality dialogue is to be established for IMPACT (and all other contact with the school), then the home/school maths scheme should be simply one of a variety of strategies utilized to involve parents in their children's education.

IMPACT maths can become a tool for developing a whole school approach to work with parents. Its introduction to the school may come from one or two teachers, but when implemented successfully, the pressure from pupils and parents alike often results in the vast majority of teachers within the school implementing the scheme. In this manner almost all teachers are drawn in to work with parents, whereas with the more traditional home/school work, which has evolved over the years, the responsbility for involving parents rested solely on the shoulders of one person, i.e. the head, a home/school liaison teacher or colleague with a similar interest. Already we are finding that IMPACT maths has awakened the awareness of many teachers, who previously were sceptical, as to the importance of a whole school policy for working with parents. Home/school work was previously seen as a peripheral activity of minor importance. Now it is becoming acknowledged as a central issue for all teachers. IMPACT maths has therefore enabled some Humberside schools to improve significantly the quality of their home/school links and particularly in a shorter period of time than by traditional methods.

Finally, the potential for utilizing parents to reinforce the work of the school is also being recognized in other subject areas. Already the home/school maths approach has led to home/school science and special needs activities. It is our aim to take this approach into other subject areas when appropriate. When such a goal is achieved, and parents, the home and community are fully acknowledged and recognized as a considerable educational force, then collectively the efforts of all concerned will help raise standards of education. Teachers in time will appreciate that they cannot undertake this responsibility alone — the support, commitment and goodwill of parents must be seen as an integral part of the educational process. Again, IMPACT is enabling teachers and parents to share the responsibility for the education of the children.

IMPACT maths on Humberside has given a fresh and radical impetus to our home/school work and teaching methodology. A small seed has been sown, which is already flourishing, but from all the indicators so far, it will bear much fruit for many years to come. The chance meeting with Ruth Merttens in Oxford has certainly paid dividends.

Reference

WIDLAKE, P. and MACLEOD, F. (1984) *Raising Standards*, Coventry, Community Education Development Centre.

Chapter 8

IMPACT in the Urban Authority

David Bristow

David Bristow provides a detailed description of the introduction of IMPACT into an urban LEA in the years 1987–89. He recalls the discussions and assumptions which were formative in setting up the project in Redbridge and analyzes the effects of the structures and mechanisms created over the two years. He talks about the 'success' of IMPACT and tries to pinpoint the ways in which it came to be judged and evaluated. Finally, he reviews the practical difficulties involved in setting up and running IMPACT as a 'steady state' mode of practice in a school or LEA.

Early Aims

When I arrived in Redbridge as the new Mathematics Adviser, I was delighted to find that the IMPACT project had already made preliminary contact with the Chief Inspector and the Principal Inspector Primary. The borough was committed to becoming one of the three founding authorities. I had only to agree that the proposed development did sound worthwhile, and take part in appointing our first advisory teacher for IMPACT.

I doubt if anyone involved in the project at that stage had a clear idea of where it would lead. In Redbridge, we joined the project because of our conviction that involving parents in their children's learning of mathematics must be a 'Good Thing'.

In less flippant terms, all involved in the primary advisory team believed firmly that home and school should form a partnership and that IMPACT had the potential for developing this beyond the shared reading schemes which many of our schools operated. From the mathematics point of view, we hoped that it would allow pupils to see mathematics in real contexts and to gain practical experiences. These experiences should be much easier to organize at home, where the adult to child ratio for this kind of work is likely to be one to one, than at school where teachers have to deal with much larger groups.

A Five-Year Development Plan

How did we envisage the life of the project would work out? We had a choice of two different approaches. Either the project could concentrate on excellence in a small number of schools — however excellence would be defined — or we could hope for a lesser effect in a larger number of schools. Most concerned in Redbridge felt that if a development of this kind were good for one school it would be of benefit for all, and no one wanted mathematics to take up a disproportionate share of curriculum and preparation time in any school, as this would distort the balance of the primary curriculum for their children.

Another factor in long-term planning was that we were determined that whatever progress was made would remain long after the original project team had disbanded. As the project was intended to last for three years, our long-term vision therefore took the form of a more or less explicit five-year plan. Our hope was that we could have all schools in the borough operating IMPACT in five years' time. This expectation was always unrealistic even before the Education Reform Act and the National Curriculum, but it did condition our thinking about the necessary scale of development, and how long each phase should take. Phase 1 — a grand title for the first year of advisory teacher work — would therefore see six schools' pilot developments with two teachers each. In the second year these phase 1 schools would then expand IMPACT within the school to take on more teachers with more classes, and another six phase 2 schools would start IMPACT from scratch. During this second year we would develop whatever packs of materials, handbooks and teachers' materials that we needed to introduce schools to IMPACT, so that in the third year we would impose no restrictions, but would take on any schools in the borough that wished to join.

How would phase 1 and 2 schools be chosen? They would clearly have to be schools which were keen to start IMPACT, but would be representative of the schools in Redbridge so that any conclusions reached would be applicable elsewhere. Their headteachers would have to be committed to the aims of the project, and be prepared to give the necessary support in staff time and other resources.

Fitting IMPACT into the School Structure

As ideas took shape over time, we realized that the kind of grass roots development the project team had in mind with teachers writing their own sheets weekly and without reference to others was not our ideal model, but that we would prefer a more formal approach. The authority had a well motivated and relatively stable staff. Nevertheless it seemed to us that teachers are entitled to a home life, and that it was up to the development team not only to try to improve mathematics teaching for the children of the borough, but to do this without expecting an inordinate amount of commitment from the teachers involved. Even if we were able to find enough teachers to make the 'total commitment' kind of model work during the development phase, this model would not be sustainable when the project expanded into other classrooms and schools. Furthermore, our aim of making IMPACT accessible to all schools in the authority conditioned our view of how ambitious we were prepared to be in asking teachers to prepare their own sheets, how often they should send sheets home, and what kind of support would be needed from the school management.

Our intention in developing IMPACT was therefore to keep it in proportion, and to make it an integral part of school life. If it were to survive as more than a flash in the pan, IMPACT work in a school would need to be more than an optional extra introduced by a small number of very keen and charismatic teachers. It would need to become embedded into the structure of the school and parents would need to hear about it not as a special development in mathematics, but as part of the school's policy for partnership with the home. If we were able to achieve this, parents would hear about IMPACT from others on the parental grapevine, and many would come to the school knowing what was expected from them and asking questions of the school if the IMPACT work they were expecting did not materialize. Likewise, teachers would view IMPACT as a standard part of the school's work and newcomers would be able to call on advice and support from colleagues in this area of work as in every other.

At this stage, I do not think we formulated our ideas more clearly than that, but that did condition our subsequent thinking about the way in which the project should develop in Redbridge, what qualities our IMPACT coordinator should have, and what arguments we would have with the central development team.

A Resource Bank of Materials or Support for Teachers Writing Their Own?

An immediate question was how IMPACT work should be generated. Ideologues of the 'best IMPACT sheet is a blank sheet of paper' persuasion argued passionately that the only way for teachers to make good IMPACT sheets was to write all their materials themselves, starting from scratch, while the opposing view was caricatured as the 'off the shelf' lobby who did not believe in teachers doing any writing themselves (see Merttens and Vass, 1990, for details of this point). The argument on the one hand was that work generated by an individual teacher would be designed for the actual class itself, would be planned more carefully and would be more related to the actual work taking place in the classroom at that time. The counter-argument was that teachers are extremely busy, and while they are quite welcome to write their own material if they wish, they deserve everything possible to be done to make their lives easy.

These apparently diametrically opposing views have gradually synthesized into the situation that we have now, where there is a resource bank of material, but there is also considerable support for teachers who wish to edit material to suit their own particular situation or to write completely new material. This situation has come about because as material has been written, it has been edited and stored, and where teachers orginally had little choice but to write their own material they can now choose from a vast bank of materials written and tried by other teachers. In addition, many tasks have been put onto discs so that editing a sheet to suit local requirements is very easy — but still comes out looking good. Different subsets of the resource bank and teachers' guides have been identified to make it more accessible to teachers who come to it fresh — there are 'starter kits' for example — and it has been cross-referenced to the National Curriculum and also collected under common primary topics. As the project has gone on, many schools are also starting to identify their own school resource banks to avoid problems where pupils could be given materials that they have used in previous years.

At the same time no one wanted to stifle teachers' creativity or reduce their ability to respond to the interests and needs of their children, so apart from the wealth of materials that are available for editing, guidance is now available for teachers who wish to develop their own sheets starting from scratch.

The Position After Three Years

Our aims as originally formulated were on a grand scale, so how have they fared? At the time when the project started in Redbridge, the Education Reform Act and the National Curriculum were just over the horizon. The turmoil caused in schools by the design and publication of weighty documents one after another at a great rate clearly diverted schools' attention away from other curriculum developments, no matter how worthy. This distraction has had a considerable effect on the take-up rate for IMPACT. On the other hand, it is also true that one of the principal thrusts of the Education Reform Act is to accept the principle that parents are entitled to a great deal more information about schools than they have been in the past, and this is very much in line with the philosophy of IMPACT.

Currently, thirty-two of the borough's fifty-seven primary schools are operating IMPACT to some extent, with eighteen of these schools using sheets with most if not all of their classes. How often sheets are sent home varies according to schools' policies, but most are sending work out at least fortnightly. The number of pupils who bring work back to schools also varies. Most teachers in most schools have returns over 70 per cent, and this goes up to neary 100 per cent in some schools which have made a strong feature of IMPACT in a whole school policy. It would be tempting to look for a direct correlation between the time spent by the borough's IMPACT coordinators in particular schools and the success of IMPACT there, but this would be spurious because schools which are having difficulties may well be the ones which ask for most help.

Factors influencing success will presumably be analyzed elsewhere in rigorous research mode, but my subjective impression is that success in IMPACT — like any other educational initiative — depends on teachers being convinced that the considerable extra effort involved is not only justified by the benefits to the children, but is better expended in this way than any other. Clearly there needs to be strong support by the headteacher. Also, as expense is an issue, in many cases the extra resources for photo-copying provided by parent-teacher associations have been essential for success. Some schools have had extra difficulties, perhaps where there has been a particularly high staff turnover or where there is not a strong tradition of contact with parents. Nevertheless, the experience overall suggests that no factors preclude success on IMPACT if it is introduced with sufficient will.

Two-Way Learning Processes

One of the most important features of IMPACT for me has been the number of different two-way learning processes that have been taking place. As a new adviser, my own involvement with the IMPACT team has enabled me to develop expertise in primary mathematics education much more rapidly than would have been possible otherwise. On the other hand, in the early stages the central IMPACT team seemed to be unaware of the monster they would unleash as they set about converting the whole of three authorities to their way of thinking about IMPACT.[1] This process, however, proved merely to be a curtain-raiser to the attempt to take the whole country by storm with the IMPACT National Network. I suspect one of the qualities that has carried the team through has been an unerring skill for bringing things down to earth — who else would have thought of naming the three reports of the Task Group on Assessment and Testing 'Daddy Bear, Mummy Bear and Baby Bear'?

At another level, the relationships between parents and teachers have been changing the perceptions of many members of both groups. On the one hand many teachers have seen IMPACT as a way of showing parents the kind of maths that is taking place in school, and of convincing them how valuable it can be. As an adviser it has not been my function on the project to collect evidence systematically, but if the large number of anecdotes of the type 'I knew he could do sums but I never realized that he wouldn't know what sum to do in a real situation' can be accepted as evidence, then this approach has met with considerable success. Many parents are much better informed about the need for practical experience, the power of games to motivate practice in arithmetic, and the importance of paying attention to their children's attitudes to the subject. Teachers have also learned a considerable amount directly from parents. In some cases this has not been a happy experience for them — some parents are not as diplomatic as colleagues in school or members of the advisory service — but there are some teachers and schools who are now more systematic about their planning for progression and continuity as a result of starting dialogue with parents via the medium of IMPACT.

One of the original aims of the central team was that IMPACT would provide a mechanism for in-service training for teachers. The 'third person' idea was that an advisory teacher who comes to assist a teacher prepare sheets for sending home should find it easier to influence practice than one who comes with the overt aim of directly changing what the teacher does. This aim was not one which we adopted explicitly in Redbridge, though we did generally hope that teachers might shift their practice more in the direction of practically based group work. In fact, there have been considerable benefits from this kind of in-service training. It is notoriously hard to quantify the effects of in-service training, particularly from the point of view of cost-effectiveness, but it seems likely that this type of approach has paid dividends (see Chapter (16) for details of third person INSET).

What Has Changed as a Result of IMPACT?

The crucial question is what has changed for the children as a result of introducing IMPACT to the borough? It would be tempting to look at the current practice in IMPACT schools and classes and to ascribe all the changes to IMPACT. This conclusion would not be fair because IMPACT is only one of a myriad changes over the last three years, and teasing apart the different causes and effects is almost impossible.

Nevertheless, from my own visits to schools and discussions with colleagues in schools and in the advisory service it seems that the most far-reaching change to take place over the period of the project is that schools now pay much more attention to planning, plan with more rigour, looking at concepts and skills as well as content areas, and plan over a longer time scale (up to seven years in some cases!). IMPACT has certainly not created this effect on its own, because much of the impetus has come from the National Curriculum and the training that the whole of the advisory service has provided, but it has reinforced this trend and gained momentum from it.

Looking at particular schools and trying to analyze changes, those that have espoused IMPACT most wholeheartedly and have gained most from it seem to be middle-of-the-road schools with steady management. These schools had no difficulties with the mechanisms of home/school liaison, with planning requirements or with the routine of preparing pupils for taking work home or following it up, but seem to have gained a great deal from the stimulus of IMPACT and the advisory teacher input. They have produced some exciting work as pupils do more adventurous and practically based work at home and bring their results into school for teachers to follow up. It is also very pleasing to see the realization of our aim that IMPACT should become a natural part of the work of these schools with, for example, questions being asked routinely in selection interviews about home/school liaison, including PACT and IMPACT.

Some other schools which have produced exciting IMPACT work have been ones which have previously relied very little on published schemes but have had the confidence to develop mathematics themselves from other resources and real situations. The effect here, partly as a result of feedback from parents, has been to tighten up their programmes and to pay more attention to continuity and progression.

Overall, the general effect in all schools has been for teachers to gain confidence in their own abilities to plan relevant mathematics activities for their children without the mechanical routine of a published scheme, and that schools have become much more autonomous and independent of the assistance of the advisory teacher. Turning to children's direct experiences outside mathematics, there is considerable anecdotal evidence that children have become better able to give instructions as a result of the responsibility thrust upon them to explain their IMPACT sheets to their parents or others at home.

Why Has It Worked?

The success of the project has been considerable, and it is worth trying to analyze why this is the case. The main factor is that teachers have seen the benefits of trying to extend their partnership with parents into the area of mathematics. They have not only seen IMPACT as a way of increasing the learning that pupils can achieve in mathematics, but also as a way of educating parents to see the importance and difficulty of helping young children to understand concepts rather than to learn by rote. More prosaically, they have also seen it as a relatively painless way of introducing more practical experience of mathematics into the curriculum. (As IMPACT support teachers point out, how many teachers could cope with a classful of children measuring the girth of their budgerigars or using Persil and cornflakes for measuring volume!)

Headteachers have seen IMPACT as a way of influencing practice in their schools, and some schools have seen it as a way of giving coherence to their curriculum. Parents on the other hand seem to have welcomed the chance to see at first-hand what their children are expected to do in mathematics, and to engage in dialogue with their children's teachers.

The introduction of the National Curriculum could have destroyed the impetus of IMPACT developments. The fact that it did not is partly attributable to the quick reaction of the team in ensuring that IMPACT materials were cross-referenced to the National Curriculum, and partly because the philosophy of IMPACT was in tune with the spirit of the National Curriculum as embodied in the non-statutory guidance. Attainment Target 1, for example, requires children to apply mathematics to real situations and to talk about their mathematics. This kind of experience is very difficult to provide in a classroom with large groups of children, but is much easier to organize via IMPACT materials at home with individual attention from an adult. At a more strategic level, the moves towards structure, accountability and openness implicit in the Education Reform Act also mirrored and reinforced the aims of IMPACT

Conclusion

The conclusion does seem to be that children can gain a good deal when their schools take part in IMPACT, and that in a steady state, the amount of extra work for teachers will not be prohibitive. Nevertheless all concerned in the development phase in Redbridge have been very committed and as a relatively minor contributor I would like to acknowledge the privilege I feel from being involved with a group of teachers who have been prepared to give their time so willingly for the benefit of their children.

Acknowledgments

Finally, the success of the project is a very great tribute to the charisma of the central team and the dedication of our IMPACT coordinators in Redbridge, Peter Huckstep and Su Bloomfield. All those involved with IMPACT in Redbridge owe them a great debt.

Note

1 In fact, the three piloting LEAs were very strong supporters of the developing IMPACT philosophy. Frequently the IMPACT team was simply required to suggest possible strategies rather than to convert unwilling disciples.

Reference

MERTTENS, R. and VASS, J. (1990) *Sharing Maths Cultures*, London, Falmer Press.

Chapter 9

IMPACT: Changes in a Support Teacher's Role

Margaret Williams

Margaret Williams, an advisory support teacher in Devon, outlines how working with IMPACT has changed her role. She describes how she sets up IMPACT in Devon schools, the difficulties attendant upon working with a large number of far-flung schools, and the nine-point plan she has adopted to cope with these problems. She suggests that IMPACT has also changed the teachers' perceptions of her work, and Margaret explains how she feels this has improved the quality of the support she is able to offer.

The names of teaching schemes range from the corny to the obscure, passing through the pretentious on the way. IMPACT is aptly and descriptively named. In schools where it has been adopted it makes differences which can be seen and felt.

Devon is a large authority with around 450 primary schools. A substantial proportion of them have one or two teachers only and many are village schools. The schools are 'clustered' into academic councils, which consist of about eleven or twelve primary schools, who usually, but not always, feed one secondary school. The county is divided for administrative purposes into four regions — North, South, East and West. The two primary maths advisers have two regions each, one dealing with the East and South, and the other with the North and West. There is a variety of provision across Devon with some middle schools in Exeter (5–8 and 8–12), and Tiverton (5–9 and 9–13). In Torquay, Plymouth and parts of East Devon there is an 11-plus and some 25–30 per cent of the children go to grammar schools.

Advisory Support Teachers

A team of five advisory support teachers exist to support primary maths in schools. Each member of a team works in a particular region: one in the South, one in the North, one in the West and two in the East. By comparison with some other authorities, there is a degree of flexibility in how the support teachers' time is allocated. Schools request time, which may involve anything from a one-off session, to a term's regular and sustained work in a school. The support teachers respond to needs, not only from individual schools but also from the academic councils. Advisers oversee timetables which are supplied once a week, and there are comprehensive end-of-term reports.

Home Involvement Before IMPACT

As part of the PRIME project, South Devon schools in which I was then working had already been actively engaged in looking at ways of involving parents in the maths curriculum. Some of the outcomes of this work had been very exciting. Some parents of children with special educational needs came into school at 3:30 p.m. and worked alongside their children. Another group of parents joined in with a regular Monday morning maths club. In many schools, parents designed and made games for their children to use at home. This particular idea was so successful that in one school, having re-viewed the 100 games made, parents decided to organize a games work-shop in school, which they ran themselves.

There were numerous other examples of good parental participation and many teachers who were happy about parents helping with the maths curriculum — the climate was right . . . but we had not yet met Ruth Merttens and IMPACT. After hearing Ruth's exposition at the Bath MATHSWEST Conference, I came back full of enthusiasm to get IMPACT launched in Devon. After meetings had been arranged between the IMPACT team and senior advisers, I was delighted to hear that Devon was to be included in the IMPACT network. This decision was not a surprising one in that IMPACT represented a natural extension of the work we were already involved with in Devon. IMPACT:

— followed up our specific work involving parents and National Curriculum delivery;
— provided a means of focusing the INSET provision in Devon schools;
— was perceived as a means of raising parents' awareness of the nature and purpose of the maths INSET in Devon.

Getting IMPACT Started

Coercing or choosing schools to be IMPACT schools would not, in Devon, have been an appropriate method of obtaining the required six or ten schools to start the project off. We therefore asked the IMPACT team to provide a series of awareness-raising sessions to which all schools in the area where a session was held would be invited, enabling schools to make their own choice as to whether to opt in at this early stage. Many schools adopted a policy of 'wait-and-see', but I was pleased that we found fifteen, (seven in West Devon and eight in the South) initial project schools without difficulty.

Allowing schools to 'opt in' rather than selecting them has had many advantages. We were never in a position of having to decide upon the criteria as to whether a school would be an IMPACT school or not. The policy in Devon has been that as schools express interest in joining IMPACT, we have a system of induction in which they are free to participate, and thereafter it is up to them. A limited number of schools receive substantial support in terms of help with planning the curriculum, assistance with parent meetings and so on. Some schools get a small amount of help and some schools basically go it alone with only the odd telephone conversation. All schools participate in the IMPACT INSET programme, provided by the IMPACT team. I have been surprised at the steady stream of schools who have wanted to be added to the list of IMPACT schools in Devon.

Acceptance of IMPACT depended to some extent on the established attitudes and methods of the teachers. Some found it easy to make the necessary plans while others frequently expressed doubts about the level of cooperation which would be forthcoming from parents and concern for those children who would not get the opportunity to take part in the home-based activities. Many teachers felt sure that some parents — and they often said that they could predict which ones they were — would not take part, or that the quality of support at home would not be very high. Some teachers were of the opinion that if all the children were not able to share the activity at home, if was unfair to build classwork around the IMPACT activity. Some were concerned that IMPACT would further disadvantage children already disadvantaged because of their parents' attitudes.

However, other schools took a more positive view and were less sure about which parents would and would not participate. They felt that it was worth giving IMPACT a try and they were convinced by the argument put forward by the IMPACT team that it was unprofitable, even dangerous, to make too many assumptions in advance. They were determined to look for as much support from parents as possible and to value any work the children were able to bring into class from home. Some schools are working with 100 per cent involvement throughout the schools, while others have accepted a more gradual start.

The question also arose as to which teachers were to be involved in the IMPACT schools. It has to be admitted that in those few schools where some pressure has been exerted on particular teachers to participate, the results are less encouraging than where teachers have expressed a willingness or enthusiasm to opt in. Some teachers became defensive when set tasks were queried by parents. Typical comments from such teachers included, 'I am the professional, I do the teaching', or 'Parents can't teach'. On the other hand, many teachers overcame or did not share these reservations.

Planning IMPACT in Schools

Soon we were ready to plan our IMPACT activities for the first half-term. I was surprised by the detailed plans which each teacher had made for their term's work, and even more surprised that they were opening their books and saying, 'Take a look'. Planning became a shared activity where teachers freely contributed ideas to each other. The extent to which IMPACT is an 'added extra' depends upon the school and the individual teachers' approaches, which is also true of the extent of the support with planning that is requested and given. It is true that planning can be with individual teachers or with the whole staff. We usually start in a group together, discussing topic work and suggesting a variety of tasks and we then move into smaller groups, and/or individual classrooms, to discuss specific detailed plans. In this situation, my work is more on a consultancy basis than a constant presence.

Because of the slow but steady drift of schools into the IMPACT project in Devon, I have had to devise a nine-point plan of campaign for the introduction and running of IMPACT in any one school. It works as follows:

1 A member of staff, or sometimes two or three, have come to an awareness-raising session provided by the IMPACT team in Devon.
2 I then follow this interest up with a staff meeting so that all the teachers in a school can get to hear about IMPACT and ask any questions.
3 I leave the school for a couple of weeks to let them discuss IMPACT among themselves at leisure.
4 The school then gets back in contact with me to tell me if they have decided to go ahead and with which classes.
5 I attend a second staff meeting, the purpose of which is mainly organizational. We agree how we shall plan together, with individual teachers or in groups, and when this will take place. We decide on the format and number of the initial parent meetings, and which staff will attend.
6 We meet to plan IMPACT and the maths curriculum for the next six or so weeks.
7 We have a launch day when we hold three or four parent meetings.
8 Sometime later I will return to the school for a 'How's it all going?' meeting. Quite often we will be in touch by telephone before this meeting, especially if there are any particular hiccups or surprising events.
9 About a term or a term and a half after IMPACT first started, we will hold a follow-up parent meeting. This is to enable the parents to let us know if there are things they find particularly rewarding, or other things which they would like to see adapted or changed.

This system is not a rigid one, and adaptations are made according to individual schools' needs. Sometimes a teacher or a school will have heard about IMPACT indirectly rather than through an awareness-raising session, and my staff meeting will have to be more informative than discursive. Sometimes a school will feel that they would prefer to plan without any outside support and will simply request a bank of suitable materials to help them with ideas. Other schools prefer to run their own parent meetings, and so on. However, the structure outlined above has worked insofar as it has enabled me to give varying levels of support to a large number of schools.

Introducing IMPACT to Parents and Their Responses

Once schools had accepted their role, the next stage was the introduction of IMPACT to parents. At this point I and many of the schools were surprised at the magnitude of the response. In most schools the turnout at meetings far exceeded that customarily received in both numbers and enthusiasm. Many parents already help their children, managing as best they can — and were therefore pleased to be better informed about what we do and reassured that their participation was welcome. Even at initial meetings, parents showed a willingness to undertake the tasks prescribed and seriously considered the possibility of increasing them. One father said he thought there should be an IMPACT activity every other evening! Other comments reflecting the level and degree of parental support were:

> We are willing to pay each week for the photocopying of the IMPACT sheets even though we are poor.

> I will do all the photocopying of the sheets.

and in one school,

> I will do all the photocopying at home on my machine for nothing.

At subsequent meetings, after their experience of IMPACT in their homes, comments ran as follows:

> IMPACT gives us good quality time spent together.

> There is better communication between us now.

> At last we have something we can sit down and do with the youngest of our children.

Other parents felt that they could help the teachers with drawing up the actual IMPACT sheets and drafting a sentence explaining the area of work to be covered that week. In one school, parents were invited into schools to be part of the process by which IMPACT activities were planned and selected.

This is not to say that there have been no alternative viewpoints:

> My child will only learn to be numerate if she does the same sort of sums that I did [said by a parent of a nursery child].

Most children have responded with enthusiasm. They are happy to take their IMPACT tasks home and clearly enjoy the shared experience of their completion. They feel a sense of ownership for this work and gain a feeling of status from organizing their own education. Even judging from the simple criteria of the IMPACT comment sheets, there has been a steady change from, 'Went well, learned a little', to 'Went very well, learned a lot'.

Effect Upon My Role as Maths Support Teacher

I find that IMPACT has altered considerably how I work in that it has enabled me to provide maths support for teachers within the context of a much less threatening situation than previously existed. Through IMPACT, I am invited to plan with teachers which means that I am able to have an input at a crucial stage in the teacher's work. The teacher and I are jointly focusing upon the specific details of the involvement of parents in the maths curriculum. We are *not* concentrating upon her/his adequacies or inadequacies as a teacher of maths. This enables the teacher to share ideas, ask for assistance and express areas of uncertainty in non-threatening situations. This ease was brought home to me when one teacher actually commented upon how comfortable she felt in the planning situation with me because it was so 'non-threatening'.

Too often support teachers have, rightly or wrongly, been perceived in the past as coming in and telling the teacher how to teach, but I now find that teachers actually start asking questions. The IMPACT materials act as a starting point for the teacher's own development. We study the materials, often together, and jointly construct a suitable scheme of work, which generates a feeling of security rather than danger, and the teacher gains in confidence as a result.

IMPACT has enabled me to be far more responsive to individual needs and schools' or teachers' particular contexts. I have found myself much less inclined to make general statements and more able to be specific in referring to the details of the situation, which I believe has improved the quality of the support that I am able to offer to teachers.

Of course, it is true that I am myself committed to the aims and philosophy of IMPACT. As time has gone by, the development of the three-part relation between parents, teachers and children has proved its worth, not only in terms of the mathematical progress of the children, but in the broader aspects of interpersonal relationships. Children, parents and teachers are conscious of a partnership which all find meaningful, successful and rewarding.

Chapter 10

Child-Centredness, IMPACT and the National Curriculum

Ian Lewis

Ian Lewis, a curriculum development officer in Wales, looks at the National Curriculum and at the effects it is having on teacher's conversations, the accounts they have to produce and the assumptions they make explicit. He discusses the difference between the view implicit in the National Curriculum and those justifications explicitly given by teachers who describe themselves as operating a 'child-centred curriculum'. He argues that many of the practices which teachers have come to adopt in order to fulfil the requirements of the National Curriculum may not be those which the exponents of parental partnership programmes such as IMPACT most want to see.

I recently reread an article (Kelly, 1986) which recalls many of the concerns which I have about primary education at this moment. One paragraph, amusingly, summarized my greatest worry:

There is one shoe manufacturer whose television advertisement reveals more awareness of the individuality of children's feet than most current political pronouncements on the curriculum reveal of the individualities of their minds or personalities. Education is at least as personal and individual a matter as health or diet.

I wish that I had penned that comment, particularly after some recent visits I have made to schools.

I suppose all education advisers have schools which they enjoy visiting more than others. I certainly have! These schools, if they are like those on my list, are generally characterized by the warmth of their welcome, by the vitality and fizz which emanates from them, by the understanding they display of the way in which children learn and by the fact that parents are as welcome as professional colleagues and are treated with the same respect. As Kris William wrote in *Child Education* in October 1987,

> When I go into my ordinary village primary school which my two youngest children attend, I am treated as a senior partner in the team responsible for their education; a team which includes teachers, family and friends, and of course, the children themselves.

I wonder how ordinary a village primary school that really was! I visited such a school recently. It was a large infant school with twelve staff, one which I had visited many times before. Sited on a large estate, which could hardly be described as stimulating, the school itself has always provided a haven of culture, security and colour, and had provided a succession of quality experiences all designed to encourage the children's educational and social development. Staff had taken care to identify children's needs and to respond to them. The fact that the children were open and honest in their relationships with all adults in the school (including visitors) was a tribute to their teachers. On this occasion, however, I was able to relate only briefly with the children. I was at the school for a staff meeting. The agenda read simply 'Reviewing Implementation of the National Curriculum'.

I sat and listened to the staff for awhile as they discussed some of their successes and failures. It became very clear that their real concerns were two-fold — how to implement the new science curriculum and how to organize the reception classes (three of them) which contained 4-and 5-year-olds. In discussing the latter issue they were concerned that they should be effectively meeting the demands of the National Curriculum.

As the conversation developed my spirits sank lower and lower — a staff which had always identified the needs of the children had been changed into one which seemed more concerned with the National Curriculum. They were not discussing *teaching* young children, simply *delivering* the National Curriculum and meeting its demands. After awhile I could listen no longer and reminded them that the National Curriculum is not set in stone, that it will have to be modified in the light of experience and that they (good practitioners) should be the very people to modify it in order that it accommodates more closely the needs of children.

On another occasion recently I met a teacher with whom I had taught for several years. She had always displayed real originality and creativity — a person of considerable talent and flair. I enquired how she was coping with the new arrangements only to be told that she had been to the local career office and was searching for a post outside teaching. Her comments were illuminating. She stated,

> I do not think that I can deliver all that I am being asked to deliver but above all I cannot work under all these restraints with the feeling that I am constantly tied down.

Ian Lewis

The Early Effects of the National Curriculum

Personally, I find this type of experience alarming, suggesting, as it does, that the National Curriculum, which was supposed to lead to a raising in the quality of children's educational experiences, seems instead to have altered the focus of school provision to narrower curriculum demands. Orienting to narrower demands can, ironically, shift attention away from teaching in-depth, as I shall argue below. We must examine the consequences of this shift on an approach that has been dubbed 'child-centredness'.

It is fair, however, to point out that the early effects of the National Curriculum are not all bad. In particular, there was been a dramatic change in the level of whole school planning which is going on. In fact, the National Curriculum has achieved more in six months than many years of exhortation had managed in this field. There are obviously considerable benefits which come from this amount of planning:

— The likelihood of pointless repetition of work should be decreased;
— There is the opportunity to build on previous experiences and extend them;
— Staff are able to share information, skills and resources more easily;
— Resources can be managed more effectively.

In addition, the focus on assessment and record keeping has meant that some teachers, perhaps for the first time, have had to focus attention on individual children and their needs. They have, as a result of this pressure, also focused their attention on the ways in which classrooms are managed and organized to allow for all modes of teaching — class, group and individual. Long-advocated collaborative groupwork is, in some classrooms, becoming reality for the first time, and many teachers are enjoying the experience.

What, therefore, are the dangers in the current situation? I believe that this question can be answered quite simply: The subject documents of the National Curriculum (the Statutory Orders) were initially prepared by those with great subject expertise with very little advice from effective practitioners. As a result of this subject-based 'expertise' approach (alien to the primary school) we may see a fragmentation of the curriculum, leading to:

— A level of content or knowledge which is far too great and much of it irrelevant to the primary child,
— A level of record keeping which is too detailed and inappropriate with this age group,
— An overburdening of primary school teachers who are required to introduce too much, too quickly,
— A level of training for staff which is highly disruptive for children.

All of these pressures could mean that effective practitioners might resort to the 'stuffing in of knowledge' with less attention given to the provision of appropriate, demanding, effective and exciting learning experiences for children.

It is important, at this point in time, for people in primary education to restate what they mean by good primary practice and to convey this to themselves and the public at large. In a perhaps necessary and certainly an understandable move to reappraise educational methods, much of the work of the last twenty years is being rubbished. Those decades were times of considerable experimentation and innovation, a remarkably creative and lively period in education. However, the move to jettison in their entirety any methods or styles which evolved throughout this period smacks strongly of repression rather than a genuine desire to improve children's educational experiences or to raise standards, and almost certainly involves throwing out the baby with the proverbial bathwater. There is no unified or uniform pedagogy common to the approach which came to be known as 'child-centred', and any attempt to suggest that this is so ignores the variety and diversity of the strategies and skills which teachers have developed over this period of time, some of which are likely to more than prove their worth as we move into the next century with a National Curriculum. It seems important to make two statements.

— A curriculum is not necessarily broad, balanced, relevant or differentiated simply because it contains elements of all the areas of experience described in *Curriculum Matters 2* (DES, 1985). All of the areas of experience also need to contain content which is broad, balanced, relevant and differentiated;
— A curriculum which is broad, balanced, relevant and differentiated may not be effective if it lacks depth and it is this aspect of the curriculum which may be most damaged by the National Curriculum as teachers respond to the pressures of time.

When the experiences children are provided with are poor it is often because they lack depth. In science, for example, this often means that they only develop the skills of following instructions, observation, measurement and recording. They are not encouraged to develop the higher skills of controlling variables, making fair tests, predicting and hypothesizing. In music they may listen to music and sing but are not encouraged to compose. In mathematics they may not apply what they have learned to real life situations or in problem solving or investigations. They may not develop the ability to think mathematically, logically and coherently, to structure their findings and systematize their investigations. In English, they may learn to read, but may never choose to do so. They may decode words but never read a book. They may copy lines of writing but never write for themselves. It is in planning and providing a curriculum which displays depth that we encourage children to think for themselves by providing experiences which are intellectually challenging.

The *mode* of delivery of the curriculum is vital to its success. This point was highlighted fairly recently in an HMI Report on the quality of educational provision in my own authority which reiterated a number of truisms about teaching and learning. They included:

— The need for the child to be actively involved in his/her learning;
— The need for the work to be matched to the ability level of the child;
— The need for teaching to be responsive to individual needs;
— The need for children to work collaboratively in groups as well as individually and in a whole class;
— The need for a range of experiences which are innately interesting or made interesting for the child in order to maturate learning.

The Welsh Office Publication *Curriculum and Organisation of Primary Schools in Wales* (1984) summarizes much of what is worth saying about the primary curriculum in these three paragraphs:

'The way in which children respond illuminates the quality of the provision. Their response will be wholehearted (or whole-minded) only when they recognise that they are in with a chance — in other words, that care has been taken to match their activities to their abilities, experiences, interests and aptitudes. Such opportunities occur within a climate where communication flourishes and where relationships are such that errors are not regarded as deadly sins but as guides for future learning'.

Developing Personal Qualities

Primary education, at its most successful, is based on the characteristics of the children it seeks to serve. The personal development of children has to be viewed alongside the needs of contemporary society, recognizing that the development of personal qualities affects the quality of life in society. Schools therefore, should be so organized as to allow (indeed, stimulate) scope for the development of personal qualities in children, to promote the refining development of their gifts and graces, to encourage belief in themselves through a building-up of their confidence in themselves and their abilities, while at the same time providing a secure ambience within which respect for each other underpins the work they do and within which the children themselves feel that their dignity is respected. It follows, therefore, that education within this phase should be primarily *cooperative* and not primarily *competitive*.

The child should be personally involved in her/his learning; much of her/his work should demand something of her/his very self and the exploration of ideas, emotion and experiences should be the basis of what is done. What the child learns should help her/him think for her/himself and convey meaning clearly, make reasoned judgments and choices in a rapidly changing world, and become aware of her/himself as a unique individual, but one having responsibilities towards others. It is this emphasis on the individuality of the child that we are currently in danger of diminishing. Richard Pring (1986) recently written:

> In the more utilitarian ethos of the present times, where the value of teaching lies in the economic and social purposes that it serves, we are in danger of forgetting the person to be educated.

Discussing the Curriculum with Parents

What has all this discussion to do with IMPACT? It is my opinion that the work of those involved in this project (and that which has developed at Haringay, Kirklees and others) which have involved parents and teachers working together in a close professional partnership, have helped to create the climate in many schools where a dialogue about the nature of the curriculum has already developed. Those schools are now in a very strong position to take part in the debate about education and to motivate parents to contribute. In the continued discussions, I believe, parents are likely to be a key force in influencing decisions for better or worse. IMPACT and other projects like it can ensure that this influence is far the better and I will offer one or two examples of how this has happened.

At a recent joint meeting of parents and teachers to discuss the introduction of IMPACT into a school, several parents were questioning the schooling they had received and asked about the place of learning tables and doing sums. The headteacher tackled this in an interesting way. She posed the question 'How do you best learn?' and split the parents into groups to provide the answer. (Teachers worked in their own groups). It was interesting that all groups, teachers and parents, having been asked to do so, produced a very similar list of factors which helped them learn. These included:

— a clear explanation of what is required,
— the opportunity to do it for myself,
— the chance to talk to somebody else about it,
— the opportunity to reflect on what I have done (to let it sink in) and to come back again and try again,
— the opportunity to apply what is being learned in a different context,
— the need for time to learn — without being rushed,
— the need to enjoy the experience,
— the need to feel successful.

It was then pointed out to parents that children learn in much the same way and that effective teachers create the opportunities described above for them. It was also pointed out that, time-consuming though this is, it is well worth the effort

Later in the evening one of the parents again raised the question of tables implying that they should be 'chanted until known'. The need for children to learn their tables was agreed but the parents were fascinated when staff went on to explain the need for practical activities which involved the grouping of numbers, the building of number staircases, the drawing of graphs and so on which would build the necessary understanding for effective learning (at the same time they emphasized the fact that some children will need more and some children less of these activities). They also explored some of the algebraic work which could follow on from learning tables, e.g. The digital roots of the numbers in the 3 times table are obtained by adding their digits: thus the digital root of 12 is $1 + 2 = 3$. A pattern is obtained which is distinctive to this table.

3	6	9	12	15	18	21	24	27	30
			3	6	9	3	6	9	3
				3	3		3	3	

Figure 10.1   Digital Root Patterns.

Many of them spent some time working out the patterns involved in other tables. All agreed that this approach was more likely to produce children who were interested in mathematics and enthused by their learning than would the traditional approach. Again, staff emphasized that these activities, while time-consuming, were worthwhile.

Discussions of this nature, brought about in many cases through the IMPACT project, are helpful in giving parents an insight into how teachers work and why they work in the way they do. This was also illustrated in early work in my authority related to parental involvement in children's reading. The following comments came from parents in the valley of the EBBW Fach:

We were guided as to when and where to listen.

Catherine is now a keen reader and all stories hold her interest.

I am amazed at her knowledge of unusual words.

We all thought this was a smashing funny book.

The children have also enjoyed these activities:

> When I read to my mum I like the book better — it seems to make more sense.

> I'm learning things when I read at home. There is more time and we often have a laugh with a book.

Since introducing IMPACT there have been similar comments relating to mathematical activities. One involved parents in making lanterns. Parents are always asked to record any problems they encounter. The following note was received: 'Mammy didn't know how to make a lantern'. (They had nevertheless produced an excellent one which presumably involved parent and child learning together.)

Another activity involved the child in working out how many candles he/she would have blown out on all his/her birthday cakes — and to do so for another member of the family. The problem identified on this occasion was:

> James cannot count beyond twenty without help. He understood the exercise, he drew a candle for each year of his birthdays and then counted them all up. He also did this for Shep, the family dog, aged eleven.

This appears to be a case of parents being as ingenious as teachers in attempting to extend learning situations.

On other occasions the activities have involved the measurement of feet and heads in the family. One return described the difficulties of measuring the budgerigar's feet and the head of the goldfish which has to be constantly returned to the tank for reasons of survival!

All of these activities, and others like them, are important in helping to foster home/school insight and awareness mentioned above. IMPACT, however, takes matters a step further. The directors of the project have insisted, and teachers have wholeheartedly agreed, that the activities which the children take home are not seen as something separate, an extra or a bolt-on, but as an integral part of what goes on in the classroom and a natural extension of it. The need for careful planning of these activities is therefore obvious, as well as the need to communicate the outcomes of this planning in terms of objectives and activities. Advance planning and prior information are prerequisites of the IMPACT approach (and of the National Curriculum).

A further spin-off from this work is that it can also help parents form a clearer perception of their child's ability and achievement. 'James cannot count beyond twenty without help' was, in all probability, a realistic assessment of what the child could and could not do. A parent who has made such a statement is unlikely to claim that the child is at a higher level when the school reports the level a child has achieved to his/her parents.

Conclusion

The National Curriculum has endeavoured to incorporate two educational traditions. The first of these traditions lays emphasis on the processes of learning. The second tradition lays emphasis on the acquisition of knowledge. As a result there are tensions within the curriculum which will have to be resolved in the near future. The challenge of the next few years will be to ensure that we do not disconnect the acquisition of knowledge from the processes of its application or utilization. In order to achieve a reasonable synthesis it will be important for teachers to plan their work carefully, to communicate with parents and the wider community effectively and to protect the quality of children's learning tenaciously. I am sure that IMPACT has a major role to play in this debate.

References

DES (1985) *The Curriculum 5–16: Curriculum Matters 2*, London, HMSO.

KELLY, G. (1986) 'Knowledge and Curriculum Planning', London, Harper and Row.

PRING, R. (1989) 'Parental Views on TVEI', in MACLEOD, F., *Parents and Schools: The Contemporary Challenge*, London, Falmer Press.

WELSH OFFICE (1984) *Curriculum and Organisation of Primary Schools in Wales*, London, HMSO.

WILLIAM, K. (1987) Letters in '*Child Education*', October, Leamington Spa, Scholastic Press.

Chapter 11

IMPACT at the Core of the Curriculum: The Work of a Primary Maths Adviser in the New Era

David Owen

David Owen was a member of the National Curriculum Working Party on Mathematics. He is here discussing the National Curriculum in mathematics and setting out his views on how it should be monitored and its effects assessed. David describes his fears concerning possible directions in which strict adherence to an over-rigid model of the National Curriculum could take us. He also mentions the role of parents and the wider community in helping teachers to interrogate their own practice and explore its effectivity.

Local Education Authorities have for many years made links with the curriculum of individual schools in two ways. First, LEAs have monitored quality through systems of inspection and second, they have supported schools by providing advice and in-service education. These two functions have been, and to some extent still are, the responsibility of LEA advisers and inspectors.

Making judgments and providing advice cannot, sensibly, be separated. It is not possible for an adviser to provide useful advice unless he/she first of all finds out what teachers are doing and what they are thinking. Conversely, there is no point in inspecting unless one can provide pointers for future development. How advisers might best find out what teachers are doing and what they are thinking is a complex matter but it is perhaps helpful to consider some ideas about formative assessment and examine how they might look in relation to the adviser as 'teacher' working with the teacher as 'pupil'. This is not as patronizing as it sounds — rather it is recognition that we are all life-time learners. While it is to be hoped that the teacher always has something to offer the pupil, the relationship is not simply one-way. The teacher will also learn from the experience.

A concept fundamental to formative assessment is that a teacher will ask himself or herself in relation to an individual pupil, 'Where is this child now?' and 'How can I help this child towards further meanings of some value?' The adviser or inspector should similarly be asking, 'Where are these teachers (or headteachers) now?' and 'How can I help them to move their thinking forward so that the quality of educational provision for the children continues to grow?' More powerfully, the adviser/inspector might ask how he or she might foster the development of 'questioning cultures' within schools, where approaches to teaching are constantly examined and re-examined by the teachers themselves. This requires that individuals recognize that not only is learning life-long, but that it takes place best within a community of learners, where each one learns from the others. These approaches are at the opposite end of the continuum from one which is concerned with telling people what to do. Telling teachers what to do is as unlikely to meet with success as its parallel when employed with children, although, as with children, it is possible for those working in schools to 'learn the tricks' and give the impression that they are doing the right things. With so much on teachers' plates at the moment this method, of course, is a natural survival technique.

Changes to the Advisory Role

Local Education Authorities have, in the past, normally appointed two main types of adviser. First of all is the generalist who is usually concerned with issues relating to the whole curriculum, the management of schools, the appointment of staff and the supervision of probationers. Second, LEAs have traditionally had subject specialists who have been concerned with the development of their subject and considerations of how it relates to other subjects and to the curriculum as a whole. These specialists will also be deeply concerned with how learning takes place, with common patterns of development in their subject, and the way in which these developmental patterns relate to assessment.

The advent of the Education Reform Act (1988) has brought increasing demands on both types of adviser, particularly with LEAs having had a major responsibility for monitoring the work of schools in relation to the demands of the National Curriculum. Some authorities have used the introduction of the National Curriculum, coupled with the devolvement of funds to schools, as an excuse to reorganize the inspectorate so that the traditional divisions no longer apply. However, in this chapter I will be concentrating specifically upon the work of specialist mathematics advisers. Some of the challenges for mathematics advisers and primary school teachers are discussed below.

The National Curriculum is, in fact, concerned with telling teachers what to do in the sense that it provides maps for various areas of the curriculum. In mathematics these curriculum charts are mainly concerned with content, and in style they are closer to London Underground maps than to the Ordnance Survey. Some stations are clearly specified but in between we are left in the dark. There is also little indication of how the Underground systems relate either to the road network or to British Rail! This skeletal approach has a number of fortunate outcomes, the most important of which is the fact that it provides for individual initiative in relation to both content and method (within a useful national framework). However, since the National Curriculum is not, and cannot be, the final word, schools need and want help from those whose knowledge of individual subjects extends beyond the National Curriculum to fundamental principles underlying it. I believe that it is difficult if not impossible for mathematics advisers to provide this alone and that they need to be supported by teams of well-qualified and experienced advisory teachers.

The existence of the National Curriculum does not make adults or children learn in different ways. Those working most closely with teachers and headteachers will need to recognize this, take on board the issues raised early in the chapter, and examine their own 'teaching styles' in relation to their work with teachers. For example, do teachers, like children:

— need to be motived?
— learn best from first-hand experiences and reflection on these experiences?
— need to construct their own meanings?
— learn best when they have the opportunity to discuss issues with others?

The Education Reform Act emphasizes the fact that the child and the teacher are simply a part of a much wider whole. In particular, it is essential that headteachers and teachers become more concerned with the part to be played by both parents and governors in the education of children. It is here that the IMPACT project can be very powerful in helping schools to:

— articulate the mathematics curriculum for parents, teachers and the wider public,
— provide a sense of continuity between home and school in relation to children's learning,
— help teachers and parents to understand that children are not merely empty vessels waiting to be filled,
— fulfil the statutory duties in relation to reporting, but making this part of a continuous process of keeping parents informed rather than a 'one-off' event.

The National Curriculum itself, through both the Statutory Orders and Non-Statutory Guidance for mathematics, provides a national framework to set against the positions adopted by segments of the press in relation to various aspects of mathematical education. This framework can be most helpful to headteachers and staff when trying to explain to parents that children should not spend their time solely on the number aspects of maths.

Probably the biggest challenge of all is to try to keep track of what the National Curriculum is doing to mathematics education and which of the effects seem to us to be good and which look as if they are undesirable. This is clearly a job for researchers, HMI, LEA advisory services and for the NCC. As a member of the National Curriculum Mathematics Working Group, I am particularly interested — since I can be held partly responsible for things which go wrong! It is, however, unlikely that I will be applauded for the things that go right! There is no question that there is a great deal of work for teachers and advisers to do in the coming years to ensure that British primary education maintains its position as a system widely admired by educators in other countries. During the next few years I will be on the lookout for the following:

1 Are children's mathematical experiences in schools derived solely from the National Curriculum Statements of Attainment?
2 Are children being 'pushed' by the National Curriculum specifications and by the demands of reported assessments, into mathematics at a high level too quickly?
3 Is there a growth in 'base-line' assessment at the age of 5? If so, are these assessments damaging?
4 Is there a growth of 'setting by ability' in mathematics? What are the effects of this upon the mathematics curriculum, the curriculum as a whole, and the children?
5 Is there any damage to the provision being made in schools for particular areas of mathematics? For example, is measurement receiving only the cursory attention apparently demanded by the National Curriculum?
6 Are teachers being fooled into thinking that the National Curriculum can be 'delivered' merely by purchasing yet another textbook?

On the positive side I will also want to know:

7 Are there firm moves towards the learning of mathematics in contexts which make sense to the children?
8 Are children being given the opportunities to formulate questions and are they being encouraged to search for answers to these questions?
9 Are the children being provided with the freedom to develop their own strategies and are these strategies and the children's solutions to problems being used as starting points for teaching?
10 Are children being provided with the opportunities to work co-operatively with others in mathematics?
11 Is talk recognized as important to foster when learning mathematics?

12　Are calculators and computers finding their proper niche in the teaching and learning of mathematics? Is 'mental' mathematics receiving appropriate attention?

13　Are teachers writing guidelines and policies ranging beyond the demands of the National Curriculum Statements of Attainment? In other words, are they filling in the gaps?

14　Are particular areas of mathematics previously not common in primary schools developing because of the National Curriculum? Has work in probability taken a firm hold, for example, in primary schools?

In these busy times it is most important for all of us involved in the education of young children to keep in mind the fact that children have rights. Every individual child has the right to ask:

Do I have access to the full curriculum in mathematics?

Are resources allocated throughout my school according to learning needs, and are my learning needs being met?

Do I, whatever my age, sex, race, religion or social background, have access to the use of high profile equipment such as computers?

Do I have the opportunity to make decisions when learning mathematics? Is anyone responding to my questions?

Do I receive a broad and balanced mathematical diet?

Can I participate in self-assessment and the recording of my achievements?

Am I experiencing the full range of teaching styles?

Does my teacher have realistic and positive expectations of what I can achieve?

The above are all independent of the National Curriculum and, together with the checklists in this chapter they can be used to make judgments on its effects.

Finally, it would be as well for us to remember that the main function of mathematics in schools should be to help children to make sense of the world around them or as Simon Jenkins (editor of *The Times*) once put it, 'Mathematics: an essential tool of democracy'.

References

DES (1988) *Education Reform Act*, London, HMSO.
DES (1989) *Mathematics in the National Curriculum*, London, HMSO.

Part IV

Research in the Area

Chapter 12

Parents in the New Era: Myth and Reality?

Martin Hughes, Felicity Wikeley and Tricia Nash

Martin Hughes and his colleagues at Exeter have been engaged in an extensive research project which explores the ways in which parents see schools, teachers, the curriculum and indeed their own role within the education of their children. Here, some of the findings of this research are published and discussed. The ways in which parents' ideas and perceptions match or conflict with the assumptions underlying the recent legislative changes in education, particularly those that affect or are justified by reference to parents' wishes or requirements, are analyzed in some detail. The chapter illuminates many of the conflicts and misapprehensions which serve to complicate the establishment of better interpersonal relations between actual teachers and parents in individual schools.

Introduction

The idea that schools should build productive partnerships with parents is hardly new. During the past few decades it has been put forward many times by a variety of educationalists, theorists and practioners. While the basic message remains the same, however, the form of partnership being advocated and the reasons given for building partnerships, have varied widely, reflecting the dominant concerns of the day.

In the 1960s and early 1970s, for example, there was a strong emphasis on 'compensatory education'. There was concern that children whose parents were less interested in education were performing less well in school, and so schools were urged to seek the involvement of such families. These compensatory ideas lay behind the advocacy of parental partnership in the Plowden Report (1967) and also motivated the work of Young and McGeeney (1968), the EPA (Educational Priority Area) projects, and various home-visiting schemes (e.g. Raven, 1980). In the late 1970s and 1980s, the emphasis shifted towards involving parents more directly in the curriculum. Pioneering projects such as the Haringey Reading Project (Tizard, Schofield and Hewison, 1982) and the Belfield Reading Project (Hannon and Jackson, 1987) established that parents could be directly involved in children's reading, while the highly successful IMPACT project has shown that parents can be similarly involved in the primary mathematics curriculum.

As we enter the 1990s, the educational climate is changing yet again. The growing emphasis on accountability, parents' rights and consumerism during the 1980s culminated in the 1988 Educational Reform Act and the introduction of some of the most sweeping changes ever undertaken to the British education system. Many of these changes have been introduced with the suggestion that they are what parents want; indeed, one major feature of the current scene is the insistence that the wishes of parents 'should be paramount' (to use a notable phrase from the 1980s). But what these wishes actually consist of, and how far parents themselves want their wishes imposed on schools, are by no means clear. Few systematic attempts have been made to discover the true nature of parents' desires and beliefs, and instead, assumptions about parents' views are rife.

In this chapter we will first outline five major assumptions which are currently being made about parents. We will then look at data from our current research to see how far these assumptions are justified.

Five Assumptions about Parents

One of the most important assumptions which is currently being made about parents is that they should be seen as 'consumers of education'. Quite what is meant by this term is not clear, as it has never really been spelt out. Nevertheless, it fits with the current government's ideological position that services, such as health services and care for the elderly, should not, as a matter of principle, be provided by the state. Rather, the argument goes, the quality of such services will be improved if they are subject to market forces. The suppliers of the service will therefore be required to provide a service geared more to what the consumers actually want, while the users of the service must be given the opportunity to take their custom elsewhere if they are not satisfied. In the case of education the picture is slightly complicated by the fact that the users of the service are actually children between the ages of 5 to 16. While it could be argued that the pupils are the real consumers of education, it is their parents who at present are seen in these terms, presumably because they are considered to have control over, and responsibility for, their offspring.

The second assumption about parents, which is central to their role as consumers, is that they should be given a large degree of choice. This assumption has already been enshrined in legislation; the 1980 and 1988 Education Acts have given parents, in principle, the freedom to send their child to the school of their choice. Whether parents actually want a large degree of choice, and how they choose to exercise it if they do have such choice, are questions which have so far been relatively ignored.

The third assumption which is frequently made is that parents are not only to be seen as consumers of the education service — they must also be regarded as dissatisfied customers. Again, this assumption has only rarely been made explicit, but it is implicit in many of the remarks which are publicly made about parents. Indeed, the 1988 Education Reform Act can be seen as resting on such a premise — if parents were totally satisfied with the education service, then one major plank on which the reforms rest would be immediately removed.

The fourth assumption about parents is that they want a much narrower form of education than that which is currently on offer in schools. Parents are frequently portrayed as wanting a much greater prominence given within the curriculum to basics, such as literacy and numeracy, and an increased emphasis on traditional topics such as spelling and knowledge of multiplication tables. The introduction of a National Curriculum, based around the three core subjects of English, maths and science, is thus seen to be providing the kind of education which parents want.

Finally, it is also assumed that parents are in favour of the regular testing of their children and the publication of results, so that they will have objective evidence on which to judge schools. Thus the introduction of standardized assessment of all children to national standards at the ages of 7, 11, 14 and 16 is seen as providing precisely the kind of information which parents need. This assessment, and particularly the publication of assessment results, is a vital element in the attempt to improve educational standards by introducing market ideas. The assumption is that schools will have to raise standards, and make public the fact that they have done so, or parents will take their custom elsewhere.

These five assumptions form a coherent picture of how parents are currently to be viewed. This is not to say that any one individual actually holds all the views put forward here — indeed one of the more interesting features of the current scene is that such views are rarely made explicit. Nevertheless, it would be hard to deny that these assumptions are an integral part of the current educational climate. If they are true, then the kinds of partnerships which schools will be required to make with parents will be radically different from those that have been advocated up till now.

Research on Parents' Views

Our current research on parents and the National Curriculum has provided a valuable opportunity to gauge the extent to which the five assumptions outlined above are in fact shared by parents themselves. The research is part of a long-term study in which a cohort of young children are being followed through the first years of the National Curriculum. The overall aim of the project is to monitor the changing relationship between parents and schools as the 1988 Education Reform Act is implemented.

As part of the project, we carried out in-depth interviews with the parents of 141 children in year 1 (aged 5–6 years) at the end of their first term of the National Curriculum. The sample was drawn from eleven contrasting schools in the south-west of England, and consisted of parents in widely differing socio-economic circumstances. The interviews took place in the parents' homes at the end of 1989, and the interviewees consisted of 119 mothers and eighteen fathers (on four occasions both parents were interviewed together). The parents were interviewed on a range of issues concerning their children's education, of which only a small proportion will be discussed here (more details of the study can be found in Hughes, Wikeley and Nash, 1990).

Parents as Consumers

At one point in the interview the parents were asked directly how far they saw themselves as 'consumers' when thinking about their child's education. The most striking feature of their responses to this question was that nearly half the parents (45 per cent) found the question puzzling or difficult to answer. Typical responses included 'what do you mean?', 'in what respect?', 'I don't understand the question', 'I don't think like that' and even 'I'm a farmer simple as that', as well as various puzzled looks. Clearly the term was one which a large number of parents found difficult to relate to how they saw themselves as parents.

Having established some sort of consensus as to what the term meant, we were then able to classify parents according to how far they saw themselves in those terms. Nearly half the parents (49 per cent) did not see themselves as consumers at all, giving reasons such as 'parents don't know enough to be consumers', 'you take what you get with the state system', 'with the National Curriculum parents have no say', and 'I hate the whole idea of thinking about education as a commodity — it's about creating people and personalities'. About a third of the parents (34 per cent) regarded themselves to some extent as consumers, making comments such as 'will expect to [regard myself as a consumer] more because of the National Curriculum but still find it hard to use the term', 'to a certain extent in that parents must keep an eye on what is going on, but on the other hand I regret the passing of trust between parent and teacher' and 'not entirely like buying a packet of biscuits, you're putting in as much as you're taking out'. Only a small minority (11 per cent) unequivocally saw themselves as consumers: '[sending a child to school is] like going out and spending your money on something — are you getting value for money?' and 'if I only had one school to choose from I might not have thought of myself as a consumer, but as I had choice I did'.

It could be argued that while parents might not see themselves as 'consumers' they would in fact be prepared to behave like consumers in certain circumstances. For example, one aspect of being a consumer is that you have the right to chose another product if you are unhappy with the one you are currently using. We therefore asked parents whether they would consider moving their child to another school if they were not happy, and what would make them do this.

Over half the parents (58 per cent) said they would consider moving their child if necessary. The main reasons given for this were if their child were unhappy or if he/she were not making any progress. Around a third said they would only move their child as a last resort, typically pointing out that they would first try to sort out the problem with the child's teacher. However, a small number of parents (11 per cent) said they would not move their child in such a situation, typically commenting that it would be too disruptive for the child, that there was no guarantee it would be any better elsewhere, or that there was no real alternative.

The relative importance to parents of factors such as their child's happiness was further emphasized by their answers to another question, 'what makes for a good school?' This question elicited a wide range of responses from the parents, with many mentioning several features. The most frequently occurring features, which were mentioned by between a third and a half of the parents, were 'the relationships between parents, teachers and children', 'the staff', 'the atmosphere' and 'the ethos'. In contrast, 'academic results' were only mentioned by 11 per cent of the parents, while physical features such as 'resources' and 'facilities' were mentioned even less frequently.

The responses to these questions reveal a slightly different picture of parents as consumers than is commonly supposed. On the whole, parents do not see themselves as 'consumers of education'; indeed, nearly half of them found the term puzzling. Nor do they seem likely to move their children from one school to another simply on the strength of a school's academic results, for this was relatively low on their list of priorities. At the same time, they are naturally concerned about the happiness and well-being of their own children, and if their child is not happy or progressing they reserve the right to do something about it.

Parents' Choice of School

The second assumption made about parents is that they will appreciate and make use of the increased choice of school provided for them by the recent Education Acts. In order to see how the parents in our study were making use of this increased opportunity we asked them how and why they had chosen the school which their child attended, whether they had visited the school before making their choice, and whether they had considered or visited any other schools.

When asked why they had chosen their child's school, the parents produced a wide range of reasons. Most parents gave more than one reason, and many gave several. The most frequently mentioned reason was the 'locality' of the school, mentioned by over half the parents. The school's 'reputation' was the second most frequent factor, mentioned by nearly half the parents. Other factors which were frequently mentioned included 'impressed on visit', 'size of the school', and the 'ethos' of the school.

In view of the importance attached to locality, we looked at how many parents sent their child to the local school (i.e. the one geographically nearest to them) and whether locality was the only reason for their choice. Over two-thirds (69 per cent) of parents in fact sent their child to the local school. Some of these parents felt they had no choice — other schools were either too far away, were full, or refused them entry. Other parents chose simply on the grounds of locality. However, the majority of parents who chose the local school did so for positive reasons other than it locality, e.g. 'told it was a very good school, and in the area', and 'because we live in the village, my father had said it was a good school'.

Just under a third of the parents (31 per cent) opted for a school which was not the one geographically nearest to them. Some of these parents had been unable to obtain a place at the local school, while others considered the local school unsatisfactory in some way. The majority of those choosing a non-local school, however, had made a positive choice, often because they were seeking a particular type of school: 'catchment area [of the] school [was] good but too large for [a] timid child' and 'the school chosen was caring — there was one in the village but [it was] very church-oriented — because of my background [I] didn't want it'.

Over half the parents (56 per cent) visited the school before making their choice, while most of those who did not visit had found out about it through other sources, such as visiting with the playgroup or asking friends and relations. Those who chose a non-local school were more likely to have visited the school than those who chose the local school.

The parents were also asked how many schools they had considered or visited in coming to their decision. Nearly half the parents (47 per cent) had only considered the one school, and virtually all of them had chosen the local school. Parents who chose a non-local school were much more likely to have visited more than one school.

Taken together, these findings indicate that the majority of parents are not exercising a great degree of choice. Their first preference is for the local school, and if this seems to be a good school, according to their own particular criteria, then they will look no further. A minority of parents, however, appear to be more consciously 'shopping around' — possibly because they are looking for something different from what the local school has to offer. These parents are much more likely to act as 'consumers', by considering or visiting more than one school before they make their choice.

Parents' Satisfaction with the School

The third assumption which is frequently made about parents is that they are to be regarded as dissatisfied customers. We therefore asked the parents whether they were happy with their choice of school and whether they thought that on the whole the teachers in the school were doing a good job. We also asked them what sort of relationship they had with the school, and whether they thought this would be affected by the changes currently being introduced into schools.

The parents' answers to these questions make clear that they are by no means dissatisfied with their children's schools or teachers. The overwhelming majority of parents (86 per cent) said they were happy with their choice of school, although a few of them expressed some reservations. A similar proportion of parents (83 per cent) thought that on the whole the teachers were doing a good job, with nearly a quarter of them being particularly enthusiastic: 'very good', 'very impressed' and 'brilliant under difficult circumstances'. Over two-thirds of the parents felt they had a good or reasonable relationship with the school, with many of the remainder feeling that the limitations in the relationship were due to them (for example, because of younger children or work commitments) rather than the school. The majority of parents felt that their relationship with the school would remain unchanged over the next few years, and most of those who predicted a change thought it would change for the better.

These responses make clear that the parents in our study were overwhelmingly positive in their attitude towards the school and the teachers. Indeed, we were impressed throughout the interviews with the considerable respect shown by parents for the teachers' professionalism, and the sympathetic awareness of the considerable demands being placed on them. Of course, this response does not mean that the parents had no complaints at all, and indeed a number of concerns were raised about what was happening in the schools. But overall, there is little support here for the view that parents form a large mass of disgruntled and dissatisfied customers.

Parents and the Curriculum

The fourth assumption about parents is that they favour a narrow curriculum with an emphasis on the 'basics', together with a return to more traditional teaching methods. Several questions in our schedule aimed to test these assumptions. Parents were asked what they thought were the advantages and disadvantages of the idea of a national curriculum, as well as whether or not they approved of the National Curriculum which was currently being introduced. They were also asked whether they thought that the three core subjects of English, maths and science were the most important aspects of the curriculum and whether they approved of the six foundation subjects (history, geography, design and technology, art, music and PE) being introduced at this level.

On the whole, the parents gave qualified support to the changes currently being made to the curriculum. They were more likely to mention advantages than disadvantages of a national curriculum, typically pointing out that it would give a standard range and level of subjects to be taught in every school, and that it would make it easier if children had to move schools. Nearly half (43 per cent) said they approved of the National Curriculum, compared with only 6 per cent who disapproved, although a large minority (28 per cent) felt they didn't know enough about it to give an opinion. Many parents were concerned, however, about the way the National Curriculum was being introduced, and over a quarter expressed sympathetic concern for the extra work it was creating for teachers.

The majority of parents (62 per cent) agreed that the three core subjects of English, maths and science were the most important areas of the curriculum. Those that disagreed were divided roughly equally between those who wanted more emphasis on other subjects ('they're basic but not overriding') and those who wanted less priority given to science ('English and maths come before any Bunsen burners'). There was also general support for the introduction of the six foundation subjects at this age level.

For each of the three core subjects, the parents were further asked what they thought children of this age should be taught, and whether they thought that it was already being taught. These questions were intended to elicit any strongly held dissatisfactions with the current curriculum. In fact, very few dissatisfactions emerged. In the area of mathematics, for example, the main topics which parents thought *should* be taught were addition (71 mentions), subtraction (56), basic numeracy (53), concepts (28), counting (22) and tables (22). When asked what they tought was *already* being taught, the parents came up with a virtually identical list, namely addition (65 mentions), subtraction (50), basic numeracy (46), concepts (28), counting (24) and tables (13). Indeed, what came over most strongly from this line of questioning was that the parents had few preconceived ideas about what children should be taught at this age, and based their opinions on what they thought their child was already being taught.

Parents and Assessment

The final assumption to be examined here is that parents strongly support the regular assessment of children and the publication of assessment results, so that they will have objective criteria on which to base their choice of schools. Several questions in our interview explored these issues.

Over two-thirds (70 per cent) of the parents thought that the assessment of 7-year-olds was basically a good idea, compared with only 16 per cent who did not. These figures, however, need to be seen in the context of what parents thought was the purpose of assessment. For the most part, parents approved of assessment on the grounds that it would provide both parents and teachers with information about what children could or could not do so that appropriate help could be given: 'Yes [to assessment] — if problems [are] known [about] before [it is] too late and [we] can give more help'. Only a small minority (9 per cent) saw assessment as a means of evaluating schools, and even fewer (5 per cent) saw it as a means of raising standards.

At the same time, the parents raised a large number of concerns about the way assessment was to be carried out, and about the effects that publication of results might have on children. A quarter of the parents (25 per cent) expressed concern that 7-year-olds would have to take 'exams', frequently mentioning fears about a return to the 11-plus. Concerns were also expressed about the possible pressure that assessment might place on children, and that it was wrong to label children as 'successes' or 'failures' at such an early age. These concerns, it should be noted, were usually voiced on behalf of all children, rather than just for their own child. Finally, nearly three-quarters of the parents (74 per cent) were opposed to the assessment of children at a younger age than 7 years. These responses suggest that while parents are in favour of assessment as a means of diagnosing how individual children need help, they are opposed to assessment as a means of grading children and schools.

Conclusions

In considering our findings, a number of qualifications must be made. The sample (141 parents) is by some standards relatively small. The parents were all from a single county in one part of England. Their children were relatively young, and at the very start of the National Curriculum. All these factors may have influenced our results, and any generalization to other groups of parents must be made with care. Nevertheless, having made these qualifications, the findings still give us important insights into the views of parents at a crucial period in their children's education.

Taken together, our findings give only limited support for the assumptions outlined at the start of the chapter, and suggest that the introduction of 'market' ideas into education has not yet had a major impact on parents' perceptions and attitudes. For example, the majority of parents did not see themselves as consumers of education, although they reserved the right to move their child if necessary. The majority of parents were not 'shopping around' to any great extent — if the local school met their requirements then they did not look further afield. The overwhelming majority of parents were happy with the school and thought that the teachers were doing a good job. The majority of parents were in favour of the National Curriculum, but showed some concerns about the way it was currently being introduced. The majority of parents approved of assessment, but more as a means of helping children than as a means of grading schools. Indeed, several questions revealed that parents were much more concerned about children's happiness and general progress than about narrow academic results.

Our findings suggest that the consumerist model of parents which is currently being advocated does not, at present, fit closely with reality. Our interviews have instead led us to put forward an alternative model. While there are obviously many differences between parents, the vast majority are concerned about their children's happiness and well-being, are respectful of teachers' dedication and professionalism, and are deeply interested in their children's education. Instead of being consumers of some narrow educational product, they would rather be partners in the exciting business of helping their children learn. Supporters of schemes such as IMPACT, which aim to do precisely this, can take much heart from our findings.

Acknowledgment

We are extremely grateful to the Leverhulme Trust, the University of Exeter Research Fund, and the School of Education Research Fund for their financial support of the research described here, and to all the schools and parents who have helped us with this research.

References

CENTRAL ADVISORY COUNCIL FOR EDUCATION (1967) *Children and their Primary Schools* (The Plowden Report) London, HMSO.

HANNON, P. and JACKSON, A. (1987) *The Belfield Reading Project: Final Report*, London, National Children's Bureau.

HUGHES, M., WIKELEY, F. and NASH, T. (1990) *Parents and the National Curriculum: An Interim Report*, University of Exeter, School of Education.

RAVEN, J. (1980) *Parents, Teachers and Children*, Edinburgh, Hodder and Stoughton.

TIZARD, J., SCHOFIELD, W.N. and HEWISON, J. (1982) Collaboration between teachers and parents in assisting children's reading, *British Journal of Educational Psychology*, **52**, pp. 1–15.

YOUNG, N. and McGEENEY, P. (1968) *Learning Begins at Home*, London, Routledge and Kegan Paul.

Chapter 13

Parental Partnership: Comfort or Conflict?

Richard Border and Ruth Merttens

Richard Border was the home/school liaison advisory headteacher in Oxfordshire who was mainly responsible for the introduction of IMPACT into Oxfordshire primary schools. Here, he and Ruth chart the parents' reception of IMPACT as their children began to bring home maths activities on a regular basis. The results of the detailed monitoring of the parents' meetings are presented and these findings analyzed. The authors then go on to suggest that initiatives in parental involvement can be classified under two headings — those that allow parents access into the curriculum, and those which preserve the more traditional roles of 'teacher' and 'parent'. They argue that the first type of initiative, of which IMPACT and PACT are exemplars, carries an inevitable risk or 'disruptive' element and results in the creation of dilemmatic situations or conflict.

IMPACT was introduced into Oxfordshire in 1987, as one of the initiatives funded by the Parental Involvement Group under the chairmanship of Bill Laar, the then chief adviser. Unlike the other two pilot authorities, Oxfordshire had taken on IMPACT specifically as a parental involvement initiative, rather than as a form of maths in-service training. The pilot schools in Oxfordshire were therefore schools which had successfully bid for money for resources and support for parental involvement. All of these schools were given five days' of supply time and a little money for material resources to use as they needed in order to support the setting up of IMPACT.

IMPACT was generally introduced into schools in the following way. The IMPACT team, plus the Oxfordshire advisory headteacher for home/school partnership, visited each school for an informal chat with the head and the staff. We then came back for a further meeting at which we arranged when and how to plan the first few weeks' IMPACT activities. We also fixed the times and dates of the introductory parents' meetings, which always consisted of a day of meetings. A letter was sent home to parents explaining that the school was now part of a scheme, IMPACT, and that we needed to speak to all the parents about it. It was stressed that the meetings would be short, and that there would be a series of alternative meetings so that parents could pick the most convenient time.

These meetings were extremely well attended, and in five out of the six pilot schools, the percentage of parents who turned out and came into schools was greater than 80 per cent. In the sixth school, some home visiting was felt to be appropriate, and the parents were also invited back for a further series of meetings.

IMPACT was then underway in each of the schools, and the IMPACT team spent half a day per fortnight in each school in order to support the teachers by discussing the IMPACT sheet, designing the next week's activity, developing and integrating the IMPACT sheets into classroom practice, and assisting with any problems which seemed to have arisen.

After a period of between a term and half a year, each of the schools held follow-up meetings in which the parents were invited back to discuss how they felt IMPACT was going. These meetings were almost always organized to the same pattern:

1   The chairs were arranged informally. Tea and biscuits or wine and crisps etc. were provided.
2   As parents came in they sat around the tables and they were given a pencil and a piece of paper per group.
3   The parents were then welcomed and they were initially asked to work in pairs or small groups, discussing in general their feelings about IMPACT — points that they felt positive about and other points which gave rise to concern and could be improved. A list was compiled under each heading.
4   After about fifteen minutes, the parents were asked to join forces with the group sitting nearest them, and to combine their lists so as to come up with a jointly agreed set of three positive aspects of IMPACT and three negative aspects.
5   The headteacher a member of the IMPACT team would then lead a feedback session in which the groups put together their comments, and the various points raised were discussed in an open forum.

This method of organizing the parent meetings had the great advantage that no one parent or set of parents could dominate the meeting. It was genuinely possible to find out what different parents were thinking and for those who were reluctant to speak in front of a meeting to air their views and have them heard. The lists were always kept as a form of record of the meeting, and any agreed changes to IMPACT practices — e.g. to change the day on which a sheet was sent out — would be noted and included in a newsletter so that those who were unable to attend the meetings also had a record of what was said.

As a matter of routine, the IMPACT team attended all these parent meetings in the pilot schools, and kept records of what was written. By recording the follow-up meetings over a period of two years — and then longer once the pilot phase of IMPACT was over — it has been possible to monitor in some detail the changes in parents' concerns over time. As IMPACT gets underway, are there any common concerns voiced by all — or most — parents? How do the comments change, if at all? We were interested to find answers to these questions by recording these meetings.

First of all, we noticed that certain comments came up in both categories (the 'positive' remarks and the 'negative' remarks) in every single school. This has continued to be the case with surprisingly little change throughout the last three years whatever the catchment area of the school, the ethnic background of the parents, or the age of the children doing IMPACT. The only exceptions occur at meetings held for the parents of nursery children, who do appear to have different concerns. In the first two years when we monitored the pilot schools, we were able to list the comments in order of frequency of occurrence:

Positive Comments

— Enjoyable — helps children to enjoy maths and not to be frightened
   ... makes maths fun (48 mentions);
— Shows parents how children learn maths (46);
— Provides opportunities for children and parents to share maths and
   talk about it (45);
— Helps parents to know what is going on in school (43);
— Helps parents to see how the child is progressing ... 'We can start to
   see what they can and can't do' (36);
— Helps develop a good attitude in the child (36);
— Shows children and parents that there is usually more than one way
   to do something or to solve a problem (21);
— Teaches parents maths and helps them enjoy it (20);
— Relates maths to real life (18);
— Good training for parents ... good preparation for when the children
   are older and have homework or GCSE course work (12);
— Children like filling out the comment sheets (12).

Negative Comments

— Sometimes the instructions are not clear.... Sometimes he/she
   doesn't seem to know what to do and we can't seem to make it out
   (49 mentions);
— Can't see the point of the activities ... How do they help maths
   learning? (46);

— Would like to see where the activities fit into the teacher's overall scheme ... Need to see how the activities are followed up back in the classroom (45);
— Level of the activities is sometimes wrong ... they're often too easy (38);
— Parents find it difficult to explain maths to the children because they aren't trained ... my children won't listen to me ... sometimes I'm not sure if I'm getting it right myself (21);
— Sometimes the activities are boring ... not much fun (19);
— There aren't enough suggestions for how to extend an activity ... We don't know how to make it harder — or easier — to suit our child (14);
— Pressure on time ... Don't like the mess or the preparation ... sometimes too much work involved (11);
— Teachers don't listen to parent's ideas (9).

These comments were collected from twelve parent meetings. There were an average of four to five groups commenting in each meeting. Any comment mentioned in only one meeting is not included. Typically such comments concerned particular school arrangements such as the means of giving out IMPACT — i.e. in a folder, or on its own, the day of giving it out, and how many IMPACT sheets were sent per term.

Surprisingly, we found that the comments changed very little as IMPACT continued over time. Where schools or teachers took pains to alter IMPACT or adapt it, some of the comments were made less vociferously or even less frequently. For example, many schools adopted a policy of putting a short 'rationale' on the bottom of the IMPACT sheet. This explanation then reduced the number of comments concerning 'not seeing the point'. It did not eliminate them, however, and it seems clear that what is a justification for a teacher in terms of what the activity achieves, may not necessarily satisfy a parent, or may leave the parents still mystified. (With the advent of the National Curriculum, this problem has somewhat altered since it is now possible for teachers simply to make reference to the National Curriculum Maths Document, for example, by naming the attainment targets and levels addressed by the activity, providing a justification apparently accepted by both parents and teachers alike).

In some schools, there was a noticeable lessening in the number and force of parental objections to certain types of open-ended, more problem-solving or investigational tasks, possibly suggesting that parents began to see the value of them. Indeed, some of the comments made at subsequent follow-up meetings do point us in this direction:

IMPACT gives me a small insight into my daughter's progress in maths ... rather than her just saying that she's moved up a book, I can actually see how much she's learning ...

We can actually see that there is maths there even though it doesn't look like it at first . . .

We were surprised how much maths there was in that activity . . .

The children enjoyed IMPACT, finding things out for themselves, doing maths wihout realizing it almost . . . one project a fortnight was about right . . .

In other schools, attempts were made to allow for parents to come in and ask for help if the instructions were not clear. IMPACT was routinely given out on a Thursday rather than Friday, so that parents could pop in on the Friday and check out anything which didn't seem to make sense. However, concern with the clarity of the instructions continued to be expressed at parents' meetings, suggesting that either the parents who found instructions difficult were unwilling to come in and admit to this, or that the difficulties only emerged in the actual doing of the IMPACT task.

A few schools decided to send home a simplified form of their scheme of work for the term. This was to enable parents to see where the IMPACT activities fitted into the more general maths plan. Where this was done, the comments relating to wishing to see 'where IMPACT goes' or 'how it fits in' did decrease or even cease altogether.

Research Conclusions

It appeared that parents at all the pilot schools generally raised very much the same sorts of concerns and also found the same pleasures in IMPACT when asked to comment at follow-up meetings, which could suggest that the mechanisms of IMPACT insertion into school practices themselves encourage or enable certain responses and discourage or even disallow others. Thus parents may actually be presented, under the guise of an open meeting, with very few options as to what they are 'permitted' to say or not say. For example, there would be a strong case for suggesting that many parents might like to say that they find IMPACT time-consuming or a bother, but they are only too aware that articulating this grievance will make them out as a particular type of parent — maybe as 'lazy', 'can't be bothered', 'unsupportive', or even 'uncaring'. Therefore they restrict themselves to those comments which can safely be made while continuing to present a positive image of themselves as parent *vis-à-vis* the school. This view as to the constrained nature of the options parents are actually presented with receives further support from the fact that the type of parental comments made at IMPACT follow-up meetings change relatively little over time.

Home Involvement

In this section of the chapter, we would like to contrast two types of home-involvement or parental partnership schemes. We shall then argue that the first type has within it the seeds of contradiction and inevitably leads to conflict. This conflict is manifested either as a disputation between the separately positioned participants, e.g. between parents on the one hand or teachers on the other, or through the production of dilemmatic thinking within individuals, that is the emergence of contrary themes into the realm of explicit argumentation or conscious thought. Thus, teachers and parents may enter a series of discussions *vis-à-vis* the curriculum or related pedagogical issues, the outcomes of which may be that the position of each group becomes over-determined in relation to the other. Alternatively, the teacher may become aware of the conflicting demands made by adherence to the dominant educational orthodoxy on the one hand, and the strongly held belief that parents should be able to influence the curriculum and its teaching on the other. Thus we shall conclude that the first type of parental involvement initiative inevitably risks disruption by making manifest, through the forms of social interaction instigated by such schemes, those oppositions previously camouflaged by accepted modes of rhetorical and behavioural strategies. The second type, by contrast, allows the preservation of the ideological values reflected in everyday situations unchallenged by the disclosure of discordant elements.

Curriculum-Based Parental Partnership Schemes

The first type of home/school initiative depends upon an overt invitation being issued to parents to participate in the curriculum, which happens inevitably as a result of IMPACT processes, and contingently as a result of shared reading programmes, such as 'paired reading'. Since reading and maths are the only two areas of the curriculum in which curriculum-based parental partnership has been extensively essayed, it is helpful to consider these separately in some detail.

Shared reading
Many, if not most, schools now claim to engage in a programme of shared reading. The term is notorious for covering what might be described as a multiplicity of diverse and different practices. In some cases, shared reading means very little other than that the children are allowed — or perhaps required or encouraged — to take reading books home. Here, the school is effectively operating a library system. Children take home books, perhaps in folders marked (misleadingly) PACT or 'Shared reading', but no regular or sustained dialogue between the parents and the teachers — or indeed, the children — is expected or developed. There may be an exercise book which

travels back and forth with the child, but any comment written by the parent remains isolated, unresponded to, and certainly does not form part of any reading record.

By contrast, shared reading can involve the parent in contributing, on a sustained and regular basis, to the child's learning to read and the records kept of this process by those teaching her/him. The book is taken home, any reading is recorded along with any comments about that reading made by the child or the parent. The teacher will then respond to the comments, and the diary — or card — which passes back and forth in this dialogue is itself the reading record for the child. The teacher and the parent are partners in the sense that they are both part of the process of teaching the child to read. We do not mean to imply that the partnership is necessarily an equal one, or that the two parties occupy the same roles within it in relation to each other. Clearly the relationship is not a symmetrical one; there will be a very real sense in which the teacher remains the 'expert' and the parent is, in some sense, a 'novice' (at reading pedagogy rather than at reading itself). Nevertheless, a partnership is established in which each feel they have a role which is played out *in communication with,* and *in direct relation to*, the other.

In these situations, shared reading becomes a means by which parents can, metaphorically speaking, insert a probe directly into the curriculum or into classroom pedagogy. Thus, it is possible to study the outcomes in terms of changes in the types of social interaction and behaviour patterns brought about as a result of such intervention. Once it is an accepted and 'normal' part of school life that children's reading is discussed by parents and teachers and a jointly constructed record is maintained, both parents and teachers must in some sense reconstruct what can and can't now be said or done. For example, is it permissible for a parent to suggest that the child should move two books ahead on the reading scheme? Or must such a suggestion come from the teacher, who 'knows best'? Can the teacher imply that the situation in which the child is being asked to read at home be modified — e.g. that the permanently 'on' television should be switched off for the duration of the reading? Or would we all agree that this was unwarranted interference by the teacher as a professional? The rules in this new situation have to be redrawn. Through the processes of negotiation and social argumentation we have to establish what is and is not allowed, what can and cannot be articulated, what must remain hidden, which information the teacher guards from the parents and those things the parent makes sure the teacher doesn't find out about.

Our experience of shared reading initiatives suggests two patterns of parent–teacher interaction. First, we have observed that if parents are dissatisfied with a child's reading responses on a particular occasion then it always remains open to them to lay the blame on the text rather than at the feet of either the teacher or child. Thus both teachers and parents can absolve themselves from the responsibility for an unsatisfactory situation by mere virtue of the fact that the book itself was produced by neither. That the production of the actual reading text does not rest with the teacher comes to be an important factor when we compare shared reading schemes with shared maths schemes such as IMPACT.

Second, it appears that many parents do see it as their role to help teach their child to read. Evidence from both research and practice would tend to suggest that parents read with their children whether the school encourages them to do so or not. Many parents also feel that they are qualified and able to help their child read simply by virtue of being parents. Once again this is an important difference between shared reading and shared maths to which we shall return.

Shared maths

There have been various attempts by schools to share maths activities at home with parents, including libraries of maths games, Hackney 'maths-PACT', and Kirklees, paired Maths. The largest and most widely disseminated of these schemes is IMPACT. With IMPACT, parents are involved in sharing weekly or fortnightly teacher-designed maths tasks with their children, commenting on them and sending the results of their work at home back into the classroom. In contrast with the shared reading described above, through IMPACT parents have an automatic input into the classroom curriculum which is not dependent on how 'well' or 'badly' IMPACT is done in the school. Furthermore, something always comes back into the classroom — whether it is a game, an 'object', data, or simply the comment sheet. There is, therefore, an 'object' which is transferred from classroom to home and back again, possibly, or even probably, undergoing some form of transformation in the process. This 'object' becomes the subject of overt discussion and covert negotiation between the three parties involved, the parents, the child, and the teacher.

Also in direct contrast with the shared reading, in IMPACT the teacher is perceived as responsible for the text which comes home, and by which what is to be done is (partly at least) conveyed. The activities are teacher-productions, at least as far as the parent and the child are concerned. Therefore, if something is unsatisfactory about the maths activity as it unfolds at home the teacher can be held responsible. This can obviously include matters as trivial as parents complaining about a spelling or typing error, or as serious as a child's distress because the activity is 'too hard', seems to underestimate the ability of the child, or seemingly, does not make sense.

One further point which can be made about both the shared reading and the IMPACT maths is that a parental response can itself constitute a threat as far as the teacher is concerned. The nature and gravity of this threat will vary according to the substance of the comment and the situation and identity of the teacher. Some responses may make explicit antithetic assumptions which hitherto coexisted without conscious formulation. Thus a comment may have the effect of causing a controversy through which contradictory positions are taken and ascribed. Alternatively, it may cause a teacher to be placed in a dilemma, since previously unchallenged 'common-sense' assumptions have been illuminated through contradictions being revealed or demonstrated. Thus curriculum-based parental partnership initiatives can be a risky business for all concerned. We shall return to this conclusion at a later point.

Extrinsic Parental Involvement Schemes

These schemes are methods schools adopt for involving the parents without at any point allowing the disruption of curriculum or pedagogic control. Examples of such initiatives include:

— Setting up parent or family rooms in schools,
— Running after-school groups or clubs,
— Holding curriculum meetings or workshops,
— Giving parent interviews,
— Baseline assessment,
— Parents assisting on outings,
— PTA and other similar associations,
— Parents working in the classroom.

With the possible exception of the last mentioned item, all these ways of involving parents position parents firmly outside the locus of control of curriculum or pedagogy. Although curriculum meetings give information, they do so in a spirit of 'telling the parents how we do things here.' There is no sense that the parents may have a right to put contrary views as to how the curriculum should be managed or the classrooms organized. Family rooms, after-school clubs and PTAs are all firmly extra-curricular and historically have developed this way for reasons which make them likely to remain so. Baseline assessment, a new idea currently being much spoken about and trialled (see Wolfendale, 1990) is also extra-curricular and it can be persuasively argued that the ownership of any assessment record in fact remains firmly with the professionals. Parent interviews are 'information-giving' or at best, 'information-sharing' sessions (see ILEA Primary Language Record, 1989) and once again, there can be no dispute that the locus of control rests firmly with the teacher.

Parents working in the classroom do have the potential to be disruptive in terms of curriculum management and control. However, because of the asymmetry in the relationship between the teacher and her/his parent helper(s), such a threat is rarely, if ever, realized. The teacher controls what tasks the helper may undertake and which are deemed to involve too much 'teaching'. Any criticisms or even suggestions the helper may have are unlikely to be voiced, at least not to the teacher her/himself. The only occasions under which these constraints may not be is where a teacher and a parent have been working together for many years, and a relationship has grown up of mutual respect and goodwill. However, the transitory nature of individual parents' involvement with any one class or school mitigates this being more than a very exceptional circumstance. (Of course, there will be occasions in which a 'parent' helper is also, and in another context, a 'teacher'. This may produce problems as to relative positionings and identity-constructions, but negotiated settlements will need to be found if a workable situation is to result).

What Price Safety?

We have tried to show how categorizing home-involvement initiatives in this way produces a reading which illuminates certain features — the 'risk-elements'. Where teachers or educationalists instigate curriculum-based parental partnership schemes, they open the door to perhaps inevitable conflict or disruption. It should be emphasized that such conflict does not necessarily — or even commonly — emerge between the groups of participants, such as parents versus teachers. The contrariety may be manifested in a multiplicity of ways. Particular teachers may find themselves in dilemmas. They may have come to recognize opposing tendencies or polarities within hitherto tacit assumptions. Or one teacher may find her/himself in the firing line on the question of a specific educational practice. A strongly held educational belief may be in direct conflict with an equally strongly held position on the rights of parents. Such oppositions, whether interpersonal or private, are intrinsic, we believe, to the social situation of schooling itself, but, they normally rest undisturbed within the web of social interactions and relations afforded by the more traditional school/home division.

Manifestations of Conflict

Over the first two or three years of IMPACT we had the opportunity to observe at close quarters and in some detail how teachers cope with the introduction of a curriculum-based parental partnership scheme. We found that certain patterns seemed to be emerging. While our own observational data was comprehensive, it encompassed a relatively small number of schools and it would be unwise to draw anything other than tentative conclusions from any analysis of these observations. However, this work at least serves to indicate possible directions in which further study could be profitable.

We found that the insertion of IMPACT became most problematic after a time in a school in which the staff were apparently unified in a strongly held and well-entrenched belief in a 'child-centred' curriculum and a pedagogy which had moved away from formal and rote-learning to encompass an integrated day. Such schools could be characterized by a lack of dependency upon any commercial maths scheme, a reliance instead upon a great deal of planning, usually as a team, and an emphasis upon the creative and investigative abilities of the children. In the schools of this type which we observed, the fervour with which this style of pedagogy, frequently referred to as 'child-centred' (a term which apparently needs no justification), is adhered to and described is matched by the strength of the conviction that parents should be involved in their children's schooling.

The first result of working in any school and observing closely what occurs on a day by day basis, is that we can see that 'the staff' is not in fact a unified object. There were some members of staff who believed fervently in the 'doctrine' of child-centred education. Other teachers seemed much less comfortable, and would, in private, express reservations, especially once they had ascertained, through a series of exploratory and tentative statements, that the listener might not be unsympathetic to an alternative viewpoint. The IMPACT activities obviously reflected the curriculum and pedagogical style of the school. When it came to defending 'unpopular' activities with parents, we noticed that it was the less dominant, relatively 'unconverted' members of staff who found themselves most vulnerable to parental criticism. They appeared to attract more unfavourable comments than the other members of staff, and were less able to muster the appropriate rhetoric in defense of the activities. The uncomfortable analogy which suggested itself to one of the authors was that of the hockey pitch. Those members of the team who are keen and convinced about hockey do not come to grief. The attack tends to focus, or to be most effective, against those players who are hesitant.

Several schools of this particular type had said that they had decided to do IMPACT because they felt that it would help to convince parents of the right ways of working, to 'bring them round' to a more 'open', broader view of teaching and learning. However, if IMPACT failed to do this, then these strongly held beliefs proved apparently impregnable. In this sense, the teachers could be accused of wanting to involve parents but refusing to *listen* to them. For some teachers, this posed a dilemma. Some solved this problem by attempting to adapt the curriculum in ways which went towards what the parents — or some of them — had suggested, but not sufficiently to lose those aspects most clearly signalling child-centred learning and most dearly adhered to by its proponents. In other words, they tried to have their cake and eat it too. Others decided that a school should reflect its community and that they must interrogate with more vigour previously uncritically-held beliefs about teaching and learning.

We also observed, however, that parents cannot be considered as a homogeneous group. There was no identifiable unity of opinion about anything other than the vaguest generalities. One of the functions of IMPACT practice as it inserts itself into everyday school life is to illustrate how often a parent's educational principles (or a teacher's) can remain comfortably in place only as long as they remain untested by the specific demands of particular circumstances. Thus, it is easy to maintain in abstract that children should concentrate more on written arithmetic and not 'mess about' with all this practical equipment. When an IMPACT task requires that a child produce certain written symbols or uses numerical operations, however, many parents have realized how essential it seems to be to have some practical apparatus at hand or to resort to finger counting.

Conclusion

Shared reading and the introduction of IMPACT into Oxfordshire schools has enabled us to explore curriculum-based parental partnership schemes in practice. Through observing and noting the detailed manoeuvres, strategies, negotiations, and rhetorics which make up the web of social interactions created by such schemes, we have been able to chart differences and op-positions as they emerge. This investigation has enabled a reading of this type of parental involvement in which conflict is posited as an almost inevi-table constituent of the insertion of such 'collaborative' practices into the social institutions which comprise schooling today. We suggest that further exploration of shared reading and maths programmes could further illumin-ate contradictions previously camouflaged.

References

ILEA Primary Language Record, 1989, London, ILEA.
Wolfendale, S. (1990) *All About Me*, Nottingham, NES/Arnold.
Woods, P. (1990) *Teacher Skills and Strategies*, London, Falmer Press.

Chapter 14

IMPACT and Cultural Diversity

Deborah Curle

Deborah Curle is one of the researchers employed by IMPACT, and in this chapter she discusses her research into the effects of IMPACT in schools where much cultural diversity exists. Working within the theoretical frameworks of thinkers such as Billig, Harre and Shotter, Deborah analyzes some of the findings from her research, exploring the ways in which the mechanisms inserted into the social world of the school by IMPACT can illuminate the dilemmas faced by the participants. Similarly, she argues that the sites of exchange can be those in which particular forms of rhetoric come to be exposed and which then provide a forum for argumentation by which and through which new identities might be asserted or constructed.

Overview of 'Ethnic Identity'

There was a tendency to view the cultures of ethnic minority groups as static. Much of the literature on minority groups from the 1960s onwards represented minority cultures in simplified ways, construing them as changeless wholes nestling within the larger framework of the dominant culture. The literature has freely made use of such stereotypical views and labels like 'Asian' and 'West Indian' which effectively obscure the diversity of backgrounds covered by these terms. The traditional cultural backgrounds tended to be emphasized, ignoring the dynamics of what is happening today in Britain, and studying minorities as if they were living in isolation. By stressing the gulf between minority and majority cultures, we have ignored the important, complex and changing interactions taking place in those situations that provide for routine contact between peoples of different cultural milieux. The assumption that sets of cultural values are fixed with no possibility of adaptation now has generally given way to a view which sees ethnic identity as a fluid product of social interaction. Certainly the more interesting and illuminative recent research bears this view out, for example, the work on Asian adolescents (Weinrich, 1979) and the changes between first and second generation immigrants (Ballard, 1979; Saifullah-Khan, 1979). The idea that second-generation immigrants are undergoing 'culture conflict' is somewhat crass — implying a straightforward tug-of-war between East and West, traditional and modern. On the contrary, it is not a situation that can be so neatly disposed of. Ethnic minorities have difficult 'dilemmas' to resolve in those myriad situations where different sets of values appear to apply. In resolving them they work towards new syntheses of British and other cultures.

'Identity', or even the various 'identities' we appear to use in different situations, appear to be as much products of those situations as of 'socialization' within a particular milieu. This view is held by writers such as C.H. Cooley (1902) and G.H. Mead (1934). A person's identifications in different situations may be incompatible with each other. These views of identity tie in with those of Shotter (1989) and Harré (1989), who also stress the importance of social context in the formation of 'identity'. There is no such thing as a stable object 'I', which is separate from everything else; we come to know ourselves as a particular person by being addressed as 'you' in certain circumstances by certain people. The importance of language in the social contexts where identities are manufactured has required that we turn our attention more and more to the 'rhetorical' and 'persuasive' uses of languages in social interaction.

The rhetorical approach to social psychology has been developed by Billig (1988, 1989) who discusses at length the dimension of argumentation to social situations. His analysis of the nature of attitudes and thoughts is substantiated by empirical work on the subtleties of 'ethnic identity'. Billig emphasizes the importance of the social nature and context of thought. Knowledge is seen as being socially shared. Yet socially shared beliefs, or 'common sense', contain contradictions, giving rise to dilemmatic thinking in individuals. This view contrasts with traditional psychological notions which have not been able to articulate socially situated thinking without recourse to, and over use of, the purely logical aspects of thought. Rhetoric and argumentation have been ignored or misrepresented in the zeal to see everything from the point of view of logic. However, ideology is dilemmatic as well. It is useful to see ideological values reflected in everyday situations, not as a closed, coherent system, but as an incomplete set of 'contrary themes' continually giving rise to dilemmas in the interactions in which people find themselves. Hence, people are not to be seen as driven by pre-programmed plans of actions and ideologies, but as constantly reacting to and dealing with dilemmas.

This view has implications for the way we look at attitudes. In traditional psychological theory, the notion of attitude implies an organization of beliefs, a sense of consistency which is detected in psychological terms like 'attitudinal/value system'. Thinking is seen as a need for attitudinal harmony. In the 1950s Festinger (1957) claimed that attitudes are altered to enable people to have a consistent outlook on life. However, in the rhetorical approach outlined above, attitudes are seen as 'positions' taken in matters of controversy, held within a social, argumentative context without which they would not exist. It has been found (McGuire, 1964) that people possess few arguments for unchallenged assumptions. When people *are* challenged, however, they develop defences, and thereby what we call attitudes. Previously unchallenged common-sense assumptions develop into attitudes when people are under attack. This is a stance which Billig develops. It is interesting to consider the implications of this view in the present case of IMPACT operating in multicultural schools, with teachers and parents being directly confronted with and challenged by different cultural and educational practices than what they are used to.

Sherif and Howland (1961) noted that people possess 'latitudes of acceptance' — i.e. they will agree with a whole range of statements on a subject. In the rhetorical approach, since people are seen to respond to the rhetorical context, they can find themselves arguing against different positions, depending on the context. This response has particular relevance to our present consideration of looking at people who shift their identities between different groups. They will take up different positions depending on the context and when they do not identify completely with a single group.

Billig looks at the example of a study of second-generation Irish adolescents living in Britain, and shows how the sense of one's identity can emerge within a context of argumentation. These youths often switched their loyalties in order to react against their social circumstances:

> When you're in Ireland, you find yourself sticking up for England —
> they call you English. Then when you're over here, they call you
> Irish. So you find yourself sticking up for both sides, and you can't
> feel you're either (Ullah, 1985, quoted in Billig, 1989).

Hence, a change in the rhetorical situation is the setting for the testing of a previously unchallenged attitude expressed in a different context. Billig calls attitudes 'essentially unfinished business'. Every attitude is incomplete since future circumstances may pose limitations and the possibility that counter-attitudes will be put forward.

Looking at IMPACT, we are tapping into fluid and ongoing processes. Not only do the parents have complex, conflicting and changing views, but so do teachers, perhaps particularly when put in situations like those implied by projects like IMPACT where they are becoming closely involved with parents of different religious and cultural backgrounds.

Terminological note
For the rest of this paper, I will be concentrating on groups from the Indian subcontinent, mainly Gujarati, Punjabi and Hindi speakers.

I will be referring to children and parents by their linguistic groupings for convenience, although this is in some respects unsatisfactory in that these groupings can collapse important religious and nationality differences (not to mention differences in world views within speakers of the same language, religion and nationality).

I will also be using the terms 'ethnic minority' and 'bilingual', and, occasionally, 'Asian', again for convenience. I will be taking the term 'bilingual' in the sense of the ability to use more than one language. This usage, of course, does obscure a whole range of degrees of bilingualism.

The Background of Ethnic Minority Parents

There has been relatively little research into the views of minority parents on education. Studies examining the attitudes of parents from different cultural and religious backgrounds have come up with some interesting comparisons (Ghuman and Gallop, 1981; Gupta, 1977; Rex and Tomlinson, 1979). However, it is increasingly recognized that it makes no sense to view parents' attitudes out of context. Their perceptions of education cannot be divorced from their own background; their culture, religion, country of origin, class, whether they come from urban or rural settings, will all influence their views on education and their expectations for their children. There have been several illuminating studies of the background of parents (Ballard, 1979).

Despite their cultural diversity, many ethnic minority parents have gone through colonial education systems and have drawn their educational attitudes and expectations from them. Colonial schools on the whole were based on the old British system, with an emphasis on learning English, rote memorization, and examinations, a system which benefits the children of the better-off with middle class aspirations (Curle, 1986). Lack of funds tends to result in large class sizes, few textbooks or resources, and hence rigid teaching techniques. Given this background, it is not surprising that parents' expectations will differ vastly from the reality of education in Britain.

Knowledge of parents' geographical and social background is also important. For example urban parents with some education may expect their child to do well in school, but for a rural peasant, the fact that the child is in school in the first place may be a major achievement. Minority parents of relatively affluent middle-class background are often relegated to low socioeconomic status in Britain. The class position of ethnic minority parents is complex and cannot be easily equated with the class position of white parents.

However, while an understanding of the legacy of educational experience is important for understanding parents' attitudes, it must be remembered that these attitudes will not be static, but will be argued through situations and experiences in the British education system.

Ethnic Minority Parents and the British System

'Because we do not know exactly what or how they teach in schools here, we cannot help our child at home. Even if we want to coach them at home we don't know how' (a Bengali mother; Ghuman and Gallop, 1981).

The above quotation encapsulates poignantly the sense of frustration with and ignorance of the education system which many minority parents feel. A number of recent reports on attitudes of Asian parents towards education show a degree of dissatisfaction by the parents with the level of communcation between home and school (NFER, 1989; ILEA, 1985).

Research does indicate that most minority parents are very keen for their children to do well and acquire useful skills and qualifications, irrespective of their class and background. (Saunders 1973, 1977; Midwinter 1977). Margaret Clarke *et al.* (1986) and Tizard *et al.* (1981) found that for many parents the wish to get a good education for the child was a major factor in coming to the UK in the first place. It has also been found that minority parents exert a strong influence over the child's educational life (Gupta, 1977).

Studies that have sought the views of parents indicate an overall satisfaction with education (ILEA, 1985). However, this view could be because their knowledge of the school system is sketchy, and they rely a great deal on schools to inform them of their processes, which schools do not always do. They may also sometimes be reluctant to admit their ignorance.

Overall, there is undoubtedly room for improvement in home/school relations as far as minority homes go. Research shows that by the early 1980s, there had been efforts to improve contacts, but on a rather limited *ad hoc* scale. Improved home/school contact with minority parents was largely regarded as a matter for liaison by professionals (EWOs, etc.). As far as the parents were concerned, this attitude tended to seem like just another layer of professional bureaucracy.

Parents' and Teachers' Expectations of School

A mismatch of expectations between teachers and minority parents of what schools can offer does exist. This mismatch is partially explained by the parents' very different experience of education in their own country, as discussed above. Parents may expect school discipline to be more authoritarian, and rote learning to be the main teaching method. They may find it difficult to accept some practices in school. Tizard *et al.* (1981) found that Asian parents put high value on cleanliness and hard work and found difficulty in understanding the 'messy' and culture-specific sand, water and paint activity. Tizard *et al.* also found that minority parents' expectations and views on parental involvement differed from those of the staff.

Another possible reason for mismatch of expectations is that the multi-cultural education movement has focused mainly on the curriculum as a target of reform, whereas it seems that the curriculum is not the prime area of concern. Asian parents in particular appear to be more concerned that schools should recognize cultural diversity, and are anxious about religious teaching, education of girls, dress, food, etc. (Ghuman, 1980; Tanna, 1981).

There may be a clash between the values put over in British education and those of certain ethnic minority parents. For example, the individualistic nature of learning, the relatively competitive nature of British education, and girls' education may worry some Muslim parents.

Another basis for the mismatch may be the inequality of opportunity within the education sytem. The inner-city schools which ethnic minority children largely attend are perceived not to offer opportunity equal to more affluent, suburban schools, and do not offer the traditional 'grammar school' type of education that parents may expect.

Finally, the 'disadvantage model' has arguably clung on longer with regard to ethnic minority homes than in other cases. There has been a tendency for educators to stress 'cultural deficits' to explain failure rather than racism, which may be of far more pressing concern to the minority families. Teachers have perhaps viewed their work as being more in the pastoral care than in the academic domain although it may be the latter which is of greater importance to parents. Some of the mismatch has been helped by the move in education over recent years towards accepting alternative values in schools and cultural diversity, increased awareness of equal opportunities, and improved teacher-training in these areas and in home/school links generally.

I carried out a series of open-ended, semi-structured interviews with teachers in five IMPACT schools in three outer London boroughs. Some were established IMPACT schools, having been doing IMPACT for the duration of the research project (two years, two and a half terms at time of writing), some were relative newcomers, having done IMPACT for two and a half terms. All the schools had a high number of children from the Indian subcontinent, mainly from India and Pakistan.

My main concern was to elicit teachers' views on how IMPACT, an ongoing negotiable process, engages with the home, which is also in constant flux. I wanted to see whether any particular issues, problems or benefits arise from doing IMPACT with minority children and parents. As discussed earlier, attitudes are likely to alter in different contexts, and it seemed to me that in the IMPACT situation, parents, teachers and children are particularly exposed to different schemata or 'rhetorical settings'.

I was aware that this exercise was exploring the perception of only one group of protagonists. However, this approach was necessary for practical reasons, and for a preliminary study, it was important to tap teachers' views, as they are the ones in the position of implementing IMPACT.

For the sake of clarity in discussion, I have divided up the themes that recurred thus:

1 language,
2 relationship with parents,
3 teachers' perceptions of parents' views on IMPACT,
4 cultural diversity.

The data discussed was selected for their illumination of the conflicts the teachers themselves made explicit.

The Schools

School A: 'established' IMPACT school:

> 33 per cent Gujarati,
> 10 per cent Muslim (mainly Pakistanis, some Arabs and Moroccans),
> A few West Indian, Tamil, Sikhs, Greek,
> No mother-tongue support in school,
> Have English language support.

School B: 'established' IMPACT school:

> 80 Punjabi-speaking,
> 48 Gujarati speaking,
> a few Urdu, Hindi, Bengali, Tamil and Somali speaking,
> Mother-tongue teacher — speaks Urdu, Punjabi, Hindi.

School C: 'established' IMPACT school:

> Languages mainly Urdu and Hindi,
> A few Chinese, Greek, Turkish,
> ESL teacher in twice a week doing groupwork,
> No mother-tongue support.

School D: recent IMPACT school:

> main language: Punjabi, Gujarati, Hindi,
> a few Chinese, Bengali, Tamil,
> Mother tongue teacher support in shcool.

School E: 'established' IMPACT school:

> main languages: Punjabi, Urdu, Gujarati,
> a few Hindi, Bangladeshi,
> No language or mother-tongue support.

Language

A recurring theme concerning language was parents' attitudes towards use of mother-tongue languages. Teachers had varied perceptions of this issue; a brief consideration of these views shows the complexity involved.

Several teachers felt that parents were reluctant for their children to speak in their mother-tongue. In School C, it was felt that parents did not want work translated in the home language, and were keen for their children to learn English. When it was suggested once that notices go up in two languages, an Asian father came in and protested.

In School A, the reluctance to speak in the mother-tongue was also noted with concern. A teacher said that she had to tell parents to do IMPACT in their own language, but did not feel that the message was getting across. She felt that many bilinguals believe that teachers demand English in school, and that this inhibition was affecting children detrimentally. With IMPACT, many parents would feel unable to help because of the language involved.

An interesting slant was put on this issue by a mother-tongue teacher in School D; although she speaks the main languages of the school, she reports that parents are reluctant to speak to her in these languages because they are unsure of what her reaction might be. Although they may speak the same language as her, they may be of different regions, countries, or religions. This can be off-putting and worrying for parents, and the consequent reluctance to speak in the mother-tongue spreads to the children.

In School B, on the other hand, the mother-tongue teacher did not note any reluctance of parents to communicate with her in mother-tongues. She felt that as there was not enough scope for mother-tongue speaking in school, many children and parents, wanting to keep their own language alive, communicated mainly in their own language at home. This situation contrasts with the opinion expressed in School C that families largely speak English at home.

In School E, it was felt that the children quite happily spoke in their mother-tongue at school without inhibition. As there is no mother-tongue teacher there, it was not possible to gauge how parents would feel about speaking it themselves.

From these observations, it can be seen that attitudes towards mother-tongue speaking amongst parents (and children) are varied, probably very much affected by the overall context. It was been found in recent research (Rees, 1983) that it is overly simplistic to say that Asian parents don't want the mother-tongue introduced into school. It is a complex issue, and needs full parent and teacher understanding of the issues involved; factors are likely to include broader sociological ones (e.g. migratory history, environment, racism, etc) as well as educational ones. For example, in the present case, the difference in attitude towards speaking in the mother-tongue between parents in School B and School D may be related to the fact that

School B is an established IMPACT school, small, approachable, with a strong tradition of parental involvement. School D, on the other hand, is large, rather physically off-putting, and is a very recent IMPACT school. An interesting remark by the mother-tongue teacher at School D suggests that attitudes towards language may be closely tied up with lack of confidence:

> The tragedy is that those who don't understand [i.e. English] are not much in communication with us at school. They feel inhibited to come to school and make conversation with the teachers in front of other people. They think they will be laughed at.

This opinion is echoed by a comment made in School E, where it was noted that parent's confidence is more important than English or lack of it in communicating with the school. If parents come in to school and see teachers regularly, they talk about IMPACT. Weak English is not necessarily a barrier. Like School B, School E is an established IMPACT school, and is a physically approachable building.

The issue of speaking in mother-tongues suggests a serious dilemma for bilingual children and their parents. The children are caught in between different attitudes about the use of their own language, with teachers on the whole encouraging its use at school (and at home), while their parents seem sometimes to urge them to speak only in English. Parents face the dilemma of whether they and their children should speak in their mother tongue or not, torn between the desire to maintain their linguistic and cultural identity, and for their children to become conversant in English. Ballard (1979) makes the point in her study of second-generation South Asians that children born and educated in Britain have greater communication skills than their parents, who often feel threatened as their children gain confidence and occasionally destablize the family structure and hierarchy. So, while wishing their children to do well in the English educational system, parents may also fear its effects.

In this discussion, both 'explicit' and 'implicit' dilemmas can be detected. In an explicit dilemma, both sides of an argument may be reasonable, and people can adhere to difference stances. In an implicit dilemma, contrary themes are detected within a particular stance which seems to be consistent (Billig *et al.*, 1988). The parents above adhere to two stances: the desire for their children to learn English, and for them to keep up their own language. Yet within the desire for them to learn English is an implicit dilemma: on the one hand, learning English will help them to get on in society; on the other, it may undermine family structure.

With respect to language, teachers are caught between their own views and those of parents. They too are aware of the need for children to maintain their linguistic and ethnic identity, and many IMPACT teachers have come to recognize the value of mathematical work at home conducted in the mother-tongue while at the same time becoming conversant in English.

Teachers also may have to compromise their educational ideals; there is little mother-tongue support available, so the teacher, while believing in the efficacy of mother-tongue teaching, may have to compromise in practice.

Teachers had different opinions on the issue of children having to translate IMPACT work at home. In School C, it was felt by one teacher that the process of a child doing IMPACT in school in English, translating it at home, and then retranslating in school could present a problem as the teacher would not know how the parent was explaining the activity. In School A, it was felt that English children had IMPACT reinforced at home since the parents would know what was expected of them, whereas ethnic minority parents would be less likely to have come to meetings, and to understand what was going on because of the language barrier. In School E, language was not really perceived as problematic. A teacher mentioned that the fact that children translate IMPACT activities into their home language and then back again into English is an advantage; the home is reinforcing a concept in the child's own language; and it is 'reinforcing the concept' which matters, not so much the language. A contradiction which is present for IMPACT teachers emerged; fear of relinquishing their control over the activities (by handing control over to parents) and yet feeling that parental input and involvement is valid and important.

One point which teachers in all five schools made was that older siblings often help children to do their IMPACT at home in minority homes. This was seen as on the one hand positive, with other members of the family getting involved, but on the other hand as worrying since it shows that parents feel unable to get fully involved. A couple of teachers said they would like for parents to feel more fully involved, rather than passing IMPACT on to older children who are more competent in English. It was mentioned several times that older siblings of English children did not seem nearly as involved.

Children come to perceive and use languages in different ways, which gives their language different meanings in their eyes. Language use can be seen as a product of a network of social relations. The transition from the culture of the home to the culture of school is not just a shift in patterns of language use, but is an adjustment to new sets of social relations and values.

The issue of language use is particularly pertinent for IMPACT, which was originally set up to provide a site of exchange between the languages of home and of school (Vass and Merttens, 1987). The language in which children choose to carry out work with their parents is significant, reflecting the constant interplay of attitudes of child, parent and teacher touched upon above. There is a paucity of research into language use in informal educational situations; IMPACT has provided a unique arena in which to examine this issue in more detail.

It was been suggested (Hornby, 1977) that language use is closely connected with a sense of ethnic identity, that threat to ethnic identity may alter the motivation to become bilingual, and that language learning patterns may be affected by social pressures within the home group. Hence use of language is an interesting indicator of the attitudes prevalent within the group and between the minority and majority groups. Language is thus an important factor when looking at an area of crucial importance in IMPACT — that of relationships between schools and parents.

Relationship with Parents

A teacher at School B saw IMPACT as being useful in breaking down parents' preconceptions about what their children should learn at school, and likewise teachers' preconceptions. However, in other cases (e.g. School D), it was felt that the overall situation (size of school, etc.) was not conducive to establishing dialogue, and it was felt that bilingual parents were daunted by approaching teachers.

An interesting observation made by a teacher at School B was that in the present economic climate, with mortgage rates going up, increasingly both parents in Asian families need to work. This tendency has meant that mothers are less able to come into school now, and have less time for their children at home. It has also led to a decrease in the number of Asian helpers in school.

In School A, it was felt that parents are in awe of school, and are put off by the language barrier, so parent meetings are ill-attended. However, another teacher at School A felt that IMPACT was helping to build relationships with parents, that parents were becoming less diffident, and more worthwhile dialogue was going on.

The lack of translation was also mentioned as a problem in School E. Certainly, having a mother-tongue teacher to translate seems to help, as in School B. However, as mentioned previously, the mother-tongue teacher in School D encountered reluctance by Asian parents to speak to her in their mother-tongues; more is involved than just providing a mother-tongue speaker.

Several teachers (in Schools A and D) mentioned home visiting as an important aspect of building up relations with parents. As a teacher at School D said: 'Visiting homes is ... important ... asking parents to take teachers as friends, not as someone who is going to assess them'. A teacher at School A said: 'There's a whole structure in schools. . . . to approach this sort of thing we should have a lot more home visits'.

The overall feeling was that it is the ethos of the school rather than IMPACT *per se* which affects relationships with ethnic minority parents. In schools which have established good relationships with parents and involve them in other initiatives, parents are already used to participating in school life.

The above observations highlight the necessity of taking account of the overall context of people's lives, the economic and educational climate, personal backgrounds and experiences. These aspects will all contribute to the formation of attitudes and opinions.

Adapting to Cultural Diversity

One of the main points of concern to come up amongst teachers was the need for sensitivity to the cultural diversity of the children to make activities relevant, to consider parents' attitudes towards the activity, and to consider the resources available in the home. For example, many of the Asian children would have showers instead of baths, making a bath displacement activity impossible. IMPACT was seen as being greatly facilitative in educating teachers about different cultural backgrounds. One example of exploding cultural assumptions was a tea-making (sequencing) activity, when the teachers first became aware that many Asian parents don't make tea in a teapot. As a result of this, they altered the home corner equipment, and when subsequent capacity activities were sent home, teachers were now sensitive to the fact that children may not have teapots at home. Hence, through sending work home, teachers became more aware of cultural diversity in the homes and altered and re-evaluated what happens in the classroom accordingly. In this way, a two-way flow of information between teachers and parents, learning about each others' cultures and child-rearing practices can be established.

Another example of assumptions altering through IMPACT practice was in connection with games. A teacher at School B found that Asian children on the whole did not seem to play structured games at home, and so were not used to the rituals of taking turns, scoring, etc. She found that the children who were more conversant with games were those with older siblings who had been through the English school system. It was also suggested that there might be an economic factor, as, increasingly, both parents have to go out to work, children are left watching TV more.

As well as IMPACT helping to increase the two-way flow of information between school and home, teachers claimed to be able to see the richness of resources in the home; for example, when children were asked to bring in a potato recipe in School D, the bilingual children brought in an exotic selection of recipes, getting away from the perennial chips! This might be placed alongside my comments in next section concerning the 'disadvantage model'; when the teacher becomes aware of the resources available in the home, and not just lack of 'western' resources, she/he is less likely to attribute failure to children's disadvantage. Billig *et al.* (1988) found that teachers, while espousing the child-centred, discovery philosophy of education, would also espouse the disadvantage model: any failure must be due to a lack in the child's environment or capacity. He terms this an 'implicit dilemma'; these two beliefs seem contradictory, yet can be held by one teacher. The distinction between them is less clear in practice than in theory. Billig suggests that rather than springing from two separate ideological camps, they may be different expressions of one unitary, dilemmatic philosophy.

The requirements of teachers to 'deliver' the curriculum and at the same time to respect and honour all cultures equally was raised as being an important issue. Several teachers mentioned fear of offending different ethnic minority parents and, particularly, white parents. A teacher at School B had had comments back from white parents objecting to various multicultural activities. Respecting the cultures of all children is not a straightforward matter. The mother-tongue teacher at School D pointed out that although children may speak the same language, they may be of different religions, regions and/or, nationalities. They are in no way a homogeneous group.

Teachers, like everyone, are affected by the social climate in which they live. If recent events (such as the situation in Cleveland in which white parents withdrew their children from a school with a large Asian population) lead to a climate in which the customs and behaviour of minority groups are regarded as being less important and are misunderstood or perceived as threatening, teachers could face a dilemma between this climate and that of multiculturalism. However, IMPACT may have a very positive role to play in this area, as discussed above, in informing teachers and parents of each other's cultures.

This problem is linked to another point touched upon in the next section; there may be a tension between teachers and parents over the focus of multicultural reform — whether to focus on the curriculum, or on cultural factors. IMPACT again has an important part to play in increasing dialogue and enabling a forum to emerge in which these issues can be aired. It would be a mistake to regard IMPACT as purely a curriculum maths project; the wider ramifications, perhaps particularly in the realm of communication with bilingual children and parents, are important.

Returning briefly to the question of identity, a distinction has been made between cultural or ethnic identity on the one hand and personal identity on the other (Weinrich, 1979). Difficulties may arise when the two interact; to foster cultural identity may hinder development of personal identity, and vice versa, for the encouragement of personal identity in children may alienate them from their culture. The need to satisfy development of both types of identity is a dilemma inherent in British education as a whole which tends to emphasize the development of the individual. Knight (1981) says that some parents may expect ethnic identity to be developed at the expense of the child's general social and educational development.

Teacher's Perceptions of Parent's Views on IMPACT

Parents experience contradictions in their own conception of education and what they see happening in English schools. Teachers were very aware of this conflict. These contradictions encompass several areas.

Deborah Curle

Discipline of the child

One teacher feared that many of the children did not have the sort of relationship with their parents where they could say: 'This is what my teacher said; you're doing it wrong'. In other words, the fact that IMPACT children are encouraged to instruct their parents may cause a problem. It should be noted, however, that another teacher felt that the minority families got more involved in IMPACT because of the closely-knit family structures. It is possible that parents see the fact that the children are the tutors with the maths materials at home as a possible threat to family structure and hierarchy; in the education system they were brought up in, children are not encouraged to be assertive, independent and questioning. This conflict of expectations is made more acute in a situation like IMPACT when school is brought into the home, via the child.

The nature of the work the child does

It was pointed out by the mother-tongue teacher in School B that the type of work involved in IMPACT is very unfamiliar to parents used to a formal system of education. In School C an example was given by a teacher of a parent who sent her child back to school with suggestions for IMPACT sheets along the lines of: 'A is for Apple...', the type of work that the parent had been used to in her own country. Several teachers, (in Schools C and E) felt that many parents want more computation-type of activities, and had better results from these types of activity. They felt that this sort of activity is what parents understand, that they can see what is expected of them, and can see the point of the activity. It is interesting to ask whether this point is particularly true of minority parents, and whether minority parents are perhaps less likely to adjust as quickly as white parents in their ways of working. Teachers, again at Schools C and E, felt that parents often do not appreciate the difference between doing and understanding; that they see IMPACT as 'homework' that the child should do and finish, and are more concerned with the product than the process. Apparently, the parents sometimes actually do the activity for the child in order to produce a perfect result.

Comment sheet returns

The return of comment sheets is one way of ascertaining the amount of parental involvement. Overall, the trend was for returns from ethnic minority parents to be less than from English parents. A teacher at School B felt that English parents were more likely to make a comment because they know what teachers want them to write, and noted that this also happens on reading cards. She felt that the comment sheets could be off-putting as they involve parents having to write the 'correct' thing. Other teachers at the same school noted that the children who brought back the IMPACT sheets were the same as those who brought back their reading folders, and this response rate was not related to ethnic background. In School C it was noted that English parents overall made more critical and in-depth comments than Asian parents, elaborating on how they had followed up an activity. So while the level of involvement between minority and majority parents was perceived to be the same, the quality of comments received back was different. In School D, on the other hand, one teacher had had no comments back at all from ethnic minority parents. This can be related to the lack of confidence noted by the mother-tongue teachers at the same school.

Parent's role in education

The dichotomy between parents' views on their own role in education and the teacher's view of the parents' role came out in several instances. While IMPACT teachers are looking for parents to take an active role as co-educators, some parents may see their own role as fostering social and moral development rather than intellectual development. The awe in which some minority parents held teachers was brought up several times as an impediment to dialogue with parents, and many teachers felt that parents would not deem it their job to get involved in education. This reticence could account for the lack of critical and constructive comments. It is also interesting to consider it in light of the point made in School E that it is the parents who have regular contact with the school who make comments about and are more involved with IMPACT.

From the above observations, several contradictions emerge. Teachers face an inherent dilemma; within our educational ethos is the traditional desire for parents not to criticize, yet teachers doing IMPACT are now wanting parents to criticize on IMPACT comment sheets, criticism being a sign of involvement and partnership. Parents are caught in the conflict between their view of their role in education, and the teacher's view of what the parent's role should be.

Teachers face a clash of values between their educational ideals and those of the parents, with parents often wanting more formal methods of teaching. In this way, IMPACT is situated at the heart of the problem by bringing work into the home. A lot of it boils down to relationships with parents, which IMPACT is seen to be addressing in a very real and immediate way.

It is important to look at these conflicts in what Billig calls their 'rhetorical context'. As discussed previously, attitudes are not held in a vacuum; they are very much affected by one's situation. It is possible that parent's attitudes towards these aspects of education are affected by the challenge to their beliefs posed by the British system, by social isolation, lack of equal opportunities, etc. IMPACT is pitching into this complex mess of factors and is interwoven with them in its efforts to effect change.

Conclusion

By bringing school into the home, IMPACT provides specific points of contact between parents and teachers, some of which have been touched upon in this paper: parents' response/comment sheets, the activities which the child brings home, displays and notices in the school, dialogue between parents and teachers. It is clear that these sites of exchange can and do provide what Billig refers to as 'dilemmatic situations' in which parents' and teachers' views are argued through in a way specific to that situation. For example, a teacher puts a display notice up in two languages, and finds an Asian father protesting about this. Her views on 'multicultural education' and his views on what he wants for his child are both challenged and subsequently argued through. Taking the issue of language at large: in some instances, parents appear to be happy to do IMPACT activities in their mother-tongue, while in others, they are reluctant to do so, which indicates a myriad of social, migratory, psychological and educational factors of which IMPACT is one, operating in complex interaction. Likewise, issues such as the child instructing the parent, parents' reactions to IMPACT activities and parents' views on their own role in education provide a forum for argumentation about ethnicity in each circumstance. As Billig suggests, views can be contradictory within a seemingly unified stance. Examples of this are parents wanting children to do well in British society, yet not wanting family structures undermined; teachers wanting parents to get involved yet not to 'interfere'. There can also be contradictions between different stances, as when teachers' and parents' views conflict. We have seen instances of this conflict with regard to language, and the nature of the work the child does. Both types of contradiction arise when parents and teachers have to argue through the situations posed by IMPACT through the points of contact mentioned above.

The implications are far-reaching. They suggest first that we re-evaluate our views on 'ideology'. Billig suggests that ideology is not a logical, cut and dried system, but that it contains 'contrary themes', which are constantly being argued out in the arena of everyday life. The ideologies of 'multiculturalism' and of 'involving parents' are not straightforward, cohesive systems by any means. Within the ideology of multiculturalism, teachers are arguing out their values in the face of parents' attitudes and expectations (e.g. trying not to offend parents of different backgrounds) and of the general social and educational climate. Within the ideology of involving parents, teachers sometimes have to re-evaluate their methods in the face of apparent parental reluctance to get involved, and are struggling with contradictory forces; wanting parents to become involved, yet not wanting parental criticism. So, while people may adhere to a particular 'ideology', in practice they are arguing through unique social situations and reacting to them accordingly.

Likewise, the concept of 'ethnicity' must be brought into question. It was mentioned at the beginning of this paper that there is a recognition now that ethnic identity is not a static entity. It would seem that we can go further and suggest that ethnicity is being argued through in a unique way in every different situation. Parents' attitudes towards, say, use of the mother-tongue, their child's cultural identity, and the roles of home and school are argued through in accordance with their present and past circumstances. It follows that we cannot say that, for example. Muslim Bangladeshis from Sylhet in East London whose children attend a school of type X will hold the following views on Y. Similarly, we cannot say that doing IMPACT in one particular way with Tamil Indian children and parents will lead to a particular response.

The implications reach beyond IMPACT to educational policy generally. The realization of the complex dynamics and the contradictions arising out of educational life must be thought-provoking for policy makers and curriculum reformers everywhere. Rather than panicking at the lack of certainty suggested by this complexity, however, surely we should look upon it as an opportunity to look at situations in a fresh light, and accept that in giving up a degree of certainty, we are gaining a more fruitful, illuminating way of looking at the social world.

References

BALLARD, C. (1979) 'Conflict, Coninuity and Change' in SAIFULLAH-KHAN, V. (Ed.) *Minority Families in Britain*, London, Macmillan Press Ltd.

BILLIG, M. (1989) *Arguing and Thinking: A Rhetorical Approach to Social Psychology*, Cambridge, Cambridge University Press.

BILLIG, M. *et al.* (1988) *Ideological Dilemmas: A Social Psychology of Everyday Thinking*, London, Sage Publications Ltd.

CLARKE, M., BARR, J.E. and DEWHIRST, W. (1986) 'Early Education in Multicultural Schools', *Concern*, Winter 1985–86, 57.

COOLEY, C.H. (1902) *Human Nature and Social Order*, New York, Scribners.

CURLE, D. (1986) *Report on a Visit to Bangladesh*, London, Florence and Don McGregor Trust.

FESTINGER, L. (1957) *A Theory of Cognitive Dissonance*, New York, Row Peterson.

GHUMAN, P.A.S. (1980) 'Bhattra Seikhs in Cardiff: Family and Kinship Organisation', *New Community*, **8**, 3, pp. 309–16.

GHUMAN, P.A.S. and GALLOP, R. (1981) 'Educational Attitudes of Bengali Families in Cardiff', *Journal of Multicultural Development*, **2**, 2.

GUPTA, P. (1977) 'Educational and Vocational Aspirations of Asian Immigrants and English School-Leavers', *British Journal of Sociology*, **28**, 2, pp. 185–98.

HARRÉ, R. (1989) 'Language Games and the Texts of Identity', in SHOTTER, J. and GERGEN, K.G. (Eds) *Texts of Identity*, London, Sage Publications Ltd.

HORNBY, P.A. (1977) *Bilingualism, Psychological, Social and Educational Implications*, London, Academic Press.

ILEA (1985) *Bangladeshi Mothers' Views on Schooling in Tower Hamlets*, Research and Statistics Report, November.

yDeborah Curle

yKNIGHT, R. (1981) *Race Relations in Bradford*, Bradford Metropolitan District Council (mimeo).
MCGUIRE, W.J. (1964) 'Inducing Resistance to Persuasion: Some Contemporary Approaches', in BERKOWITZ, L. (Ed.) *Advances in Experimental Social Psychology* Vol. 1, New York, Academic Press.
MEAD, G.H. (1934) *Mind, Self and Society*, Chicago, University of Chicago Press.
MIDWINTER, E. (1977) 'Teaching with the urban environment', in RAYNER, J. and HARRIS, E. (Eds) *Schooling in the City*, London, Ward Lock.
NFER (1989) *Boosting Educational Achievement*, report of the Independent Inquiry into educational achievement in the London Borough of Newham, Chaired by Seamus Hegarty, London, Newham Council.
REES, O. (1983) 'Ethnic Groups, Bilingualism and Attainment', in BAGLEY, C. and VERMA, G.K. (1983) (Eds) *Multicultural Children: Education, Ethnicity and Cognitive Styles*, Aldershot, Gower.
REX, J. and TOMLINSON, S. (1979) *Colonial Immigrants in a British City — A Class Analysis*, London, Routledge.
SAIFULLAH-KHAN, V. (1979) 'Migration and Social Stress' in SAIFULLAH-KHAN, V. (Ed.) *Minority Families in Britain*, London, Macmillan Press Ltd.
SAUNDERS, M. (1973) 'Home Influences on ESN Children', unpublished MPhil thesis, Nottingham University.
SAUNDERS, M. (1977) 'A review of studies of the socio-familial background', CHILD, **6**, pp. 407–23.
SHERIF, M. and HOWLAND, C.I. (1961) *Social Judgments*, New Haven, CT, Yale University Press.
SHOTTER, J. (1989) 'Social Accountability and the Social Construction of "You"', in SHOTTER, J. and GERGEN, K.G. (Eds) *Texts of Identity*, London, Sage Publications Ltd.
TANNA, K. (1981) Gujarati Muslim Parents in Lancaster — Their Views on Education, unpublished independent study for BA degree, University of Lancaster.
TIZARD, B., MORTIMORE, J. and BURCHELL, B. (1981) *Involving Parents in Nursery and Infant Schools*, London, Grant-McIntyre.
TOMLINSON, S. (1984) Home and School in Multicultural Britain, Batsford Academic and Education Ltd, London.
ULLAH, P. (1985) 'Second Generation Irish Youth: Identity and Ethnicity', *New Community*, **12**, pp. 310–20.
VASS, J. and MERTTENS, R. (1987) The Cultural Mediation and Determination of Intuitive Knowledge and Cognitive Development, paper delivered at Conference on Child Research, 'Growing into the Modern World', Trondheim, Norway.
WEINREICH, P. (1979) 'Ethnicity and Adolescent Identity Conflict' in SAIFULLAH-KHAN, V. (Ed.) *Minority Families in Britain*, London, Macmillan Press Ltd.

142

Chapter 15

Practising Mathematics Education: A Context for IMPACT

Lin Taylor and John Smith

These authors work as senior lecturers in mathematics education. They describe here the results of a series of long interviews with teachers working in IMPACT schools. These interviews were conducted by John and Lin in schools in Barnet, Redbridge, Oxford and Newham. What the teachers said, and some of the comments they made, are analyzed against the backdrop of current orthodox post-Cockcroft ideas within the maths education community. The chapter details the reponses of these teachers not only to IMPACT but also to the effects of recent legislative changes. It concludes by setting the IMPACT practices as described above in the context of the National Curriculum and related programme of assessment.

What is good mathematics teaching? There is no single, or simple, answer to this question; there is instead a forest of ideas about the problems and potential of mathematics education. How does IMPACT guide teachers through these ideas, and support good practice?

Mathematics education always stands in danger of being reduced to an attempt to teach a set of rules, rules useful for answering the kind of question set in examinations. As long ago as 1976 Skemp contrasted such 'instrumental understanding' with the procedural understanding which is essential to mathematics. Until recently, primary school teachers have largely been shielded from the pressures imposed, for example, by an A-level syllabus, but we believe that there nevertheless exists a common view of mathematics as an evil necessity. Buxton (1981) refers to the 'panic about maths' felt by many people, including of course teachers, resulting from their own experience of a narrow mathematics education. However, good teaching relies on more than just a positive perception of mathematics; teachers must understand the psychology of mathematics learning. For example, a critical step is for children to make the links between their current understanding and the formal symbolism demanded by conventional, and more advanced, mathematics. Hughes (1986) among others, has pointed to the problems this can present children with when they begin school. Shuard (1986) cautions:

> ... children are not *tabula rasa* [sic]; they come to the curriculum with a variety of understandings and misunderstandings, and with methods and problem-solving strategies which they have constructed for themselves, and which may be different from those taught (Shuard, 1986, p. 76).

According to many educationalists, the extent to which children are regarded as *thinkers in their own right* is central to their learning.

How are teachers being guided through this forest of ideas, and supported by practical advice? Mainly, we suggest, through a number of official statements, most notably the report of the Cockcroft Committee. When '*Mathematics Counts*' (best known as the Cockcroft Report) was published in 1982 it was welcomed by many educationalists as an embodiment of good practice, and it quickly developed the status of the 'Mathematics Education Bible'. Policy documents were supported by quotations from it; it was advisable to refer to it at job interviews. It became required reading in schools, so compared with the ideas of mathematics educators, or with the findings of individual pieces of research, it made a large impact. We think this impact is still felt today. For many teachers, what constitutes good mathematics practice is what they view the Cockcroft Report as having said.

How does this practice show itself in IMPACT schools? In the spring term 1990 we interviewed a number of IMPACT teachers, using an interviewing schedule designed to pilot a questionnaire to be used in the IMPACT project. Our own research interests, however, lay in exploring the ways in which teachers regard themselves, and their schools, within the perspectives referred to above. To some extent, we were probably thought of as educationalists, and therefore expecting particular answers. Even so, we believe it was possible to gain some insight into the practices and attitudes of these teachers, and their responses have clarified the ideas we set out here.

Teachers seemed to show an awareness of the Cockcroft Report, and subservience to the 'Cockcroft Bible'. They tended to see themselves as more radical than parents. They viewed IMPACT as a way for parents to get more experience of the work children do in school: to discard what one teacher desribed as 'cross and tick' mathematics, or, as another put it, to help parents to understand the importance of practical mathematics, and to take the pressure off the demand for 'sums in books'. Teachers wanted parents to value more the ordinary things they do at home, and to see them as being valuable in mathematics learning. Parents were reported as having, in many cases, a limited view of their children's maths. Some would say of an IMPACT activity, 'this isn't maths'. Parents of the older children, it was suggested, would want a more 'nitty-gritty', 'down-to-earth' '11-plus' style. One teacher suggested that parents tend to see mathematics in terms of their own last school experiences, rather than in terms of what a child might be expected to understand, and need to understand, at their own level. It was hoped that using IMPACT would introduce parents to the idea that mathematics education is no longer just learning a set of rules. The Cockcroft Report pointed to the problem:

> It has been pointed out to us that, albeit with the best of intentions, some parents can exercise undesirable pressure on teachers to introduce written recording of mathematics, and especialy 'sums', at too early a stage, because they believe that the written record is a necessary sign of a child's progress (Cockcroft *et al.* 1982, p. 304).

Most of the teachers we interviewed were very conscious of the need for practical work. One said, 'I do more practical maths now, in a more concentrated way'.

> Practical work is essential throughout the primary years if the mathematics curriculum is to be developed in a way which we have advocated ... It is, though, necessary to realise at the outset that such work requires a considerable amount of time (Cockcroft *et al.*, 1982, p. 289).

Teachers felt IMPACT had the potential to change parent's attitudes; they felt parents needed to understand that even everyday activities are relevant to mathematics learning, and so to appreciate their children's mathematics as a practical activity. Many of the teachers reported that IMPACT gave the children opportunities to do practical work which they felt would have been impossible to provide in the classroom. In particular, there was not enough time for teachers to provide the one-to-one contact needed to support this practical approach. Several felt such support could only be offered to children who, for one reason or another, failed to do the IMPACT activity at home.

However, emphasis on practical work in itself does not necessarily encourage the understanding of the link between formal symbolism and concrete understanding. As Hughes points out,

> In order to solve mathematical problems, we need to be capable not only of operating within the formal code, but also of making fluent translations between formal and concrete representations of the same problem (Hughes, 1986, p. 169).

One way of establishing this link is to introduce mathematics through problem-solving. The Cockcroft Report suggested,

> The ability to solve problems is at the heart of mathematics.... problems [set in schools] should relate both to the application of mathematics to everyday situations within the pupils' experience, and also to situations which are unfamiliar (Cockcroft *et al.*, 1982, p. 249).

Problem-solving again was an area where the teachers felt IMPACT helped, as they were very aware of the need to develop these techniques. As one teacher said, 'With infants, even choosing a potato is a problem-solving activitiy'.

Many of the teachers we talked to emphasized the need to make cross-curricular links, and described how IMPACT helped them to do this. One said, 'IMPACT now ties into topic work, not just 'maths' maths work', reflecting the trend towards thematic approaches to mathematics, and relates to the Cockcroft Report's finding:

> The experiences of young children do not come in separate packages with 'subject labels'; as children explore the world around them, mathematical experiences present themselves alongside others. The teacher needs therefore to seek opportunities for drawing mathematical experience out of a wide range of children's activities. (Cockcroft *et al.*, 1982, p. 352).

One further area highlighted by the Cockcroft report is the importance of language.

> Language plays an important part in the formulation and expression of mathematical ideas (Cockcroft *et al.*, 1982, p. 306).

although,

> For many pupils this will require a great deal of discussion and oral work before even very simple problems can be tackled in written form (Cockcroft *et al.*, 1982, p. 249).

Only one teacher, however, reported of IMPACT, 'It helps me to realize the children's difficulties, for example, in using mathematical language'. The only other references to language concerned the problem for children whose first language was not English, and who had English language difficulties. Yet Brissenden points out,

> The role of language in the learning of mathematics has come to be seen as one of increasing, indeed vital, importance (Brissenden, 1988, p. xi).

This is one important aspect of the Cockcroft Report that still seems to be neglected, as is mentioned for example by the Welsh Inspectorate report,

> In many schools the reliance placed upon published schemes, through which pupils proceed at their own pace, tends to diminish the opportunities for group discussion . . . (reported in Brissenden, 1988, p. 5).

We feel this lack significant, in that IMPACT *should* be a useful vehicle for helping develop children's use of language in a mathematical context. We are unsure why this appears not to have been taken up. One reason could be that educationalists, and research in the field of mathematics language, do not put over a concerted view, but we consider a more likely explanation is the very difficult nature of dealing with language in the classroom. For example, we need quite radical thinking about the way in which children are perceived as learners, and indeed viewed as people. The children's language needs to be given more time and importance in what is probably an already crowded classroom; when class numbers get bigger this treatment is made even more difficult. Also, to some extent, cross-curricular approaches negate the idea of areas of the curriculum being, as it were, intertwined; we may present topics as cross-curricular, yet separate out the language aspects and mathematics aspects when planning and assessing. Language and mathematics are thus viewed as separate entities. Yet several writers have pointed to the crucial *interrelationship* between mathematics and language. Suggesting that many natural languages have a mathematics *register*, in which mathematical discussion takes place, Pimm says,

> *Learning to speak, and more subtly, learning to mean* like a mathematician, involves acquiring the forms and the meanings and ways of seeing enshrined in the mathematics register (Pimm, 1987, p. 207 our emphasis).

One consequence of teachers taking on board the responsibility for children learning mathematical language is that this inevitably affects their role. Teachers need to negotiate meaning with the children, and to be flexible in their responses; this is difficult for teachers who lack confidence in their mathematical ability, who have a negative attitude towards mathematics, or who have an otherwise limited view of mathematics education.

It seemed to us that some of the teachers we spoke to were not prepared to loosen their control, and perceived IMPACT as only an addition to the curriculum. As one teacher put it, 'IMPACT was going to *help* my curriculm, not alter it', for another, IMPACT 'is one of the added extras that makes it all worth while'. On the whole, teachers we interviewed did not consider IMPACT to affect their own attitude to the mathematics curriculum.

Nonetheless, all the teachers we talked to reported some positive attitudes in their children towards mathematics. Although some attributed improvement to IMPACT, others said this attitude reflected the general ethos of the classrom, or suggested the children were too young to have been disillusioned by their experiences of mathematics teaching.

The role of parents is of course central to the success of IMPACT in their children's learning.

> We believe it is therefore important that schools should make active efforts to enlist the help of parents by explaining the approaches to

mathematics which they are using for the purposes of mathematics activities which parents themselves may not have undertaken while at school (Cockcroft *et al.*, 1982, p. 207).

We found it impressive that *all* the teachers we interviewed saw IMPACT mainly — and sometimes exclusively — as a parental involvement project. This involvement was important to them for several reasons. Many felt it was an extension of their school's existing policy of involving parents. Sometimes it helped in the day to day contact in that it gave a focus, a reason for a parent to see the teacher. Although this content was generally regarded as a good thing, one teacher remarked that she felt IMPACT made her more susceptible to parents' comments.

So the role of the teacher can be seen as under further threat from the changing roles of parents. If parents are to be involved more directly in their children's education, how does this affect the role of the teacher? We found expressions of dissatisfaction with parents, which may suggest there is reluctance to give up aspects of the teachers' role to them.

One teacher did not use IMPACT work at all to introduce new mathematical ideas, in case some children would be disadvantaged through lack of home experience. In that teacher's view, IMPACT was to be used only to follow up work already well established in school. It was the general experience that some children regularly did not do the IMPACT activity adequately at home, often through the lack of allotted time. There was concern that some children ('those you want' as one teacher put it) regularly failed to receive support at home. Teachers could argue with parents that their children would lose out, but this was ultimately unsatisfactory and seems to run counter to the spirit of IMPACT. Many said they spent time making up this deficit in school. One said, 'My role is to compensate, but not ignore those who get a good dialogue at home'.

Some teachers enlarged on their difficulties in communicating with parents. One suggested there should be a form for teachers to fill in, in reply to the form parents complete after their child's IMPACT activity! There were concerns about reaching households in which English is the second language. More fundamental, however, is the view that parents are able to provide only limited support to their children's mathematical education. One teacher said, 'I think sometimes that we expect too much from parents'. There is a general fear that what may be obvious to the teacher as an opportunity for mathematics learning may not appear so to parents. Although parents take account of what children say, some regularly were thought not to listen to their explanations and to ignore their opinions. When asked whether parents on the whole listen to their children, one teacher put it, typifying the rest, 'Some do, some don't — not *carefully*'.

The experience received by children doing their IMPACT activities at home was varied. Some were given the IMPACT sheet to colour in or draw on, irrespective of the sheet's intentions. For example, a sheet on which children were intended to draw items that would fit into a yoghurt pot, had been returned with a host of inappropriate drawings which the child clearly knew would not have fitted. Some parents seemed to use IMPACT as a last-minute item before bedtime, reducing the activity to a perfunctory carrying-out of the instructions, but losing the purpose. One sheet called for children to examine the clothes in a wardrobe; a teacher reported that one parent had simply used the set of clothes the child was wearing at the time, devaluing the sorting and matching activity which was the underlying aim of the sheet. At the other extreme, the activity could be taken out of the child's hands altogether and carried on by the parent at an adult level.

Sheer presentation was found to influence the way IMPACT was valued by parents. Where occasional mistakes in grammar and spelling had been found in materials sent home, teachers reported complaints. One school, which had gone to some lengths over presentation, had received enquiries from parents about where this scheme could be bought; the parents were then positively impressed to hear that the teachers themselves had produced the sheets sent home. It may be that experiences of this kind have a disproportionate, although understandable, effect on the way mathematics is represented by IMPACT schools as part of ordinary, everyday activity.

There were other, more positive, experiences of parental involvement. For many, there was less peer pressure for children and a view of maths as a more enjoyable activity. Friendly neighbours could join in with IMPACT, so that it was not seen as an imposition. One teacher felt parents had become better at listening to their children, and working with them at home, as a result of using IMPACT. Another teacher said that it was the children, rather than the parents now, who would protest that IMPACT was not 'real' maths and that they therefore 'hadn't done any maths today'. In many schools, the most important contribution made by parents through their involvement with IMPACT was the time they gave to the children; it was this personal attention the teachers felt they were least able to provide at school. IMPACT was thus a way of extending the classroom into the home. As Shuard says,

> Schools will need to take parents into their confidence and help them to understand the need for new ideas and new methods if their children are to succeed in mathematical thinking. Moreover, parents will themselves need to be involved in mathematical thinking if their attitudes are to change ... (Shuard, 1986, p. 136).

Assessment was a difficult area, and most teachers found it hard to put into words how they assessed, although they were aware that IMPACT helped with the process. Typical comments were, 'IMPACT helps me to realize the children's difficulties' and 'IMPACT reveals new things about the children', but assessment of how well the IMPACT activity had been done at home was mainly by getting an impression of how quickly the forms were returned. Details on the evaluation form, and a superficial analysis of how well the child appeared to have done the task, were regarded as unreliable. Some teachers expressed reservations about interpreting the returned IMPACT work. One said, 'You never know who's done it'. Parents were seen as having an unreliable view of learning. One teacher said, 'they may not value *understanding* as opposed to *doing*'. Some teachers were clear that the assessment of what had gone on at home was to be done in discussion with the children, afterwards, back in school. Some regarded the present provision for this as enough, but one said that it was impossible to find time to do this adequately, since there is not time to speak to each child individually, and 'you can't judge by the end result' — the returned IMPACT sheet.

British education has traditionally been eclectic. At present mathematics classroom practice is no more uniform and consistent than the educational theory and research which underpins it. The National Curriculum is not based on research however; its single line is not affected by the plethora of practices and theories, and as the Cockcroft Report warns,

> We are aware that there are some teachers who would wish us to indicate a definitive style for the teaching of mathematics, but we do not believe that this is either desirable or possible. Approaches to the teaching of a particular piece of mathematics need to be related to the topic itself and to the abilities and experience of both teachers and pupils. Because of differences of personality and circumstance, methods which may be extremely successful with one teacher and one group of pupils will not necessarily be suitable for use by another teacher or with a different group of pupils' (Cockcroft *et al.*, 1982, p. 242).

Teachers try out different ideas and use what works for them; this is one reason why it is so hard to define good practice. The National Curriculum, although it nominally accepts a variety of teaching styles, may tend to reduce teaching to a single mould, simply because of the pressure to test levels of attainment.

It may be that the IMPACT schools are unrepresentative; certainly we found a buoyancy and confidence about their established mathematics policies. Taking on the IMPACT project has demanded commitment on the part of each school and its staff. It was noticeable that, in our initial questions, teachers resisted the suggestion that IMPACT was an experiment. Where reference to the 'IMPACT experiment' was made, it was seen as the Local Authority's experiment, using the schools (rather than their children) as the 'guinea pigs'. The teachers then had worked hard to develop their IMPACT materials, and had adapted IMPACT ideas to their own needs.

We are at a time of crisis in education; teachers have the opportunity to implement the non-statutory aspects of the National Curriculum and continue the practices supported by the Cockcroft Report, but they face the danger of being reduced by the burden of assessment to teaching an operational understanding which will match that assessment. In the IMPACT schools, we found a sense of ownership of the mathematics curriculum, and a feeling of robustness in the child-centred practices already established.

References

BRISSENDEN, T. (1988) *Talking About Mathematics*, Oxford, Blackwell.

BUXTON, L. (1981) 'Do you Panic about Maths?', London, Heinemann Educational.

COCKCROFT, W.H. *et al.* (1982) *Mathematics Counts*, London, HMSO.

HUGHES, M. (1986) *Children and Number*, Oxford, Blackwell.

PIMM, D. (1987) 'Speaking Mathematically', London, Routledge, Kegan and Paul.

SHUARD, H. (1986) *Primary Mathematics Today and Tomorrow*, York, Longman.

SKEMP, R.R. (1976) 'Relational Understanding and Instrumental Understanding', *Mathematics Teaching*, **77**.

Chapter 16

IMPACT In-Service Training: A View from the Centre of the Web

Ruth Merttens

This chapter provides a detailed account of the provision of in-service training on IMPACT. The project is, among other things, a major supplier of INSET and INSET materials, and much of the work of those involved on IMPACT has been concerned with the production and maintenance of change. Ruth Merttens describes how the INSET on IMPACT developed from the informal, responsive and largely personal ways of working which characterized the contact with the first pilot schools, through to the largely devolved and more inspirational styles of meeting which have been a feature of setting up the IMPACT network. She develops a new and personal theory of in-service provision in which the dominant vocabulary of cause and effect, success and failure, is replaced by a more elusive imagery.

Prelude

This chapter describes how we have tried to instigate and encourage change over the last five years. IMPACT is a large project which is explicitly concerned with the introduction of new routines, techniques and strategies into classroom practices, and with the modifications of existing behaviour patterns which are necessary in order to accommodate them. We have been concerned to reflect upon and record the effects of these changes as they have become embedded in the established processes of schooling.

Usually changes in the nature or type of INSET provision are reported as if they are the result of a carefully worked out, theoretically driven plan prepared in advance and then 'put into practice' (a telling phrase). In fact in our experience, such changes are often the fortuitous result of haphazard and immediate intuitive responses to contingent circumstances and constraining demands. Rather as Tolstoy set out to debunk the 'great man' notion of history, so there are those attempting to debunk the idea that new strategies in teaching must be the result of careful, theory-based forethought, rather than arising from a multiplicity of identified and unidentified causes both proximate and more or less contingent upon immediate circumstance. This recognition has obvious implications for the planning of in-service training to which I shall return later in the chapter.

First Movement: Beginnings

In 1985 when IMPACT started, the Cockcroft Report (1982) dissemination process was continuing apace. Members of the Committee were still touring the country giving talks, and new advisory support teachers were to be found travelling the highways and byways of Great Britain to spread the word. It was not for nothing that the term 'Maths Missionaries' was coined for these teachers. The prevailing feeling was of a missionary zeal to 'convert' as many classroom teachers as possible to the right ways of seeing maths and teaching the subject to children. Indeed, there were those who would have ruled out the word 'teach'. Our job, as teachers, was to *enable* children to develop mathematically by supplying them with a series of practical tasks and activities and *encouraging* them to 'investigate' why things worked out as they did, mathematically speaking. We all had to recognize that maths existed not, as had been previously assumed by a whole generation of teachers, as a dry-as-dust textbook subject of little pragmatic use yet essential for the measurement of intelligence, but as a 'Really Useful and Practical' subject which was, above all, *fun*! A teacher writing in a maths education journal at the time wrote,

> In 1982 he signed up with the Open University. He undertook 'Developing Mathematical Thinking' and to his own amazement, he passed. In 1984 he did 'Mathematics Across the Curriculum'. This course taught him that mathematics was about solving problems and explaining things. His *conversion* was complete. He was a 'Born-again Mathematician'. His task now was to spread the word (my italics, Sherring, 1985).

The metaphor of 'conversion to a faith' is an apt one. Those who persisted in holding a contrary view were pathologized as having failed to see the light. Definitions of good mathematics teaching came to depend almost solely upon the degree to which the classroom practice provided indications of compliance to the current philosophy, and upon the teacher's ability to utilize the correct terminology in their accounts and description. It is important to recognize this since the post-Cockcroft orthodoxy still to a large extent determines what can and cannot be said in mathematics education, and, more importantly, what does not need to be said. Thus some pieces of mathematics teaching do not require any pedagogical justification; they are 'self-justifying'. We all 'know' that these are 'good' ways to approach maths teaching, and there is no need to specify why. It is this assumption which leads Paul Ernest to entitle a section in his book on current developments in maths education, 'Questioning the Sacred Cows' (1989) and David Burghes to call the same set of beliefs 'The Faith' (1989).

In the mid-1980s when IMPACT began, converting the masses required not only that the missionaries were themselves 'converted' to the new ways of being and modes of operating, but that they had sufficient contact with the classroom to demonstrate the way that teaching should — in the new era — be conducted. Thus, the dominant mode of providing the in-service training at the time came to be categorized as 'classroom focused'. This involved the support teachers (maths missionaries) in working alongside practising class-room teachers. Through this type of sustained contact with 'post-Cockcroft' practice, it was believed that the teacher would be 'converted'. Many support teachers had a timetable of six or seven half-days a week in classrooms and one or two half-days for preparing materials and administration. This is a pattern of working which persists to the present time in many authorities despite the fact that the assumption that effective changes to practice are brought about through working alongside the 'expert' has recently been sub-jected to sustained criticism on a number of fronts (see Easen, 1985; Stow and Foxman, 1988; Burghes, 1989; Brown, 1989).

The more conventional maths education 'courses' were greatly reduced in number, time and importance as part of the whole INSET scene. The methodology of taught courses was itself under fire as the impetus for 'learn-ing through doing' came to occupy a more consolidated position as the dom-inant ideology of primary practice. Teachers, like children, it was argued, could only come to *learn* and thereby to change their approach to primary maths if they were able to *do*. i.e. to try out the new methods for themselves in the classroom.

Where taught courses still existed, an ideologically more compatible pedagogy was developed. This involved the idea of 'workshops' rather than lectures. Through practical group sessions teachers could *do* and thereby learn. Thus, any lecturer actually 'lecturing' on the subject of primary maths practice, or providing lists or descriptions of a variety of suitable maths activities or possible teaching strategies, ran the risk of being described as old-fashioned or unorthodox at best, or incompetent at worst. Rather, teachers had to be given the chance to try out any activity which was being suggested for classroom use. This dramatically reduced the number of activi-ties and the quantity of information it was possible to cover in any one session, but it did mean that teachers got what later came to be called, in a computer metaphor, 'hands-on' experience of the 'new' maths.

Starting Off...

IMPACT began somewhat as a hobby since I was employed as a full-time lecturer in maths education in a teacher-training institution. All the in-service work on IMPACT therefore had to take place in the late afternoons and evenings or in the early mornings or lunchtimes. The teachers and I became expert at slotting INSET sessions into the crevices of our working day. However, it is fair to say that a very small proportion of the initial INSET of IMPACT was classroom-focused. With the exception of one school, in which I worked two sessions a week as part of my 'recent and relevant' experience, I was simply not able to work alongside the first IMPACT teachers in their classes. With the benefit of hindsight, I can see that what occurred as a result of pragmatic considerations was formative in breaking with current beliefs about effective in-service training.

IMPACT was a new idea. It was the first time that anyone had attempted to involve parents in the maths curriculum through take-home activities. When I was looking to discuss the initial ideas I found that within the world of maths education many were wary of working with parents, believing that this would imperil the new ways of teaching maths. Parents were widely credited with being the reason why some teachers expressed a reluctance to abandon their commercial maths schemes or move away from rote-learning or skills-practice exercises. Notes taken at a large meeting of the maths advisory support staff from several LEAs reveal the strength of the feeling that parents were responsible for the failure to implement some of the recommendations of Cockcroft. There were no dissenting voices to the view that parents in general represented a force for the worse in the maths education of their children, despite the fact that many — perhaps even most — of the professionals in the room were themselves parents.

IMPACT in general, and myself in particular, borrowed a great deal from the experiences of those involved in the shared reading initiatives (see Merttens, this volume). I decided that weekly maths activities, designed with the specific week's work in mind, taken home by the child and shared with the parent, sibling or anyone else at home, would replace the book in the shared reading. Because I presumed a higher degree of uncertainty on the part of the parents with regard to maths than existed with reading, I designed a simple 'box-ticked' form to act as the comment sheet on IMPACT. This was the basic model of parental involvement in the maths curriculum which, with remarkably few adaptations, has survived until the present day (see chapter 1 for a full account of IMPACT pedagogy and practice).

The in-service training on IMPACT with these first teachers largely consisted in talking through some of the issues raised by the idea of involving the parents and then instructing them in the procedures described above. The bulk of our time and energy was devoted to two aspects of the process described:

1   The designing and drafting of suitable sheets each week;
2   Instructing them in the procedures described above.

Much time and energy was devoted to the designing and drafting of suitable sheets each week. Each teacher and I would spend a great deal of time discussing where the children had got to each week with their maths. We would often focus on individual children as well as considering the class as a whole in these discussions. We would then put our heads together and see if we could think of a suitable activity for the children to do at home. This sometimes meant thinking of several variations in order to accommodate the different levels of ability within the class.

Several important precedents were established through this way of working.

— the activity had to be closely related to the immediate classwork experiences of the children;
— it was sometimes necessary to send more than one activity to accommodate different levels;
— what the activity should be was finalized only in the week it was sent out. This allowed for the parents' (or children's) comments to be taken into account.
— the activities were specially produced for those particular children in that class at that time.

The Responses from Parents

Many parents not only completed response forms by ticking the boxes to answer questions like, 'Did you enjoy this week's activity?' or 'Did you think it was too hard, too easy or just right?' They would also write a comment in the space provided. Still more parents actually came in and discussed the activities with the teachers. Both the teachers and I found these conversations enlivening and illuminating. It was the first time the teacher had been able to discuss a child's progress *on specific tasks* with someone else. Also, parents would sometimes modify or adapt an activity, or they might even be stimulated by a particular game or task to create a whole new activity. On one occasion an Indian mother described a game, similar to one sent home, which she used to play as a child in the village in India where she was brought up. The teacher then used that game as the following week's activity.

INSET Identification

The in-service training we did on IMPACT in the first two years did not really feel like INSET at all. There were no courses, no conferences and very few meetings. I did very little classroom-focused work, which up until that time I would have regarded as an essential prerequisite for implementing any changes in practice. Most of our work in schools was characterized by a lack of any defined or overt structure, and an informality of approach. We shared an image with the teachers as to a possible new way of *being* in relation to parents and children's learning. Together with the teachers, different strategies and patterns of behaviour were jointly constructed and new routines introduced, as the means of realizing this image in practice came to be generated.

More serious still was the absence of any predefined objectives. We knew we wanted to bring about changes in the ways teachers were then working, but how these changes would specifically manifest themselves, in what particular routines and behavioural strategies they would be evinced, was left to become clear over time. This is important, since in-service training is usually presented in advance as a given text. This sets up a sort of 'before and after' picture of INSET, reminiscent of those adverts 'I used to look like this *before* I started using ———, now I look like *this*!' Before the in-service training, the teacher's practice looks like this ———, afterwards, it should look like this ———.

It was not until others, outside IMPACT, started to enquire about how this in-service training had been so effective, and wanted to know the methods by which the changes had been so successfully implemented, that we began to produce *post hoc* accounts of what we had done. As always, such rationally produced, theoretically-framed, accounts bear only a tangential relation to the experiences they purport to describe. The processes of generalizing from specific experiences in particular schools give grounds for further suspicion as to the validity of these accounts. In any event, the amorphous and tentative nature of the practices I have described above cannot be captured in the terminology of 'success' and 'failure', of 'objectives' defined and met, which is traditionally available to us for the production of such accounts.

During the first two years on IMPACT we allowed the INSET to be almost wholly responsive. It was, as much as anything, *a part of the development* of change and not the *means* of implementing that change. This view of in-service training, once accepted, has important repercussions for how we think about change and development in education. It is a topic to which I shall return later in the chapter.

Second Movement: IMPACT Underway

IMPACT was set up as a jointly funded project with three LEAs, Barnet, Redbridge and Oxfordshire. There was an IMPACT support teacher in each authority.

The necessity to train support teachers was a major factor in the formalization of the mechanisms which had been developed on IMPACT during the first year. The movement from working in a fluid, responsive, and relatively informal fashion with our original schools, to the explication and exposition of the INSET methods on IMPACT in a systematic and fully articulated form, is one which too often implies not only a necessary and beneficial reflection, but a distancing from the practice itself and a focus upon the *packaging* of that practice. The fact that, surprisingly, the IMPACT project mainly resisted this process of commodification was due, in large part, to the nature of the experiences in the first two years of IMPACT.

We set about the implementation of IMPACT in six schools in each LEA in September 1987. In Barnet and Redbridge we were working constantly with the IMPACT support teacher in the authority, but almost in isolation from the other maths support staff, other than coincidental meetings and friendly chats over tea or coffee at the Teachers' Centre. In Oxfordshire, we worked in a coordinated fashion with the maths support staff since initially we had no IMPACT coordinator. We also worked very closely with the liaison officer for home-school partnership, with whom we shared the responsibility for all the parent meetings.

Since I had developed an informal way of working week by week with the teachers in the north London schools, we started by working in a similar fashion with the schools in Barnet, Redbridge and Oxfordshire. We agreed on a rota system whereby I visited schools in Barnet and Redbridge one week, and schools in Oxfordshire the next, and the alternate weeks in each area were covered by the IMPACT support staff or by the other advisory maths teachers in Oxfordshire. This support was intended to assist teachers in planning and designing their individual IMPACT activities and ensuring that they related directly to the immediate classwork. It was primarily assistance with maths, and the maths curriculum. Further, it was agreed that we would make sure that at least one member of the IMPACT team was at as many parents' meetings as possible, and we would guarantee to be present at two, at least, of the IMPACT launching meetings in every school. (There were normally three 'launch meetings' on one day).

Over a period of about half a term it was clear that both the teachers and the advisory support staff preferred to plan a little further in advance than one or two weeks, and we moved to a system of half-termly planning meetings thus pre-empting the planning requirements of the National Curriculum which was soon to arrive on the scene. Although the general maths curriculum is planned in some detail in advance, together with an outline of each week's suggested IMPACT activity, the precise details and design of the activity are drafted week by week to allow for modification in response to parents' suggestions or classroom contingencies. The structure of half-termly plans which can then be adapted is one which has remained in place on IMPACT ever since.

The same two aspects of IMPACT necessitated the vast majority of the INSET time available — namely the designing and drafting of the actual and specific IMPACT activity each week, and the management of the feedback from parents. However, I recorded in my INSET notebooks at the time that the nature of the queries posed by the teachers appeared to depend upon two factors:

— which LEA the school was in, and under what umbrella IMPACT had been introduced by that LEA;

— which support teacher (local or myself, maths or non-maths) was being consulted and informed.

Dealing with the last point first, it is almost trivially true that teachers, like anyone else, will to some extent say what they think the person listening wants to hear. Certainly, it makes sense for teachers to address questions to the person they believe is most likely to be able to answer them. However, what proved to be of interest was *which* questions teachers believed I could answer, or which points could be put to me, as opposed to those they reserved for the local support teachers, and similarly, which queries were reserved for 'non-maths' rather than 'maths' persons.

Teachers very quickly realized that IMPACT provided direct support in planning the curriculum from someone who was neither enmeshed in local politics nor necessarily sympathetic to the dominant orthodoxies, in terms of the approach of the local inspectorate. This enabled conversations which were in one sense liberating, in that no particular line had to be towed, and in another sense disabling, in that they produced some uncertainty as to the basis on which judgments or comparisons would be made. I was also surprised by the extent to which an 'outsider' to the locality, who nonetheless knew the area and worked in other schools but did not have an inspectoral role, could be used as a sounding board for 'risky' ideas. I seemed to become the repository for the expression of doubts about the efficacy of post-Cockcroft 'good' practice which could be perceived as 'dangerous' or detrimental to career prospects if expressed more publicly.

The accumulation of the 'Let's face it . . .' data — the remarks made by teachers which are off the record — suggests that there is a considerable gap between what teachers do and say in public (i.e. in front of other colleagues, as well as the headteacher or others in positions of authority or influence) and what they will say in private to someone unconnected to local power structures. The exploration of this gap is of interest in establishing the teacher's sense of identity *qua* teaching and has been discussed by others (see Schon, 1983; Ball and Goodson, 1985; Alexander, 1988; Nias, 1989; Woods, 1990). It may be, however, that IMPACT accentuated the teachers' ability to distance themselves from the dominant beliefs and to question what have hitherto been implicit assumptions, in that IMPACT requires a vision of what parents rather than teachers assume is good practice.

The first point regarding the dependence of the type of query during INSET contact upon the LEA's perception and categorization of IMPACT, was one we had not anticipated. Two of the authorities, Barnet and Redbridge, perceived the project predominantly as a maths in-service initiative, i.e. as a means of changing maths practice within primary classrooms to bring it more in line with a post-Cockcroft approach. They recognized that the IMPACT activities would involve practical and problem-solving tasks, and that teachers would respond to what the children had done at home with more similar work in the classroom. Oxfordshire, on the other hand, had an ongoing and active commitment to collaboration with parents, and IMPACT was very much a part of the provision in this area, both in terms of its funding, and in terms of the personnel who were to work on it. The maths aspect of IMPACT was more or less incidental at the start of IMPACT in Oxfordshire. It became less so as the pressure from teachers for assistance with maths planning and the design of activities increased and the maths support teachers realized its effect.

In Barnet and Redbridge, the number of queries concerning the 'parental involvement' aspect of IMPACT was very few by comparison with those which concerned some aspect of the maths curriculum and its delivery. In Oxfordshire, although the reverse was not true and the majority of the queries still concerned the maths curriculum, nonetheless there was a greatly increased number of queries concerning parental feedback and responses. This topic was more often than not raised by the teachers themselves rather than the INSET worker. Furthermore, the questions and discussion concerned sophisticated points and presumed some critical analysis and discussion among staff of the feedback they were obtaining. In Barnet and Redbridge, the topic was more often raised by the IMPACT team or by the support teacher than by the teachers themselves on a ratio of 3:1. The questions teachers asked displayed the lack of any previous thought or discussion time given to this aspect of IMPACT. No value judgment is intended here or should be taken as implied. Indeed the naivety and unexamined nature of the views of many teachers may have enabled them to 'hear' what parents were saying in a way which can become more difficult once a discussion process involving the positioning and possible polarization of parents has occurred (see Brown, this volume).

Third-Person INSET

Once the IMPACT project was up and running, so to speak, a number of people and institutions, including IMPACT itself, started to produce accounts of the in-service provision. These accounts were variously produced for the purposes of evaluation, monitoring, fund-raising, and 'academic' interest. Such accounts have an effectivity which goes beyond the ability of those producing them to predict or justify their effects. As has been mentioned earlier, the processes involved in producing accounts — the selection of categories, the creation of explanatory organizational structures, the rationalization of informal procedures and their construction within a logical order — act retrospectively to legitimize particular forms of activity. They tend to prioritize rationally produced frameworks within which activity can take place over the more amorphous, intuitively enacted, informal and responsive structures characteristic of daily experience.

However, accounts have to be and are produced, and one of the most useful descriptions of the methodology peculiar to IMPACT in-service training was that of 'third-person INSET'. This phrase was coined by Jeff Vass to characterize the way in which the INSET workers supported the teachers on IMPACT. It is easiest to expand the phrase, with reference to more established modes of INSET, to reveal its descriptive force.

The traditional role of the maths advisory teachers involved going into school and working alongside a classroom teacher. The teacher's method of delivering the maths curriculum therefore becomes the focus of attention on the part of both the INSET worker and the teacher her/himself. Her/his approach to and knowledge of primary maths, manner and means of delivery, strategies for assisting children to overcome their difficulties, and management of resources (textbooks, wordcards, structural apparatus and so on) all form the object of their joint consideration and evaluation as the in-service training proceeds. Because this scrutiny can prove stressful for the classroom teacher, provision is almost always made for the teacher to develop and maintain her/his own support structures and 'help-lines'. Nevertheless, many teachers describe the experience of allowing their practice to be scrutinized in this way as a very threatening one. A variety of strategies for camouflaging unacceptable practices or for hiding non-recommended text-books are well-known by teachers and strategically ignored by INSET workers!

On IMPACT, the in-service support takes a different form. Rather than the maths practice of the class teacher, the focus of attention becomes the relation between the maths curriculum and the home. Thus both the INSET worker and the class teacher are concerned to generate satisfactory means and strategies by which this relationship can be established in a new way. How can an effective partnership with parents be forged in the area of mathematics? How can parents' suggestions be best incorporated or answered? How can those who have not had a chance to share the activity at home in any one week be accommodated within the following week's classwork without rendering what was done at home by other children invalid or peripheral? Questions like these occupy the time of both teacher and INSET worker. The ingenuity and imagination of both is employed in finding solutions and creating or selecting suitable home-based curriculum tasks.

As the teacher and INSET worker struggle with the problems posed by IMPACT, their joint concentration upon specific problems may lead to some considerable modification of the teacher's pre-existing teaching patterns or strategies. However, the disruption of 'normal' routines will not be perceived as resulting from the suggestions or ideas of the INSET worker which the teacher has had — willingly or unwillingly — to accept. They will not necessarily appear as 'authored' at all by either individual. More often, such changes are regarded as the products or outcomes of the shared conversation and joint negotiation which were necessary to achieve the stated goal of effective parental participation. The development of this form of in-service

training — where the changes in classroom practice emerge as a direct result of the focus of attention upon a 'third person', in this case the parents
and their relation to the maths curriculum — has been a major factor in
IMPACT's reputation as successful and effective INSET.

We charted the progress of each IMPACT teacher in the initial eighteen
schools on the project, and a variety of interesting findings emerged.

Practical Maths Activities

Perhaps unsurprisingly, the greatest changes in terms of the increase in the
number of practical or 'problem-solving' type tasks given to children or
to groups of children as a part of routine classwork, were observed in the
practice of those teachers for whom such tasks had been most notably
absent before IMPACT. However, an overall and substantial increase in the
amount of time devoted to practical and problem-solving mathematical
activities in the classroom was observed as IMPACT mechanisms became
established. We found that, once having started working in this way, teachers
seemed to maintain the new style even when the support teacher time in
the school was decreased or ceased altogether. This voluntary maintenance
proved to be very important and allowed IMPACT to be described as more
effective than the traditional in-service approach.

The reason for the sustained nature of the changes could be established
from the field notes of the INSET workers. Teachers were not improving or
rethinking their approach to maths in order to approximate more nearly to
some ideal of 'good practice', or to what was now required for promotion,
kudos or credibility at inspectorate level. Indeed, many of the teachers
denied that they had changed their way of working at all, and certainly did
not manifest any of the signs normally associated with 'conversion' to a post-
Cockcroft approach. The IMPACT teachers were simply 'responding' to
what the children and the parents had done at home. The maths task which
was completed at home often required a practical activity or necessitated a
problem-solving approach in its follow-up work back in the classroom. The
home activity proved to be the stimulus for work in the classroom which was
more in line with current orthodoxies in terms of 'good' maths education.
Because teachers had not been asked to improve their ways of teaching
maths by IMPACT, any changes had a more 'natural' feel to them, having
been instigated in response to contingencies arising as a result of working in
a new way with parents.

Teacher Independence

Other factors were observed, charted and came to be incorporated in the
accounts provided of the IMPACT INSET. They included a monitoring, at

the request of one of the LEAs involved, of the length of time it took before teachers working in an IMPACT-type way became relatively or completely independent of the INSET worker's support. Such independence was charted through recording:

1 How IMPACT activities are generated — whether wholly teacher-designed, partly teacher-designed, wholly INSET worker designed or selected from an existing bank of IMPACT materials;
2 The degree of integration of the IMPACT task and its follow-up work into the routine classwork — IMPACT could remain almost an 'add-on' activity, peripheral to the children's 'real' maths work, or it could be totally integrated into the classwork in such a way that it proved impossible to decide where IMPACT began and routine classwork left off;
3 Who planned and organized the preparation for each week's IMPACT task at home — totally teacher organized, totally INSET worker organized or jointly negotiated;
4 Who planned and orchestrated the follow-up work — as above;
5 Who wrote out and duplicated of the IMPACT sheet to be sent home — teacher, INSET worker, school secretary or helper.

All these factors were measured using a simple scoring mechanism and recorded each week in all eighteen schools throughout the first six terms of IMPACT. The results indicated a significant decrease in teacher dependence for all except one of the schools during the first year of IMPACT. Throughout the second year, this trend increased and in over 50 per cent of the schools, the teachers became virtually completely independent of the INSET worker, who simply retained what became known as a 'hand-holding' function. This meant that they were asked to visit or telephone the school two or three times per term simply to give a little advice about peripheral matters, reassurance, and praise. The INSET workers described these schools as requiring 'hand-holding' only, which reflected the fact that they felt that these teachers could run IMPACT entirely without help if they had to but that they liked the reassurance provided by the occasional contact.

INSET-Worker Time

As a part of this monitoring process, we noted, on a fortnightly basis, the changes in the ways in which the teachers utilized the time that they had with the support teacher, as well as recording the amount of time they took up in all and how it decreased over the two-year period. More than 80 per cent of the teachers found that they needed most help with the mathematical elements of the IMPACT task itself, or with a related aspect of the preparation or follow-up. However, 35 per cent of teachers were recorded as needing as much or more assistance from the INSET worker on the subject of handling the responses from parents. In line with the results mentioned earlier, the subject matter of the teachers' demands was related to the LEA in which they worked as well as being school-related.

The speed with which the teachers gradually came, in the words of the INSET workers, 'to assume the ownership' of IMPACT, and 'make it their own', varied from school to school. However, as each teacher took on more of the responsibility for orchestrating the task to be sent home for each child, its preparation and follow-up in class, the INSET worker would describe them as being 'weaned', and would attempt to encourage this independence. Once a teacher was writing her/his own IMPACT sheets, or at least selecting or adapting them from the existing bank of materials, s/he became a resource for other, less independent staff in the same school. Thus, the teachers in any one school would rapidly become less dependent upon ouside INSET worker support once one teacher was totally 'weaned'. Schools which were in this position were coded by the INSET worker as 'walking on their own'. At the end of the first year only four of the eighteen schools were described in this way. However, in the second year, six new IMPACT schools began in each LEA and by the end of that year ten out of the new eighteen and all but four of the original eighteen were 'walking on their own'. This trend towards a faster and greater independence of IMPACT teachers and schools from INSET worker support intensified considerably during the third year of the project with new schools learning the IMPACT procedures and 'walking on their own' within one or two terms. The reasons for this are explored in the next section on 'IMPACT: the Network'.

In summary, it seemed that the effective implementation of change was dependent upon several factors:

1   The degree to which teachers felt that their ways of teaching were the object of critical scrutiny by others (possibly in a position of influence or power), and thereby felt threatened;
2   The extent to which the 'authorship' of the changes was seen as residing with the teacher;
3   The existence of a bank of resources (IMPACT materials) to be used by teachers as starting points for their own work;
4   The conviction on the part of the teachers and headteachers involved that IMPACT was a good way of working and a desire to work in genuine partnership with parents.

This last point is raised here for the first time, but it became an increasingly important factor in setting up the IMPACT network where the INSET provision had to be much more devolved and, to some extent, centralized. I shall return to its implications later in the chapter.

In any of the team discussion with INSET workers about the progress of IMPACT we found that, as indicated above, terms such as 'hand-holding', 'weaning', 'letting go', 'walking on their own' and 'ownership' recurred with a significant degree of frequency. These metaphors are important in that they give an indication of the processes by which we may assist others to change established ways of working, which may be intuitive rather than rationally-produced sequences of behaviour and can be described as analogous to those of parenting in that they must endeavour to produce shared images of possible worlds. The onus of performing unaccustomed actions and creating new routines, of acquiring new skills, must come to rest upon the recipient of the INSET rather than the provider in much the same way as that in which the child gradually takes over the responsibility for getting a drink or eating. We are reminded of some parent-teacher strategies (see, for example, David Wood's notion of 'scaffolding', 1986). This format has repercussions for the frameworks which we construct in order to describe and generate new forms of INSET, and predicates a more holistic approach, something which became an important factor as we had to respond to the requirements of 'IMPACT the network'.

Third Movement: IMPACT — The Network

Fourteen New LEAs

If the universe were only rationally ordered as all of us would like to believe — at least for some of the time — then expanding a project like IMPACT into first fourteen, and now thirty-three, new authorities would present no difficulty. Through the processes of structured observation, generalization and construction within a theoretical framework, either explicit or implicit, we would extract a model from which a mechanism for inserting IMPACT into any LEA structure would be generated. However, when IMPACT previously expanded from being an informal initiative in a few north London schools to its status as a fully fledged educational project, one of the lessons learned concerned the impossibility of any such process, except when realized through *post hoc* rationalization for the purposes of providing accounts. We were determined to remain aware of the crucial import of contingent events and constraining circumstances, of the non-uniform factors and the inherent unpredictability of an unknown and complex situation such as a new LEA. We had also become fully cogniscent of the dangers inherent in generalization and the tendency to find an 'essential' IMPACT which could be mapped onto different situations (see chapter 1).

Therefore, we went into discussions with each LEA joining the IMPACT network on the basis that we would find, through a process of negotiation and exploration, a means of implementing IMPACT in the schools which was particular to that authority. However, financial and managerial constraints did enforce a more universal structure in terms of IMPACT personnel and materials, which had a generalizing effect in that it precluded some ways of working and privileged others.

Each new LEA became part of the IMPACT network which agreed to provide:

— Regular central courses for LEA-based INSET workers;
— A period of apprenticeship for these support teachers in which they are given the opportunity to work alongside an experienced IMPACT support teacher in another IMPACT LEA;
— A large bank of IMPACT materials for duplication and use throughout the authority. These materials are to be free of copyright, and therefore adaptable *in situ*;
— Access to new and separately packaged IMPACT materials which are not available on the open market;
— Access to the IMPACT National Curriculum planning and recording mechanisms;
— A specified amount of INSET supplied by the IMPACT central team. This INSET is to be used directly with teachers, or with other groups such as governors or parents as preferred;
— Direct and frequent contact with and assistance to the LEA-based IMPACT support staff;
— A termly update and newsletter to maintain contacts with other IMPACT LEAs and to disseminate good ideas or innovative practices.

This structure meant that as far as the central IMPACT team was concerned, the implementation of IMPACT in the network LEAs relied upon more formal mechanisms and was less a matter of intuitive response to local circumstance. The very size of IMPACT at that time — seventeen LEAs, 200-plus schools — precluded the type of informal, more amorphous, less structured approaches which we had used so succesfully with the project schools. Such methods intrinsically depend upon a familiarity with the teachers involved and a regularity of contact both with schools and with the INSET workers in each authority which were simply impossible on the IMPACT network.

We were forced to consider how best to maintain the speed and seeming effectiveness of previous IMPACT in-service training in these new and very different circumstances. Another major factor concerned the timing of these events. The setting up of the IMPACT network coincided with the introduction of the National Curriculum. This meant that the IMPACT team found itself commissioned to deliver a great deal of the National Curriculum INSET in the network LEAs, as well as struggling to implement IMPACT itself. Certain aspects of the National Curriculum were very helpful to IMPACT and vice versa. The demand for regular and reasonably detailed advance planning was one which we had been stressing on IMPACT for two years. The movement towards more cross-curricular work and the specific attainment targets on using and applying mathematics were also very much in line with the sort of approaches developed on IMPACT. The record keeping and assessment procedures developed on IMPACT found a new enhanced currency in the National Curriculum, particularly since they incorporated a parental input. A number of the directions taken by the INSET workers in the last two years on the IMPACT network owe their inception to the dovetailing between IMPACT mechanisms and National Curriculum delivery (see Merttens and Vass, 1989).

If a new LEA now joins the IMPACT network, it would be fair to say that there is a general pattern of INSET which we would anticipate delivering in order to get IMPACT up and running within a reasonable time in that authority. This time will vary considerably depending upon whether the LEA is a large rural authority, a small urban, and the number and character of the schools within it. It will differ according to the nature and quantity of the support for IMPACT from the local advisory teachers. However, certain features of the in-service training package will remain constant:

1 We will always expect to do at least one and usually three or four initial sessions in which schools are told what IMPACT is, and informed about the philosophy behind it;

2 There will then be a process of selection of the schools wanting to take IMPACT on. There are usually more schools interested than the LEA feels can be supported. Which schools are chosen and how, varies from LEA to LEA;

3 The IMPACT schools will then have their own programme of in-service training, some of which will be supplied by the IMPACT central team;

4 There will be a specific session run by IMPACT, during which the teachers will discuss what sort of mechanisms they will use to obtain adequate parental feedback on each activity, and they will often design their own diary or reponse form (see chapter 13 for a detailed discussion of this session);

5 We will offer at least one session for governors in the LEA.

The amount of school-based in-service training may vary considerably from authority to authority, as will the amount of input by myself. In some authorities, I am involved in a great deal of the IMPACT INSET, and I work in schools, run parents' meetings and do a lot of dissemination. In other LEAs, I visit only occasionally, and the bulk of the INSET work is carried out by IMPACT support staff locally.

Inspiration not Information

One of the first things we realized about working in this more formal and less responsive way with so many new schools in such different areas was that we now needed to 'inspire' teachers — and others — to take part in IMPACT. This problem exercised me more than any of the other difficulties associated with expansion to the IMPACT network. Many of them had, in any event, been solved or resolved by the changed world in which we all now found ourselves. As previously mentioned, the National Curriculum meant that all teachers were planning their curricula in advance, and keeping records. IMPACT simply became a part of these processes. Equally helpful was the presence of a vast bank of already existing and categorized IMPACT materials from which teachers could select IMPACT tasks for the children in their class, week by week.

However, the question of what amounted to the inspiration behind the whole venture was not so easily resolved. We were no longer able to rely upon person-to-person contact to enable the whole philosophy of IMPACT — the motivation behind it — that makes it worth engaging with in the first place, to be shared in an amorphous and diffused fashion over time as we all worked together. In our previous highly personalized model of INSET, the vision of how IMPACT could work was generated through practical discussions and through negotiating pragmatic decisions about parent meetings, response forms or suitable activities. Inspiration was created through joint action *in situ*, with the INSET worker and the teachers able to work closely, hand-in-hand over some time. On the IMPACT network, this closeness was no longer even possibly the case for many tens — or hundreds — of schools.

The first session of the INSET package largely took over this function. In this session, a vision had to be created which could be shared by the participants, and which would motivate a desire to work in new ways with parents and children through the use of regular take-home tasks. The details of the precise and school-specific procedures, through which this way of working can best be established in practice, are worked out later. This leads to a decentering of IMPACT itself. The processes by which IMPACT is implemented will differ from school to school but the aims and philosophy will be held in common. Its *raison d'être* becomes the glue binding the whole together. The INSET workers have then to build on the enthusiasm generated by the initial session. Of equal importance then, is the training of these local support workers who will need to be able to share and maintain the image of a new partnership with parents.

Finale: What We Have Learned

Before running IMPACT, we had to a greater or lesser extent accepted, at least tacitly, the view that INSET provision was a matter of planning for change, deciding upon aims and objectives, and working either directly in the classroom (preferable but expensive) or indirectly in teachers' centres or colleges to achieve them. Such a view of in-service training rests ineluctably upon a perception of teachers' practices as the object of INSET, and the teacher, in isolation from any particular or specific context, as the locus of change. A concomitant notion is that any progress a teacher makes is the result of the application of what has been learnt during the in-service training programme. It is by studying the *progress* that we can assess the *success* of the INSET.

Organic Growth Rather Than Designer Structures

It became important for us on IMPACT to realize that we were largely adopting a policy of *response* rather than *prediction*. We organized and ran the INSET sessions differently in each area, according to how the growth of IMPACT could be best encouraged, given the conditions available for its survival. The metaphor of nurturing a plant is more appropriate than that of constructing a scaffold. A plant may grow in unpredictable directions, it may put out an unexpected shoot, or produce an extra and surprising bud. Unlike a scaffold, its development is not entirely controlled by what we do. Furthermore, with the scaffold, we have in mind when we start an image of what the end product will look like. With the plant, we may have a vision of the plant that the seed will become but the result may surprise us, and there is never an end product. The plant is continuously growing, always changing. It is constantly becoming, never having become. The plant cannot be considered outside its ecological context. Its whole ecosystem has to be taken into account if we are concerned with nurturing the plant. A teacher is never 'context-less'. Finally, the plant is capable of reproduction, giving rise to non-identical replicas. In this sense, once nurtured, a strong plant can be the source of new growths and offspring of its own.

Further Thoughts . . . Towards a Theory of INSET?

Previous conventional theoretical frameworks in which in-service training was planned were at one time positivist in that they have assumed 'a body of knowledge' to be transmitted or assessed and a given *static* reality to be transformed. Making use of an autoplastic/alloplastic division, in which the former makes reference to an outlook, theory or ethic in which it is assumed that it is the person, the self, who must change or adapt, and the latter refers to the practices involved in changing or reconstructing the world, INSET provision was traditionally couched in autoplastic terms with the teacher being firmly located as the site of change. More recent theoretical discussions have attempted to ground INSET within an alloplastic framework in which the context or situation including the teacher, becomes the locus of endeavour.

Contemporary theory has attempted to focus to a much greater extent upon the relationship between individuals and their surroundings, asserting a causal relation between the constitution and reconstitution of subjectivity on the one hand, and social structures demonstrated through the minutiae of social practices on the other. In this scenario, the conscious implementation of change becomes not so much the transformation of a previously described 'reality', but rather the reformation of specific practices or prescribed routines within a newly constituted set of assumptions or commonalities.

Thus the task for those engaged in an intervention programme such as IMPACT, with the overt aim of instituting change, should not be thought of in terms of altering the behaviour patterns or strategies of particular teachers (or parents, or governors). A more helpful way of conceiving such INSET is to envisage it as transforming the 'teaching world' in which teachers perceive themselves to be embedded. We have to set up a new vision, an image of a possible world in which previously accepted 'givens' are no longer invisible but can be queried. In such a world, 'tacit assumptions' can be altered and new sequences of behaviour can be anticipated. The INSET worker attempts to generate this vision, which becomes, as the INSET proceeds, a shared image.

The complexity of an actual situation will inevitably defy any analysis which attempts to predict outcomes. We can never be sure what the precise effects of particular changes in a teacher's practice will be, since the factors involved are so complex and are part of a shifting field of social relations and established rituals in which it is impossible, even theoretically, to isolate specific processes of cause and effect with any real degree of certainty. It is only as we come to view the production of change as being, in effect, a reconstitution of discourse that we can simultaneously describe its mechanisms and address the question of its effectivity.

INSET into the Year 2000 . . .

The significance, in practical and pragmatic terms, of the ideas expressed above may be hard to elaborate, but:

1 In a world which is becoming increasingly obsessed with the transfer of information — information packages, efficient information storage and the like — it is salutary to remind ourselves that, if the production of change has to do with the creation of possible worlds, then the generation of these shared images owes more to the ability to make others *feel* differently and *see* differently than it does to the ability to convey information or provide data. The ability to see things from the other person's point of view, to intuit how things are for them, the knack of telling a good story, the capacity to retain and relate a series of pertinent incidents or events, the qualities of

enthusiasm and warmth, and a genuine belief in the value of the vision being presented; all these have been traditionally devalued. Their importance in the generation of productive change has been understated at best and ignored at worst. The provision of in-service training, however, depends upon just such qualities in order to create and sustain a joint narrative with the recipients of the INSET. Teachers who are inspired to go out and try something new can, quite literally, change the world.

2 Through IMPACT I came to the conclusion that a more holistic approach to in-service training was called for as a matter of urgency. I recall a traditional Chinese proverb, used as a slogan by OXFAM: 'Give a man a fish and you feed him for a day. Teach him to fish and you feed him for life'. In attempting to implement change in education it may be the case that if we try to 'teach' specific practices, to instruct teachers in the use of certain new procedures, we are, in effect giving them a fish. For these practices, these new procedures, cannot be lifted out of the context in which they are embedded. They cannot be considered outside of a specific situation. What is 'good' practice in one situation may be disastrous by any criteria in another. What is desirable in this circumstance might be dangerous or inadvisable on another occasion. If we perceive INSET rather as an attempt to enable teachers to review their world, to envisage other ways of being, and to wish *for things to be other than they are*, we allow the presently established 'truths' to be unmasked and subjected to question, and the prevailing assumptions to be revalued, which may be more akin to teaching the teachers to fish!

References

ALEXANDER, R. (1988) 'Garden or Jungle? Teacher Development and Informal Primary Education', in BLYTHE, A. (Ed.) *Informal Primary Education Today*, London, Falmer Press.

BALL, S. and GOODSON, I. (1985) *Teachers' Lives and Careers*, London, Falmer Press.

BERNSTEIN, B. (1977) *Class, Codes and Control* London, RKP.

BROWN, A. (1990) *From Notional to National Curriculum: The Search for a Mechanism*, in DOWLING, P. and NOSS, R. (Eds) *Mathematics Versus the National Curriculum*, London, Falmer Press.

BURGHES, D. (1989) 'Mathematics Education for the Twenty-First Century', in ERNEST, P. (Ed.) *Mathematics Teaching: The State of the Art*, London, Falmer Press.

COCKCROFT, W.H. *et al.* (1982) *Mathematics Counts*, London, HMSO.

EASEN, P. (1985) *Making School Centred INSET Work*, Croom Helm.

ERNEST, P. (1989) *Mathematics Teaching: The State of the Art*, London, Falmer Press.

GRIFFITHS, A. and HAMILTON, D. (1984) *PACT Parent, Teacher Child: Working Together in Children's Learning*, London, Methuen.

MERTTENS, R. and VASS, J. (1989) *How to Plan and Assess the National Curriculum in the Classroom*, Oxford, Heinemann.

NIAS, J. (1989) *Primary Teachers Talking*, London, Routledge.

SCHON, D.A. (1983) *The Reflective Practioner: How Professionals Think in Action*, New York, Basic Books.

SHERRING, P. (1985) 'A Break-time Story', *Nuffield (South East Region) Mathematics Council Journal*, London.

STOW, M. and FOXMAN, D. (1988) *Mathematics Coordination*, Windsor, Berkshire, NFER Nelson.

TOLSTOY, L.N. (1857) *War and Peace*, Harmondsworth, Middlesex, Penguin.

WOOD, D. (1986) 'Aspects of Teaching and Learning', in RICHARDS, M. and LIGHT, P. (Eds) *Children of Social Worlds*, Cambridge, Polity Press.

WOODS, P. (1990) *Teacher Skills and Strategies*, London, Falmer Press.

Part V

Reflections

Chapter 17

Parental Involvement from Policy to Practice: An Education Officer's View

Tim Brighouse

We first met Tim Brighouse when he was Chief Education Officer in Oxfordshire and IMPACT was one of the initiatives in parental participation in that county. Tim provides an historical perspective by reviewing the development of parental involvement and the various ways in which it has been construed and constrained through LEA policy, national legislation and shifts in educational orthodoxies. He describes how schools and LEAs can seemingly conspire to exclude parents and also the different, and sometimes conflicting roles into which parents are cast by those in education as well as government policies.

The Plowden Report (1967) turned an official spotlight on parental partnership in schooling for the first time. The Taylor Report (1977), a decade or so later in the mid-1970s, gave it another airing. Since the Second World War, a variety of parental initiatives in slightly different contexts in different parts of the country have spluttered unconvincingly and sporadically into life, and just as soon subsided as the composition and priorities of LEAs have changed and, more frequently, individual headteachers have come and gone.

In the mid-1970s, when one of three deputies to Peter Newsam at the ILEA, I experienced for the first time being somewhere near the apex of a large organization and discovered such a creature's most frustrating characteristic. One of the most perplexing frustrations of large organizations is frequently the inability to persuade those within it who are properly taken up with systems maintenance, to respond to changed messages from the democratically elected members or for that matter the paid senior officials who respectively seek and determine a change in policy and therefore, they hope, practice. Sir Ashley Bramall, then the leader and Peter Newsam the Education Officer, laid down a personal challenge to me to remove the last of the 'NO PARENTS BEYOND THIS POINT' signs which decorated the entrances to so many of London's schools — a legacy of an era which deliberately excluded the parents. At the time the authority was pioneering a formalized consultative process for representative parents from their divisions but, as with so many matters in that authority, the difficulty of translating new policy into practice (especially when pursued mechanistically through a top-down linear translation), failed not merely to turn the new policy to practice but tested the patience of even the most saintly. As it happens the presence of pre-war off-putting notices (sometimes recently renewed!) was understandably an unacceptable and visible sign of ineffective management to the elected members and Education Officer alike. Moreover as fast as I thought I solved the problem and removed the signs, the elected members would gleefully find another for me to tilt against.

The anecdote is not without a point. It is not so long ago that the inherited assumptions of parental involvement, notwithstanding the brave words of Plowden and Taylor (dubbed significantly by the teachers' leaders as a 'Busybodies' Charter') were very different from those articulated today. The existence of old attitudes frequently persist long after they are no longer openly expressed or legitimized. So it is best to be cautious before getting carried away with examples of good practice.

In any consideration of the progress made towards parental partnership in education, one must not forget such inheritances and the reality of flawed practice on the road between good intentions and delivery. Not only were the off-putting notices the rule rather than the exception, even when they disappeared there remained a mental 'so far and no further' approach on the part of many practitioners. Schools and LEAs which boasted parental policies theoretically designed to welcome partnership continued practices which suggested otherwise. I remember particularly the school which prided itself on its openness to parents which persisted with forbidding notices not at the school gate but inside the building at the classroom door. Nor is it entirely surprising that progress should be so slow when one considers not only the demotivating complaints heaped on the teaching profession in the popular press (which must surely have undermined the self-confidence of the most hardy and reinforced their defensiveness) but also their position as members of a profession in general with all that implies about the baleful inherited features of closed cartels which have been properly attacked by the politicians.

In any case, for many years LEAs were aware of parents as persons required by the law to exercise their duty to secure their children's education, if they chose to do so, by carrying it out themselves — the 'Education Otherwise' movement — and LEAs would need to satisfy themselves (and sometimes they took some satisfying) that the parents were doing a good job. A second manifestation of parents for LEAs were those people who were so feckless that they failed to get their children to school and required prosecution. The overwhelming majority of parents, however, got their children to school and were expected to be an uncritical and captive support group who would be content with school reports from time to time which described their children's progresss as 'C and Satisfactory' — a very 'unparentlike' comment on their child's progress by those '*in loco parentis*'! Beyond that — and the school — parents could look forward to the occasional inpenetrable communication in 'officialese', demanding payment for transport or school meals or, if they were lucky, a form of entitlement to grants of one sort or another. For the majority in that era, the school and the LEA were remembered as the purveyors of bad news, of the failure of the majority at 11-plus and the confirmation that the hopes for the next generation must be replaced by resignation to reality. Those are the parents of today's children. It is as well to remember that.

After such a cautionary preamble I would like now to analyze and underline the enormous and irreversible changes towards parental involvement which now pervades the system. As with all changes it starts from examples of good practice eventually leading to policy shifts centrally which in turn condition future general provision.

First let us be clear of the different forms of parental involvement. I have already alluded to parents as a captive support group; Indeed it was in that guise that schools and LEAs encouraged parental involvement for many years. It was in evidence in the parents' associations and, increasingly, the parent-teacher associations which spawned the money for the rash of swimming pools, minibuses and computers, which were the rage of the 1960s, the 1970s and the 1980s respectively. Parents could be relied upon for barn-dances, garden fêtes, and bingo sessions — the more so in solid working-class and middle-class areas but the less so in the deprived inner cities. More daringly, especially in the primary sector, parents could be relied upon as supplementary additional hands for classroom non-teaching, library and occasionally teaching assistance — provided it was properly organized. They could be some of the 'responsible adults' to accompany a school trip or a ready and substantial band of helpers in a time of need. The role persists today. Closely allied to it of course is the role of the school society and community itself, as a social focus for a community of adults who happen to be parents of primary-aged children simultaneously and choose to enjoy some of their recreation together.

There is also now the role of the parent as the consumer — a role greatly emphasized by the 1988 Act although probably having its first legislative boost in the Act of 1980. The 1988 Act emphasizes parental choice in a number of ways. First there is 'open enrolment' which shifts the balance of power away from the planning function of the LEA on which the 1980 Act had struck a Solomon-like compromise. Second, the publication of the results of pupils' assessment bids to encourage the parents as consumers to compare the performance of teachers and of schools; and finally the LEA is required to set up a 'complaints' body, to hear the representations of those parents who think either the school or the LEA are short-changing them on the National Curriculum or other matters.

The 1986 Act also contributed to 'parents as consumers'. Its requirement for annual meetings of parents to receive reports of school business from the governors may have turned into an expensive damp squib but its intention is clear. It is in the 1986 Act too that we see the translation of some of the recommendations of the Taylor Report in the matter of the role of the parent as a governor. For the first time the pioneering efforts of a few LEAs have been translated into the national practice of all, some of whom were belated and reluctant converts to power sharing.

There is however one further role of the parents. It is arguably more important than any of these other roles; it is that of joint even prime educators. It is not one emphasized by the legislation save in the clause of the 1944 Act which lays on the parent the duty of securing education for their child.

When Rutter and his colleagues produced the book '*Fifteen Thousand Hours*' (1979) as a thought-provoking title about the effectiveness of some secondary schools, it was possible to emphasize that if fifteen thousand hours were vital time during which a youngster did or did not acquire relevant information, practice and develop a range of useful skills, form attitudes and become familiar with a multiplicity of ideas and concepts which is simply what schooling is about, so also does the youngster, whether intentionally or not, supplement that diet of information, skills, attitudes and ideas outside school. Moreover the waking time outside school is more than double that inside school. During that time the parent has a potentially powerful influence.

At about that time, in the mid-1970s, some research on shared reading in the London Borough of Haringey (Tizard *et al.*, 1982) showed beyond serious challenge, that where parents become even minimally involved by teachers in their own children's reading, it was possible to see greater progress in the children's learning when measured against two control groups, one left with an unaltered diet and the other with extra professional teaching support. Simultaneously the Belfield School in Rochdale was making similar but researched claims of progress where parents could be involved seriously as joint educators (Hannon and Jackson, 1987). In the subsequent decade evidence appeared sporadically from Kirklees (Topping and Wolfendale, 1985) and the Community Education Development Centre in Coventry (Widlake and McLeod, 1984) in particular, but also from elsewhere to support the thrust of the proven importance of involving parents as educators of their own children.

No LEA administration should have ignored the message. Indeed many did not, although it is a missed opportunity that in all the flurry of change, national governments have yet to pick up that message. Indeed it is ironic that, as I write this, there is raging debate about reading standards of 7-year-olds with scarcely a mention of the formalized and structured parent/partnership schemes which research has shown can so affect positive performance. It is a sadness too that HMI have been relatively silent on this issue when they have commented so extensively on practically everything else (DES, 1990).

Some LEAs in the last fifteen years have tried to change the climate in their schools by a variety of methods. The best have devoted resources to back the changed practice. They have provided parents' rooms and home school 'animateurs' who have sought to encourage and facilitate good practice and made the dissemination of that practice part of the in-service training programme both for teachers and governors. The best LEAs have made an effort to spread the principle of parents as educators across the curriculum and through the age range. They have started from the promising foundation of the early years after birth when parents are the prime and often the only educators. They have recognized and accommodated to the recognition that it gets progressively more difficult in the teenage years when the combination of turbulent adolescents properly kicking towards independence and of the issue of more specialized knowledge and skills, makes real parental partnership a more subtle matter. Even there the wise LEAs and schools have seized on the records of achievement practices which have transformed home/school reporting and teacher/student/parent learning. In short there is no shortage now of examples both of LEAs and of nationally known research to back extension of good practice.

For the next millennium with its promise of substantially increased numbers in semi-retirement and the real advances in learning techniques promised by information technology, there lies much promise of real advances in the levels of achievement of generations of school pupils. It will only come however if there is a real belief in the mutual and complementary role of teachers, parents and grandparents. The former have expertise of thousands of case studies of children whom they've taught and the latter the knowledge and the time with the individual child. When that partnership is harnessed the greatest advances are secured.

This scenario will require changed institutional practices by schools and LEAs. Some LEAs, as I have indicated, tackled the issue in the 1980s. I remember clearly the battle to establish the Oxfordshire Parents Educational Newsletter with the happy acronym OPEN which is illustrated here. It was important to ensure that the LEAs' central role in this matter advanced at a pace which would be reinforced by area based 'animateurs' who spread good practice. Each issue of the newsletter was to be preceded by the circulation of a draft to schools so they could be forewarned and could plan the accompanying leaflet about their own school's practice if they wished as part of a systematic information-giving process for parents. Educational partnership must commence with open sharing of information. The series of OPEN was planned carefully to deal with major issues of partnership and the programme circulated in advance.

It is on such a firm basis that the pioneering curriculum work of the sort which the editors of this book instigated can flourish and so our knowledge of the matter is extended along with the reassurance that the extension of that knowledge increases our likelihood of developing more of the talents of our nation's children and future citizens.

Tim Brighouse

References

DES (1944) *Education Act*, London, HMSO.
DES (1980) *Education Act*, London, HMSO.
DES (1986) *Education Act*, London, HMSO.
DES (1988) *Education Reform Act*, London, HMSO.
DES (1990) *The Teaching and Learning of Reading in Primary Schools*, London, HMSO (HMI Report).
HANNON, P. and JACKSON, A. (1987) *The Belfield Reading Project: Final Report*, London, National Children's Bureau.
PLOWDEN, B. *et al.* (1967) *Children and their Primary Schools, Report of the Central Advisory Council for Education*, London, HMSO.
RUTTER, M. *et al.* (1979) *Fifteen Thousand Hours*, London, Open Books.
TAYLOR, A. (1977) *A New Partnerhisp for Our Schools, A Report of the Committee on School Management and Government*, London, HMSO.
TIZARD, B. *et al.* (1982) 'Collaboration between Teachers and Parents in Assisting Children's Reading', *British Journal of Educational Psychology*, **52**, 1, pp. 1–15.
TOPPING, K. and WOLFENDALE, S. (1985) *Parental Involvement in Children's Reading*, Beckenham, Croom Helm .
WIDLAKE, P. and McLEOD, F. (1984) *Raising Standards: Parental Involvement Programmes and the Language Performance of Children*, Coventry, Community Education Development Centre.

Chapter 18

Special Needs, Parents and the Education Reform Act

Gary Thomas

Gary Thomas argues that the category of special educational needs is a description of certain children's requirements at particular times in their school careers, rather than a means of distinguishing a particular type of child. He suggests that effective parental participation in their children's education might be one way of preventing the category from ever arising. The contention made in this chapter is that parents are as — and usually more — effective in helping children who have been classed as having specific learning difficulties as those 'professionally trained' to assist. This leads Gary to express forcibly the view that all parents should be encouraged to participate in the work of the school through a variety of means. He finally argues that the Education Reform Act, while in some respects enabling a greater role for parents, could be counter-productive in the ways that it positions and describes both parents and teachers *vis-à-vis* each other.

What Are Special Needs?

There is no unchanging body of children whom we can identify as having a condition, special needs, which we then proceed to set about curing. All children need certain things in order to be able to learn. Sometimes they will need something additional or different, and it is at these times that we say that their needs are special. Their needs are special not because of some defect within themselves, but usually because some external factor has caused difficulties. Maybe they missed an important explanation; maybe they are perpetually tired; maybe they have been unlucky enough to have been in receipt of poor teaching for the last two years. The list of possible factors is endless.

It is important to remember this wide definition because there is the temptation to think of special needs as simply a category. Indeed, the 'statementing' procedures of many local education authorities have encouraged this view. Although the 1981 Education Act abandoned the categories of handicap set up by the 1944 Act, education professionals have often simply substituted a new set of categories for the old. Where once there was ESN (educationally subnormal), now there is MLD (moderate learning difficulties). Where there was ESN(S) Educationally Subnormal (Severe), now SLD (severe learning difficulties) has taken its place. Where once there was maladjustment, now there is EBD (emotional and behavioural difficulties). The new labels seem effortlessly to have taken the place of the old.

I feel it is necessary to make this problem of labels clear at the outset of this chapter on special needs and parental involvement, because my assumption throughout is that parental involvement can prevent special needs from ever arising. I am thinking, when I assert this, of the larger body of children who experience learning difficulties at some stage (the Warnock Report, 1978, 20 per cent) rather than those who have sensory or physical disabilities. There is enough evidence available now to show that parental involvement is a crucially important factor in determining children's progress. It has to be said that parental involvement provides a far more hopeful avenue to follow in helping children with difficulties than the traditional predilection of special educators, which has been to discover ever-newer and ever-better methods of teaching these children. The kinds of specialized methods and techniques which special educators have been so good at promulgating are not, unfortunately, renowned for their success (see, for example, Cashdan *et al.*, 1971; Hargreaves, 1978; Thomas, 1985; Algozzine *et al.*, 1986). The perhaps unpalatable fact which emerges from research on various kinds of help available to children who are experiencing difficulties is that help from highly trained specialist teachers is less effective than that from children's parents.

Much research recently has shown that if parents are actively encouraged to participate in the education of their children the payoff can be enormous. Tizard (1982) and his colleagues in Haringey showed that when parents regularly heard their children read at home, and when there was good liaison and monitoring of this process by the school, the children made remarkable progress. In fact they made greater progress than similar groups of children who were having help with reading from specialist teachers at school.

Findings like Tizard *et al.*'s have been repeated up and down Great Britain. Some of the most interesting findings come from schools in areas of high unemployment and poverty. For instance, at Belfield School in Rochdale the opening up of the school to parents has seen some extraordinary progress in children's reading. This project was done in the kind of area where parents are often assumed to be uninterested in their children's education, but the Belfield project proved this stereotype wrong. What the project showed was that parents from whatever background are keen, willing and able to help their children and become involved in their education, as long as the school makes it clear that it actively welcomes this help, and as long as it actively takes steps to overcome the reticence of parents to enter school.

These studies show that children can make extraordinary progress with help from their parents, whatever the technique used to help them.

> Of much greater practical significance is the fact that teachers and parents working in collaboration did improve the academic perform-ance of the children *without the parents being given any special train-ing in the* techniques of tutoring (my italics; Tizard *et al.*, 1982, p. 13).

It seems that given a few fairly broadly defined parameters within which any reasonably sensitive adult works with an individual child (e.g. enthusiasm, patience, the ability and willingness to give encouragement), such help can hardly fail to be successful. The lesson which seems to emerge from the research is that if parents can be involved in their children's education, special needs may never arise.

Nurturing Parental Involvement

If parental involvement is so important in helping to prevent difficulties at school, how can such involvement be fostered? Most adults today have grown up in times when parents have been excluded from schools. For many parents, memories of schools are unhappy — sometimes even painful. If that were not enough on its own to deter parents from visiting their children's schools, schools are not usually attractive or welcoming places. Under-funding has meant that they are often shabby, despite the best efforts of teachers to brighten things up with children's work. Piecemeal building alterations and Portacabins, combined with the sometimes bizarre school architecture of the 1960s and 1970s, mean that it is often well-nigh imposs-ible for the visitor even to find the entrance. Smells and sounds may be redo-lent of less-than-happy times. Is it surprising, then, that a great many parents should feel real anxiety — just at the idea of going into school?

It is no use schools trying to overcome this anxiety by simply saying — perhaps in the P.S. of a letter home in the 'pupil post' — that parents are always welcome. It needs effort to convince parents — particularly those who may be most reticent about visiting — that they really are welcome. Confusing messages may reach the mother who wanders, uninvited, into the school. Busy teachers — on their way from here to there — may not even have the time to stop and say hello, and this may easily be interpreted as rejection. It needs a great deal of effort to overcome what for many people amounts to little less than a conditioned fear of school. Belfield School in Rochdale succeeded in overcoming this fear by actively making the school more welcoming — by encouraging mothers and fathers to share in the life of the school, by providing non-stop coffee, by opening the staffroom to parents.

These things may seem obvious, but many schools appear to be mystified about why more parents do not become involved in school life or why parents may help in the classroom on one or two occasions and then give up. Stories of 'unreliable' parents abound. Usually, though, reliability is not the problem. The problem is more likely to be that these parents have not felt welcome. They may have been excluded from the staffroom; there may have been inadequate discussion between teacher and parent about what the parent is supposed to be doing. The result is that parents are left feeling uncomfortable and confused, and they do what people with feelings like this usually do — they withdraw. This behaviour has little to do with 'reliability'; it has everything to do with communication.

Most teachers have changed their attitude to the idea of parents becoming more involved. For years, teachers assumed that parents had little or nothing to offer the life of the school; questions about the work of teachers were regarded as meddling. The professionalism of teachers was not to be challenged by even hinting at the idea that parents might be able to share in the education of their children. Parents could, after all, be split neatly into two categories: the pushy middle class and the couldn't-care-less working class. Anyone who had not done a professional training course could not possibly understand the mysterious and highly complicated processes of education. Fortunately, only a few teachers share such views today.

Over the last ten years a quiet revolution has been taking place in many schools. I have found (Thomas, 1987) that parents are now actually working alongside the class teacher in eight out of ten classrooms in primary schools in the enlightened education authority of Oxfordshire. The transformation in attitude which has taken place over a fairly short time has been dramatic. Once, this participation would have been denounced as the use of unpaid, untrained labour. Now, parents see it as their right to be more involved in the education of their children, and increasingly schools are accepting or even promoting this view.

People who work in the education service increasingly recognize how much parents have to offer. Certainly, they have recognized this following the results of research. More importantly, though, the recognition has come because people today are less stuffy about guarding their professional skills. 'All professions are conspiracies against the laity' said George Bernard Shaw. He was probably directing his fire more against lawyers and doctors than teachers but his sentiment was certainly true also for education.

George Miller (1975), talking, like Shaw, about the evils of professionalism, said that psychologists should 'give psychology away' instead of guarding their precious skills and barricading their professional positions. The same can be said of teaching. By sharing knowledge and ideas, by demonstrating the ways they teach, by inviting parents into the classroom, teachers can give teaching away. No one can possibly lose if teachers do this. There can only be winners — the children — and those who are likely to benefit most by this sharing will surely be those who need extra time and extra skill on the part of those who help them.

Most educationists today realize that parents, in their relationships with their children at home, provide the context in which children learn. Most children start school with a formidable ability in language, which they have learned at home. Parents are in contact with their children for longer than teachers are, and they are with their children, one-to-one, for much longer. Also, however dedicated teachers are, parents care about their children far, far more than anyone else. Given the tools, the skills and the confidence, all parents — not simply the assertive few — can play a much more central role in the education of their children.

New Legislation and Parental Involvement

At the same time that all these changes in thinking have been going on, the government has been trying to push forward the idea of more parent power in schools. Many are suspicious about the government's motives in this, seeing the push to parent-power as a way of shifting power and influence away from the local authorities, who often oppose central government policy. Whatever the motives behind it, however, if we wish to see more participation by parents in education we have to recognize that the new legislation provides a unique opportunity. It provides a framework for far more contact, formal and informal, between parents and teachers. While most schools, particularly primary schools, have welcomed the involvement of parents, others have made only token gestures, while a few remain openly hostile to the whole notion of parent participation.

In the past it has been part of staffroom folklore, particularly in schools in more affluent areas, that parents, if given the chance, will try to move against the progressive, child-centred methods which have been developing in post-war British education. Teachers often think that parents will push for the curriculum to become more drill-based, more concerned with the three Rs. Parents will oppose the efforts of teachers to make the curriculum more concerned with creativity, imagination, communication and cooperation. There may be something in this view, but my research shows that when parents are fully involved and participating in the life and work of the school, and when they understand the aims of the staff, they are far more likely to work with the teachers rather than against them.

This participation may take many forms, from helping on school outings or on the sports field or in the swimming pool, to working in the classroom alongside the class teacher — perhaps offering special skills like needlework or perhaps hearing children read. Some parents may wish to serve on the board of governors. All these forms of involvement bring a richness and a diversity to school life; parents bring to the school a variety of talents and personalities without which the school would be poorer.

Where parental participation in the life of the school works well, there is a real cross-fertilization; the school and its children benefit from the input of the parents and the parents understand more clearly what the school is trying to do. When there is involvement in the classroom, a two-way transfer of skills, knowledge and energy follows. At its best, it enables the parent to go away from the school with a knowledge of the school's methods and its aims for the children; the school and its children will have benefited by the contribution of the parent — her/his personality, effort, skills and time.

Parents can and should also be more involved in working with teachers on not only the 'helping' and extra-curricular activities, but also in planning and developing the core curriculum of the school. Indeed, the government's consultation document, *The National Curriculum 5–16*, specifically mentioned this role of parents:

> Another essential part of the monitoring arrangements will be action
> by parents, who will be able to pin-point deficiencies in the delivery
> of the national curriculum from the information about objectives
> and performance provided to them (p. 23).

However, there are surely grave dangers in using words like 'monitoring' and 'deficiencies' almost in the same breath as talking of a 'partnership' between parents and teachers. Parental involvement is a tender young plant. It is the kind of innovation which will not work unless it has the support of the teachers, and it will never develop without trust and mutual respect. Trust and mutual respect will not be forthcoming if teachers see parents in a 'monitoring' role. A broader, richer curriculum for our children will only develop in a climate of sharing and understanding between parents and teachers.

An exciting project, with this sharing in the curriculum in mind, is currently going on in Project IMPACT, but even outside the scope of a project like IMPACT it is clear that parents are becoming involved far more in a range of activities which are more closely associated with the formal curriculum. In a recent survey (Thomas, 1987) I found that the single most common activity of parents who were working alongside the class teacher was hearing children reading — one of the once-sacred three Rs with which only teachers were to be concerned. Parents were also frequently reported doing language and number games with children.

Changes in the climate engendered by legislation may also encourage other, more formal, involvement by parents. Parents who sit on governing bodies will be able to contribute, for instance, to whole school policy documents on special needs in the school.

There are good reasons for the much more widespread involvement of parents in helping to develop the curriculum. If parents are involved they will understand better the aims of the school and the teachers. If they are involved they will be better able to help their children in key areas like reading and maths. If they are participating and understanding, they are not so likely to be complaining — standing in huddles outside the school entrance while they wait for their children to emerge after the school day — that 'all they do in there is play'.

The reason parents make such familiar complaints about 'playing rather than working' if often simply because they do not understand what the school is doing. Why should they? They are not going to pick up very much from the once-a-term open day, or the once-in-a-blue-moon meeting. These are often guaranteed to befuddle rather than to clarify, and often merely reinforce the idea that modern education has gone off its rocker.

Indeed, it is probably poor communication which has opened the way for the Education Reform Act. When outsiders (and I include parents in that category advisedly) glimpse what is going on in schools, they do not like what they see. Attempts to help children to learn-through-doing are interpreted as children 'messing around'. Only through far more sharing with parents — sharing, for instance, ideas about integration, equal opportunity and mixed ability teaching — are parents likely to want to protect and develop the education of Great Britain, which, at its best, is uniquely successful. Because that sharing, that openness, has not begun to happen until very recently, there has been precious little understanding, and 'reforms' which include testing at the age of 7 are being introduced on a backlash against progressive education.

A louder parental voice in the reshaping and development of the curriculum can only be a good thing. Teachers will be able to explain through far closer contact with parents — for example through sharing the classroom with them — what their aims and principles are. If parents' questions cannot be answered with meaning or clarity or coherence it will be no bad thing if this forces a reappraisal of certain ideas or methods. Parents are, after all, part of the 'real world' in all its diversity, and greater accountability of the education service to them must be positive.

The Education Reform Act versus the 1981 Act?

So far, I have been fairly positive about the changes in legislation which have given parents more say in their children's education. I have argued that the wider involvement of parents will help prevent special needs ever from arising, and attempts through legislation to encourage parental involvement seem to me to be beneficial from this point of view. However, the wider context within which this debate has taken place seems not to have been so much one of parental involvement as parental choice, and the unfettered exercise of parental choice holds many dangers for lower achieving children.

The 1981 Education Act (Special Educational Needs) stated that as far as practicable children with special needs should be educated in ordinary schools. However, one of the stated intentions of the Education Reform Act is the promotion of competition among schools through the mechanism of the National Curriculum on which the school's performance is measured through tests. Even if the climate of competition which is currently being engendered does not actually threaten the survival of individual schools, there nonetheless seems every likelihood that a result of competition will be a reluctance on the part of schools to accept or accommodate lower-achieving children — children who are going to drag down the school's test scores.

The effects of special arrangements designed to limit the likelihood of this (through, for example, the exemption of children with special needs from the National Curriculum) will run counter to the intentions of the 1981 Act and the Warnock Committee by accentuating the differences between these children and the rest of the school population. It will create an underclass of children who are more visibly segregated from the others than ever before. Either way, it seems that the enactment of the new legislation will work against the assimilation of children with special needs into ordinary classrooms.

This situation will create dilemmas for headteachers. In a survey conducted just before the enactment of the Education Reform Act (Simmons and Thomas, 1988), most heads were clearly in favour of the increasing integration of special needs children and said that they would be unwilling to contemplate any changes which involved the exemption of some children from arrangements to which all other children are subject.

There are other effects which are equally or more serious. Local management of schools is accompanied by an ethic which places a premium on thrift, and, taken to extremes, has led some schools to replace specialist teachers with welfare assistants (who are cheaper than teachers), or to save money by failing to buy the time of specialist services (such as the psychological service). Clearly the impact of LMS is particularly hard on such services which provide such a vital role in liaison with parents when children are experiencing difficulty; cutbacks are impeding the ability of the school to involve parents effectively when problems arise.

Conclusion

Much is still uncertain about the effects that the new legislation is having on provision for children with special educational needs. Even less certain, perhaps, are the likely effects on the shape and nature of parental participation. If, through encouraging involvement, the system can be made to meet the needs of all children more effectively, well and good. However, there is the distinct probability that the legislation does encourage distinctions to be made among children, and discourages schools from accepting lower attaining children; parents are perhaps being seen as monitors of the school's performance rather than partners. The ERA coincided with a shift in the way that children with special needs were viewed in many schools, with the introduction of whole school policies in many. The closest liaison and involvement of parents has to be fostered in order that there can be a genuinely shared understanding about the aims of the school in its desire to develop a community in which it is the responsibility of all to help the less successful minority.

References

ALGOZZINE, K.M., MORSINK, C.V. and ALGOZZINE, B. (1986) 'Classroom ecology in categorical special education classrooms', *Journal of Special Education*, **20**, 2, pp. 209–17.

CASHDAN, A., PUMFREY, P.D. and LUNZER, E.A. (1971) 'Children receiving remedial treatment in reading', *Educational Research*, **13**, 2, pp. 98–103.

HARGREAVES, D.H. (1978) 'The proper study of educational psychology', *Association of Educational Psychologists' Journal*, **4**, 9, pp. 3–8.

MILLER, G. (1975) 'Psychology: The Science of Mental Life', Harmondsworth Middlesex, Penguin.

SIMMONS, K. and THOMAS, G. (1988) 'Assessment, special needs and the Education Reform Bill', *Support for Learning*, **3**, 3, pp. 144.

THE NATIONAL CURRICULUM 5–16, (1988) London, H.M.S.O.

THE WARNOCK REPORT (1978) London, D.E.S.

THOMAS, G. (1985) 'What psychology had to offer education — then', *Bulletin of the British Psychological Society*, **38**, 322–6.

THOMAS, G. (1987) 'Extra people in the primary classroom', *Educational Research*, **29**, pp. 173–82.

TIZARD, J., SCHOFIELD, W.N. and HEWISON, J. (1982) 'Collaboration between teachers and parents in assisting children's reading', *British Journal of Educational Psychology*, **52**, pp. 1–15.

Chapter 19

Participation, Dialogue and the Reproduction of Social Inequalities

Andrew Brown

Formerly a primary school teacher, Andrew Brown now works at the Institute of Education, University of London where he is involved in initial and in-service teacher education, higher degree teaching and research. In this chapter he draws on his research into the linking of home and school through mathematical activity to raise some questions about the extent to which a dialogue between parents and teachers can be achieved. His particular concern is the way in which certain social groups might be placed in disadvantageous positions in relation to schooling. He draws on data collected through his involvement in the IMPACT project over the past two years to explore the processes by which this might happen.

Introduction

Questions of the links between schooling and practices within the home have recently taken up a place high on the educational agenda. Although this tendency has led to a rapid increase in the number and variety of initiatives that attempt to foster links between school and home, there has been little in the way of theoretically informed analysis of interaction between parents and teachers, between the home and the school. Of the research that has been conducted in this area most has been concerned with the relationship between particular forms of parental participation in schooling and narrowly defined learning outcomes. Very few studies have taken as their object the relationship between forms of parental participation and the process of the reproduction of social inequalities. Certainly within the domain of mathematics education this is hardly surprising. Why should involvement of parents in the mathematical education of their children be treated with any more critical appraisal than other recent developments in mathematics teaching such as the introduction of investigational approaches, the use of calculators in early number work or even 'the existence of clear attainment targets for mathematics, known to all' (DES and WO, 1988, p. 85)? In successive innovations in the field of mathematics teaching, the benefits of new approaches, new orientations, new contents are always assumed to be of benefit to all, to bring about a universal improvement in mathematical attainment, however this might be defined. Within this context, questions of the effects of particular practices in terms of the systematic differentiation and stratification of children, in relation to mathematical attainment, along dimensions of class, culture, ethnicity, gender and so on, are rarely addressed. We can speak of 'slow learners', 'low attainers' and even 'the mathematically gifted', but we avoid looking at the social distribution of children across these categories. When we do, it is all too easy to explain distributions in terms of the qualities of the social groups concerned, often in terms of what particular groups lack in the way of specific qualities or experiences, rather than at how school practices might themselves act to produce inequalities.[1]

The point being made here is that it is vitally important, if we are to take questions of the reproduction of social inequalities and the social distribution of differential educational attainment at all seriously, to attend to questions of the effects of innovations in the field in terms of dominant social categories. The IMPACT project, with its creative combination of development work with a range of research studies, provides an ideal opportunity to carry out such an investigation. It is a considerable strength of the project that work such as this, which is often critical of and in tension with some of the practices advocated and disseminated by the project, can be carried out alongside, and in open dialogue with, other aspects of its work. This ability might act as a demonstration of how work in mathematics education might move beyond its present narrowness and enter a period of critical reflexivity.

In this chapter I am going to explore the extent to which a parental participation project such as IMPACT can provide the basis for a dialogue between parents and teachers. In the early stages of IMPACT it was clearly envisaged that the kind of interaction between parents and teachers that the project fostered might create pressure for a transformation of school practices. Merttens and Vass (1987) state, for instance, that 'genuine parental participation sets up a dialogue between teacher and parents' (p. 268) and that such a dialogue might have a number of effects. They list three. First, they claim that dialogue between teacher and parent regarding mathematical activities carried out in the home will have the effect of making the boundaries between school subjects 'naturally blurred, since the child's learning experiences cannot be broken up into these categories' (p. 268). Second, they claim that 'it becomes increasingly hard to distinguish a hierarchy of learning' (p. 268) as parents will successfully accomplish things in the home with children that might conventionally, in the eyes of the teacher, be seen as being 'in the wrong order'. The third effect is that 'once a partnership is established, teachers are not only informing parents what is happening in the curriculum, but are also having to take on board the parents' view' (p. 270).

Furthermore, it is claimed that 'this has the effect of blurring the boundaries between the role of the teacher and that of the parent' (p. 270). I wish to argue that we are a long way from establishing the basis for these kinds of transformations. There is, rather, the possibility that the kinds of interaction and the forms of participation fostered may act to maintain the power of the teacher over the parent in the domain of education and reinforce the reproduction of existing social inequalities through schooling.

I shall start by considering the manner in which particular social identities are made available to parents in teacher discourse. Having considered the effects of this manner I shall address the asymmetry of power that exists in interactions between parents and teachers, which will lead to a consideration of one particular study (Lareau, 1987) that indicates that particular forms of parental participation can act to advantage certain, already advantaged, groups. Finally I will look specifically at one aspect of the IMPACT project for indications of such a differentiating and stratifying effect. The argument that, first, the conditions do not exist for an open and effective dialogue between parents and teachers and, second, that particular forms of parental participation might act effectively to reproduce existing social inequalities, probably seems fairly depressing from the point of view of both teachers and parents involved in IMPACT. It is not intended, however, that this chapter act as a condemnation of parental participation projects. It is hoped, rather, that it might act as a cautionary note that alerts us to the need for critical work in this area if we are to attempt to sustain the kinds of ambitions for parent/teacher dialogue stated by Merttens and Vass above.

Before setting off on this tortuous journey it is perhaps helpful to make a number of preliminary points to contextualize what follows. The first is to make clear that the concerns of this work are firmly sociological. In its concern with questions of social stratification through the practices of the teaching and learning of mathematics, in general, and attempts to link home and school through mathematical activity, in particular, the chapter takes on a distinctively different focus, and draws by and large from a different body of background work from the other chapters in this book. Second, and partly as a consequence of the above, an apology has to be made for the occasionally abstract and obscure tenor of the chapter. Reference to a number of perhaps unfamiliar concepts is necessary to make analytic sense of what is being dealt with here, and constraints of space and the necessity not to stray too far from the substantive focus of the chapter make it impossible to elaborate fully and adequately on them. Finally it should be noted that the empirical work drawn on here is part of an investigation related to IMPACT (Brown, 1990b) that is in the early stages of data collection and analysis. The analysis carried out and the conclusions drawn are thus exploratory, provisional and tentative.

Teachers Talking About Parents

Looking at the relations between schools and homes in formal terms, we can consider schools and homes, under our present education system in England and Wales, as sites defined by the principles of strong classification (Bernstein, 1977, 1990). They are, in other words, clearly distinguishable from each other and with strongly defined boundaries. While it might be possible to imagine a situation where the distinction between home and school is less clearly drawn and boundaries are blurred, for instance under the conditions of some form of deschooling, the home and school are at present distinctive sites with their own distinct practices. Communication does, however, take place between the school and the home, and people (children, parents, teachers, ancillary workers and so on) pass between these sites. This communication, and the communication that takes place within the sites, can itself be defined in terms of its direction and mode of control. Thus certain things can be voiced within the two institutions, particular communications can legitimately pass between the institutions and specific identities can be realized within them. This, in Bernstein's terms, comes under the control of the principles of internal and external framing. It is on the form and content of certain communications between teachers and between parents and teachers that I wish to focus here.

The forms of communication that take place within and between schools, and between schools and other institutions, are many and varied. I wish, however, to focus initially on what I shall call teacher discourse. By this I mean that in interacting and talking to each other teachers contribute to a universe of statements which acts to constitute what it is to be a teacher and to mark out what is sayable and thinkable from that which is unsayable and unthinkable. Teacher discourse can be seen as a subset of educational discourse, which would include both classroom talk and official discourse about educational matters. It might also be analytically useful to consider there being a number of sub-discourses to teacher discourse, such as those relating to various subject affiliations (mathematics, for instance) or phase of the education system (for example, primary teachers) or any other aspect of specialized social identities within the sphere of education (for instance, what it is to be a black teacher).

The content of these communications can be drawn from a vast array. Of particular interest here, however, is the parent as subject in teacher discourse. Teachers will obviously talk about parents both in general terms and about specific parents. This talk acts inevitably to ascribe to parents particular qualities. They may be general in that they describe what all parents, most parents or typical parents are like (for instance, that all or most parents care about the educational progress of their children) or they may be more particular in that they describe what specific types of parents are like (what 'pushy' parents are like, or what white working-class parents might say or do, for example). This ascription has a number of effects. One effect is to make available to parents particular social identities, in relation to schooling, and to judge parents' actions, including communications, in terms of the dimensions and limitations of these identities. Once particular qualities have been ascribed to Asian parents, for instance, how might the actions and statements made by a parent placed in the category 'Asian' by a teacher be interpreted? What might be appropriate responses? What might be the consequences of an individual acting in a way that is perceived as being outside the expectations indicated by the ascribed identity? Thus, through the ascription of identities, both general and specific, to parents, teacher discourse acts to constrain teachers by delimiting both what it is legitimately possible to say about parents in relation to schooling and by providing the set of discursive resources (Fairclough, 1990) on which to draw in the interpretation of parental actions and communications. Through this it also acts to constrain parents in offering, in relation to schooling, a restricted range of interpretable legitimate positions.

Some examples might help to clarify the point being made here. Headteachers, being interviewed as part of a research project to study pedagogic differences between two groups of local authority primary schools with intakes which differed in terms of social composition (Brown, 1985, 1990a), made a number of statements about the parents of the children at the school.[2] The parents of children in the group of schools on the west of the borough, predominantly white working-class, were typified as having a low opinion of schooling, of generating and experiencing a wide range of social problems that impinged on the work of the school, and as tending to be aggressive in interactions with school. This view was conveyed in statements such as the following:

> ... children will have time off for no reason, really. 'Oh well, I had to go to the shops', 'I had to stay in to look after me mum' ... It rather shows the attitude of the parents towards education. That it is something, alright, that keeps the children off their hands, but if it's necessary there are other more important things, like doing the shopping.

> There's no motivation, no drive to even attempt it [academic work] and that is something we are fighting against all the time. And so I think that the school has got an important sort of social job in an area like this; learning to live together in reasonable peace.

> Ask 'em for a birth certificate round here and you get a punch in the eye.

In contrast parents of children in the east of the borough, also working class but with a high proportion of heads of household from the new Commonwealth, were typified as being pro-schooling, manifesting few social problems which impinged on the school and compliant in interactions with the school. Statements such as the following were made:

> they [the parents] are completely supportive, they are completely behind schools. They think schools are great, they think English schools are great, and they back us to the hilt.

> [the school is] very, very fortunate to pick up highly motivated Asians who are very calm anyway . . . and will accept . . . things.

> Asian parents want a straight, traditional, formal education for their children.

> Generally we tend to be fairly, touch wood, lucky in our catchment. We don't get that many problem families that we can't handle, we don't get that many problem children and we don't get very much vandalism or anything of that nature.

Here parents are being positioned in relation to the implicit and explicit demands of the school and statements are made in discussion, even though this is not the subject of the discussion, that act to fix the position of parents. A similar tendency was found by Lareau (1987) in her study of parental participation in two US elementary schools, one with a white working-class intake, the other with a white middle class-intake. The principal of Prescott, with a middle-class intake, stated that:

> This particular community is one with a very strong interest in its schools. It is a wonderful situation in which to work. Education is very important to the parents and they back that up with an interest in volunteering. This view that education is important helps kids as well. If parents value schooling and think it is important, then kids take it seriously (p. 81).

This contrasts with the image held by the principal of Colton regarding the working-class parents of the children at his school:

> They don't value education because they don't have much of one themselves. [Since] they don't value education as much as they could, they don't put those values and expectations on their kids. (p. 81)

Interestingly, this image of working-class parents is not borne out by Lareau's interviews with the parents themselves. These parents expressed concern about their child's progress in school and saw themselves as playing a supportive role. Where their expressed views differed from those of the middle-class parents was in the level of educational attainment they aspired to for their children. When, however, the level of educational qualifications attained by the parents themselves were taken into account, the relative degree of aspiration could be seen to be comparable.[3] Thus working-class parents who were high school dropouts would hope that their children would graduate from high school; middle-class parents who were college graduates would aspire for their children to obtain a higher degree. The parents also expressed differences in their views of the legitimate relationship between home and school, a point that I shall take up in more detail later.

There are, of course, numerous opportunities within the IMPACT project to study teachers talking about parents in relation to school mathematics. One part of the sequence of activities that are used when introducing IMPACT to a new LEA is for teachers representing each of the schools about to take part in the project to discuss and draw up a parental response sheet. Typically at these meetings teachers work in small groups, each with no two teachers from the same school if possible, to produce ideas for the format for the sheet on which parents and children will give their reactions to an IMPACT activity. To help in this process each group is given some examples of existing sheets. In this situation teachers from a number of different schools, with a diversity of experiences, are put together and have to talk about what parents can do, should do, might want to do and so on, in relation to responding to a mathematical activity that they have done with their child. This would appear to be a tall order given the diversity noted above. Teachers do not appear, however, to have any difficulty in discussing and largely agreeing on these questions. In a transcript of one such group of seven teachers carrying out the above activity, a discussion which lasted for one hour and which was participated in fully by all the teachers, there were numerous statements made about parents (the words 'parent' or 'parents' occurs forty-one times) in relation to what parents could be asked to do, how they might be asked, how they might respond, and ways in which their responses might be interpreted. Throughout the discussion no teacher directly contested the image of the parent put forward by others. Not only this but 'parents' were talked about as a unified homogeneous group. In only one exchange were statements made about what could be considered a subgroup of parents. In discussing the possibility that parents might, by consistently ticking a particular box on one of the response sheets, indicate that they thought their children were 'learning nothing' from IMPACT activities, the following was said:

Teacher 1: They're sort of saying 'learning nothing, wasting time' . . .
I mean I think we know the sorts of parents who are likely to turn round and say that.

Teacher 2: But those are exactly the sort of parents that you want to get in to talk about what this is all about surely.

There was no need here to elaborate what the qualities of the 'sorts of parents' being discussed here might be, or who might be a member of this group. These things are already established in teacher discourse.

There are a number of interesting points that can be drawn from this discussion. We have a situation here where the basis is being laid for a form of dialogue between the home and the school. The terms of the dialogue are, however, clearly defined by the school. The teachers taking part in the discussion described above had a clear picture of what parents could or could not comment on and of what they considered parents would or would not be willing to do. Through them, clear limits are placed on the parent in what they can legitimately say in relation to the mathematical activities they have done with their children. This restriction is not, however, limited to the framing of a particular format for responses to maths activities, nor is it limited to specific projects such as IMPACT which attempt to set up deliberate channels of communication between the home and the school. The analysis of teacher discourse, in a variety of contexts, might lead us to examine the manner in which limitations are placed on the range of interpretations that are made of parental communications and behaviours and thus on the range of possible social identities made available to parents in relation to schooling. This is a matter of great complexity and cannot be adequately dealt with here, but it is worth considering how this process might operate and what the effects might be.

Some Effects of Teacher Discourse

Through actual interactions, spoken or written, an image of 'what parents are' is built up within teacher discourse. This acts to build up a 'normalizing' image of parents and parenting practices, which in turn provides a kind of standard against which to judge 'actual' parents, or through which to interpret the actions and utterances of parents. This is, however, at a high level of generality, although the ascribed qualities might be highly specific. Generality enables teachers from a wide range of backgrounds and circumstances to discuss parents without having any particular parent or group of parents in mind. Placed in relation to this 'general' or 'normal' or even 'natural' parent are specific groups of parents who might show some of the attributes of the general parent but may also diverge in some way. At the most specific level, particular parents are placed in relation to identified groups of parents and parents in general. Particular parents can, of course, be placed in relation to a number of groups, for instance as a single parent, a black parent, a working-class parent and so on. Through this process the 'imaginary' becomes 'actual', by way of providing the interpretive framework within which the 'actual' is placed or made sense of. Thus the parent is constituted by and through discourse and the self becomes entered and defined by a range of social divisions or categories.

The effects of this process can be elaborated by reference to two pieces of research in different domains. Duxbury (1987) carried out research exploring the effects of contemporary childcare ideologies on a group of working-class mothers. These mothers reported that they felt that images of how a mother should behave and feel in relation to their children's behaviour and of the images of ideal relationship between mother and child, created an unobtainable ideal given their social and economic circumstances. In constantly falling short of this ideal they felt inadequate and guilty that they appear to be disadvantaging their children. As Duxbury states:

> the very theories and philosophies which were supposed to liberate and individualize children, and to sanctify and professionalize motherhood, have become an added constraint particularly upon the most disadvantaged groups in society. The 'ideal' created by the literature is impossible to achieve within a multiplicity of social, economic and ideological constraints and creates a seam of guilt and doubt in the mothers' role which is quickly exploited by young children via manipulation, their own conscious reaction to the contradictory position they share with their parents (p. 23).

Academic writing concerning child development and mothering is seen here as the source of these images of 'ideal' mothering practices and 'normal' child development. It is unlikely, however, that many working class-mothers come into contact with such texts. Rather, these images of the ideal parent are circulated by doctors, midwives, health visitors and other professionals in their routine interactions with mothers, as well as through the more public and general means of the mass media, including magazines specifically concerned with parents and parenting. Here the normal parent as defined, for instance, within the discourse of health professionals acts to establish the framework within which mothers feel their own behaviour to be judged and within which they come to judge themselves. Obviously there are a number of discourses that contain within them statements about what constitutes good and bad mothering, including teacher discourse. The two mentioned here, that of health professionals and the mass media, are particularly pervasive and powerful. Within these discourses there will also be a number of statements and positions that lie in tension with each other. While it is not possible to map out these relations and outline how discourses might be formed and structured, it is important to observe that the sets of possible statements made about, in this case, mothering pre-exist these mothers themselves; 'what it is to be a good mother' acts to delimit and define the discursive space in which mothers come to be mothers and experience motherhood.[4] In short the resources are provided in discourse by which membership of a particular category is defined and judged, through which people learn to be members of that category; how, for instance, people learn to be parents. It is interesting to note, in this context, the observation made by Lightfoot (1978, quoted in Levin, 1987), in a study of the tensions between mothers and teachers:

> The school is the place where mothers experience their first public evaluation and scrutiny, where their child is compared with his [sic] agemates, and where teachers and other mothers voice approval or disapproval of the mother as reflected through the child (p. 273).

The second piece of research I wish to look at in this respect concerns the role of school experience in the initial education of primary school teachers. In this study Menter (1989) explored the extent to which school experience, acknowledged as a key component of the professional social-ization of student teachers, could play a part in 'the preparation of teachers who are reflective, critical and enquiring' (p. 459). Focusing on issues of race and gender as they related to the school practice of the students, Menter found a tendency towards 'stasis', that is that despite the time spent on these issues in the college–based components of the courses studied, there was little indication of translation of these concerns into practice. This, he proposes, can be traced to the overriding concern of both students and their supervisors for not upsetting the stability of the student-class teacher-supervisor relationship. Students expressed a fear of 'stepping on people's toes' and a 'desire to fit in', and demonstrated that the aim of 'surviving' the period of school experience took precedence over all else. College supervisors also showed an overriding concern for the maintenance of good relationships with the school and teacher, not just for the smooth running of the particular period of school experience in question but also for the future placement of students. This concern led in one case, for example, to one female tutor, who had expressed a strong concern over issues of gender and schooling, to actually collude with a male teacher in making sexist comments in a discussion about a student.

This study makes depressing reading for those involved with the training of teachers who are concerned with countering the reproduction of social inequalities. It does, however, act to illustrate some points relevant to the present discussion. We have here a situation where, through the concern to maintain stability, all parties are constrained to act in a particular way and adopt particular positions. This is certainly not to suggest that all primary school teachers are sexist and racist, nor is it to suggest that students and their supervisors should go around alienating teachers. Rather it indicates that, through the anxiety of the student to 'become a teacher' and the desire of the tutor to bring the teaching practice to a conclusion that is acceptable to the teacher as a representative of the teaching profession and maintain good relations, key aspects of teacher practice and discourse are reproduced. This outcome is hardly surprising. The central purpose of school experience would seem to be the induction of the student into the practices that characterize a good teacher, however this role might be defined. There are, however, a wide range of priorities, dispositions, personal qualities and opinions, as well as specific identifiable skills, that define what it is to be a good teacher. In the cases studied by Menter it does not appear that concern over taking action on sexism and racism are among these qualities. Might not, then, a student who is seen by the class teacher as having an 'excessive' preoccupation with race and gender issues be considered unsuited to becoming a teacher? How might the student react, no matter what their own personal disposition and opinions, to the message that discussions of racist and sexist practices within the school and in their own practice are of lower priority than, say, the aesthetic quality of the display of children's work, or that such discussions are simply not welcomed. To make such considerations a high priority might seem to the student, concerned with entry to the teaching profession, as putting themselves in jeopardy. The tutors also find themselves constrained by teacher discourse in that asserting priorities that are different from those considered legitimate by the teacher might lead to them being marginalized as 'being out of touch with the realities of the classroom'. This acts to illustrate, in a small but important way, how the student learns to 'become', or 'become recognizable as', a student *teacher* by being incorporated into teacher discourse, by only being able to legitimately voice that which can be voiced, by being 'one of us'.[5]

These two studies act to indicate both the power of discourse and also asymmetries of power within discourse. In both cases one identifiable group of people is learning, or being taught, to take up a particular identity through the definitions of self — being offered to them by other, more powerful groups. Notice here that power is not being defined in terms of any absolute status hierarchy, but is related to context. Thus, while a college lecturer might be in a position of power in relation to a teacher who is enroled on a higher degree course, the teacher may be relatively powerful in terms of the continued credibility of the lecturer as a legitimate teacher educator or, as in the study above, the acceptance of the school experience placement of her/his students. This is not to suggest, however, that all groups are powerful in some context or another, but that being relatively powerful in one context does not necessarily imply power relative to the same group or groups in other contexts.

Parental Participation and the Possibility of Dialogue

To return to the question of the possibility of establishing partnerships between the school and the home we can assert that, in the context of communications between the school and the home it is the school/teacher that is relatively powerful and that it is through these communications that parents are positioned in relation to the school. Thus the position available to parents in teacher discourse, as outlined above, matters if we are to begin to talk about the possibility of dialogue between home and school.

In an article written after the two pilot years of IMPACT, Merttens and Vass (1987), in discussing the possible challenge that parents might provide to the preconceptions, assumptions and professional knowledge of teachers draw an analogy with medicine:

> Generally when we go to the doctors we have some idea not only about what is wrong with us, but also about what to do about it. We go in order to enter into a dialogue, in which on one side there will be ourselves, with our intuitions and our feelings and our knowledge of ourselves, and on the other will be the doctor with her [sic] professional expertise and knowledge acquired through training and experience. Few people would maintain today that the patient should have no say in the treatment. But, also, few could be so foolish to ignore completely the professional's expertise. For most of us in this situation it is the dialogue that is important (p. 270).

This passage obviously refers to what the authors consider should be rather than what is, both in the domain of medicine and education. Even so the scenario lacks recognition of power relations in such meetings. Numerous studies in the sociology of health and illness have indicated the asymmetry of power in medical consultations. Silverman's (1983) study of consultations at a cleft palate clinic, for example, demonstrates how, in an exchange that follows a question-answer-further question format, the questioner, in this case the doctor, controls the agenda for the consultation. He also demonstrates through the analysis of specific instances how a particular discourse is constructed which acts to constitute the patient as what he calls a 'marginalized' subject. In the light of this kind of work within the domain of medicine, it is interesting to contrast the image of the medical interview given by Merttens and Vass with that drawn by Bernstein (1990).

> In any pedagogic relationship the transmitter has to learn to be a transmitter and the acquirer has to learn to be an acquirer. When you go to the doctor you have to learn how to be a patient. It is no good going to the doctor and saying, 'I feel really bad today, everything is really grey.' He [sic] says, 'Don't waste my time,' because he has many patients. 'Where is the pain? How long have you had it? What kind of pain is it? Is it acute? Is it chronic? Is it sharp? Is it persistent?' After a bit you learn how to talk to your doctor. He teaches you to be an acquirer. But how he teaches you is the function of a much more general set of forces (p. 65).

Here the relative power of doctor and patient is more fully elaborated. The patient learns how to be a patient much as the student teacher learns how to be a student teacher and the mother learns how to be a mother. Certain positions are made available to one within the discourse in which, and through which, one is being constructed; one's options are limited. Obviously, through this process one person can be ascribed, or take up, any number of contextually related social identities. For instance, an incident was recently recounted to me by a parent, also an educational researcher, who was constructed, within the same school, as both a 'good' parent and a 'bad' parent in face-to-face interaction with two different teachers. The utterances and actions of the parent were interpreted as those of a good parent in relation to one of their children who was seen as doing well at school and was, in the school's terms, a good pupil. In interactions with another teacher, this time concerning a child seen as having problems at school, the utterances and actions of the same parent were construed as those of a difficult and inadequate parent. In both cases, however, it might be claimed by the teacher that some form of dialogue is taking place, although it can be seen from this example that in certain circumstances it is only possible for the parent to voice certain things, to be a particular kind of parent.

This raises again the difficult and complex question of the multiplicity of social identities that can be ascribed to any one person, and the relationships between them, which is interesting in the context of teacher discourse. Participating in the IMPACT meeting discussion drawn on above were a number of teachers who were also parents. Only once, however, did a teacher refer to their own experience as a parent. This comment was in the context of a discussion of what it might be appropriate for children to comment on having taken part in an IMPACT activity.

> Teacher 1:   Well, I don't like that there. I mean I accept your point perhaps about the adult writing it down, but what about the child? Well if you've got children of your own at school, you say 'what did you learn today at school?' 'Er, nothing' [laughs] is almost a standard response or something, that doesn't mean anything in itself, does it?

Thus the only reference made to teachers themselves as parents was to make reference to the behaviour of children in the home context as distinct from the school context. Interestingly there were no references in the discussion that indicated that some parents might be teachers or other workers in the educational field, and thus that the categories of parent and teacher are not mutually exclusive. What this lack indicates is perhaps that these divisions actually enter the subject themselves, that is, that there is some degree of insulation between the social identity of a person as 'teacher' and as 'parent' in terms of what might be voiced in which context. We might recall the apparent insulation between the identities 'student teacher' an 'active anti-racist' in Menter's study.

The discussion so far would seem to suggest that the possibilities of dialogue, given the asymmetry of power in the teacher-parent encounter, are fairly limited. At this point it would be useful to return to look in more detail at the study by Lareau mentioned earlier. Lareau found that the requests for parental participation made by the staff of the two elementary schools studied were broadly similar in both form and frequency. Both schools actively sought to involve parents through home reading schemes, requests to work alongside teachers in the classroom and invitations to attend a range of formal and informal events.

> At both schools, the definition of an ideal family-school relationship was the same: a partnership in which family and school life are integrated (p. 76).

There were, however, inequalities inherent in the proposed form of partnership, both between teachers and parents, and between parents of different social class backgrounds. Firstly, although all teachers encouraged parents to voice their concerns about their children not all voiced concerns were welcomed. For instance:

> Teachers and administrators spoke of being 'partners' with parents, and they stressed the need to maintain good communication, but it was clear that they desired parents to defer to their professional expertise. For example, a first-grade teacher at Prescott did not believe in assigning homework to the children and did not appreciate parents communicating their displeasure with the policy by complaining repeatedly to the principal. Nor did principals welcome parents' opinions that a teacher was a bad teacher and should be fired. Teachers wanted parents to support them, or as they put it, to 'back them up' (p. 76).

Thus the teacher has the upper hand in the partnership and the parent is, once again having to learn how to be a parent in this domain.

This discussion leads on to another form of inequality in the form of partnership, this time between parents from different social class backgrounds. Parental performance was taken seriously by teachers and was noted and remembered by them. Thus, it becomes important for the parent to be seen to participate in schooling in what is thought by teachers to be an appropriate way. There were, however, differences evident in both the levels and forms of parental participation between the two schools. Not only was parental participation at Prescott, the middle class-school, higher but parental initiated interactions were more frequent and were more likely to relate to the academic progress of their children. Parents here also tended to make more specific requests to the school regarding matters such as resources and homework and were more at ease in their interactions with school staff. The parents of children at Colton, the working-class school, in contrast initiated few communications with the school and those that did take place were more likely to be about matters such as lunchboxes or playground activities than about academic progress. These parents were seen as being ill at ease in their interaction with staff at the school. In both schools level of parental involvement was taken as an indication of the value placed on schooling by parents. Colton parents were thus perceived as being less concerned about the progress of their children at school, as noted earlier.

As Lareau points out, material, social and cultural factors differentially place parents in relation to the requests made by the school. On the most obvious level this might include the greater ease with which middle-class parents can manipulate their working arrangements to participate in day-time events or work in the classroom alongside the teacher. Less visibly it might include differences in the perception of the relationship between work and home, and thus between school work and appropriate home activity. Some of the working-class parents in Lareau's study indicated that they felt that there should be a high degree of separation between work and home. These parents, though they clearly valued education, saw schooling as work and thus felt that, like work, it should be left behind at the end of the day. A number of the working-class parents also expressed unease about the contribution they could make, given their own educational backgrounds, to the education of their children. This insecurity, combined with the desire to maintain the boundary between 'work' and home, led to a tendency to see the education of their children as strictly a school matter, something for teachers, as 'educated people' take responsibility for. This image contrasts with the views expressed by the middle-class Prescott parents who saw education as more of a partnership and scrutinized and monitored the educational experience of their children. Additionally they considered themselves to be, at least, the social equals of teachers, that is that they themselves had equal or superior educational skills and qualifications and, thus, that teachers were not doing anything they could not do; it was merely a question of division of labour.

The children of these middle-class families spent much of their out of school time engaging in organized social activities, such as swimming lessons, karate, and art and craft sessions, which also acted as a basis for a social network of Prescott parents through which information about the school, particular teachers, specific school activities, the relative performance of children and so forth circulated. Colton children, on the other hand, engaged more in informal activities such as bike riding and snake hunting. Their parents' social networks centred more on family and relations rather than involving a wide range of other Colton parents. Subsequently, Lareau argues, these working-class parents were less well informed about the details of their children's schooling as they lacked the form of social network that might provide this information. This non-interaction might not be so important if teachers were not, to return to an earlier point, to interpret the forms of participation and the types of engagement of parents as being indicative of interest in education and concern about children's progress. As Lareau concludes, the form of relations between parents and teachers expected and encouraged by both schools fits better with, and draws more heavily on, the class culture of the middle classes than that of the working classes. The school thus advantages middle-class children by seeking to establish particular forms of participation.

> Because both schools promote a family-school relationship that solicits parental involvement in schooling and which promotes an interdependence between family and school, the class position and the class culture of middle-class families yield a social profit not available to working-class families. In particular, middle-class culture provides parents with more information about schooling and also builds social networks among parents in the school community. Parents use this information to build a family-school relationship congruent with the schools' definition of appropriate behavior (p. 82).

Here teachers are defining what counts as worthwhile parental participation, what counts as real interest and involvement, what counts as good parenting. They are doing so, however, in such a way that favours one group over another by drawing specifically on the culture of that group.[6] Which raises questions about the criteria or standards that parental participation projects set which act to define what an ideal state of partnership, participation and dialogue might be.

Communications from School to Home

Might the processes and procedures associated with IMPACT be having the differentiating and stratifying effect noted above? One possible way of addressing this question is obviously to look at what it is that is being asked of parents, and how they are being asked, and to attempt to analyze the underlying class assumptions. A rich source of data on which to base such an analysis are the booklets, outlining how IMPACT will work and what the parent's involvement will be, that are produced for parents by all schools participating in IMPACT. In order to explore what we might gain from these, let us take a look at one such booklet[7] (see the following list).

Booklets such as these are produced by the school to communicate certain information to parents. High among the priorities in writing such a text is clarity, that is producing something that can be easily understood by parents. As such the booklet constitutes both an element of and product of teacher discourse. Enshrined in this product is obviously an image of 'the parent', a notion of what is understandable to the parent, what format, content, vocabulary is palatable and appropriate, what it is that the parent can comprehend, what it is that they might want to or need to know, and so on. Thus we have a text that both speaks to and about parents, both in its form and content. The text also makes statements about teachers, about children, about school, about homes, about mathematics and so on, as well as making statements about the relations between them. This chapter is not the place for a full-scale textual analysis, but it is possible to pull out some observations that are of interest in the present context.

Text of a School IMPACT Booklet for Parents

Primary School
IMPACT
Enjoying maths with your child

---

5 MATHS CAN BE FUN

Impact is a partnership between parents and
teachers. The children also gain a lot from having
to explain what they are learning. Parents have a
10 direct involvement in what is being taught in the
classroom because when the task is completed it
will be taken back into the classroom and shared
with the other children.

---

15 ENJOY MATHS

Your child will bring home a maths activity to
share with the family.
Let him/her EXPLAIN what has to be done.
20 BE A GOOD LISTENER.
Discuss the activity with your child.
ENJOY working together.

---

24 HELP YOUR CHILD

There are three main types of IMPACT ACTIVITY
1) COLLECTING INFORMATION
Your child may be doing some work on Time so
they could be asked:
30 How long does it take to do the washing up?
How long does it take to get ready for bed?
HELP your child with the information which will
be discussed in school.

---

35 WORK TOGETHER

2) DOING AND MAKING
This could be cutting out and making a box from
card.
40 Let your child tell you what to do.
FOLLOW HIS/HER INSTRUCTIONS

PLAYING GAMES TOGETHER

45 3) GAMES

The activity may be in the form of a game.
Why not sit down on the rug and have FUN to-
gether.
50 Make it a FAMILY time.
Above all ENJOY yourselves — remember
MATHS CAN BE FUN

You will be able to let us know how well the
55 activity went by filling in the response sheet
e.g. The CHILD'S response could be

I did not enjoy/I did enjoy the activity.

60 The PARENT'S response could be
This activity went
very well/had problems/no problems.

There will also be regular meetings to discuss
65 IMPACT with the teachers.
Research has shown that WORKING TOGETHER
really does help your child!

We at [X Primary School] welcome this parental involvement and
70 hope that you will feel free to work with the
teachers and discuss with them any problems that
might arise. We hope that by doing this we can
continue to give your child the best in education.

First, the text can be seen to make a number of statements about what good parents do or should do. They are good listeners, discuss activities with their children, work with their children at home and enjoy doing so (3–22–24). They are members of a distinguishable family unit that has identifiable family time together (3–52), that shares activities from outside (3–17), that has fun together (3–50–51). They are involved in their children's schooling (3–12–13–66–67) and work with and discuss with teachers (64–65). In the light of the discussion above it can be seen that even such a simple communication contributes to the setting up of a normalizing discourse. It acts to produce truths about parents and families against which, in the significant domain of schooling, parents are, or feel they are, evaluated. Obviously it can be seen that some groups, through economic, social and cultural circumstances, might be less favourably positioned in relation to this ideal. In relation to these statements it is also worth considering the way in which statements are made about parental behaviour. In the case of this booklet there is a predominance of imperatives: 'Let him/her EXPLAIN . . .',

BE A GOOD LISTENER, 'HELP your child...', FOLLOW HIS/HER
INSTRUCTIONS, and so on. This very much a case of the school telling the
parent what to be and what to do, but not, noticeably, how to be, or, in all
but the vaguest terms (19–20), why.

This problem leads us on directly to a second observation. There is little
indication of what the school considers valid and worthwhile mathematical
activity to be. Instead we have examples of types of activities that might be
considered mathematical: timing home events, making a box, playing a
game. Thus the parent is put in the position of not being given access to the
criteria by which teachers judge mathematical activity. This is likely not to be
a deliberate and calculated move on the part of the school to disempower
parents, but rather an indication of the diffuse and inexplicit nature of the
means by which the quality of a mathematical activity or experience is
judged by teachers. Because of the complex of theories and professional
knowledge on which such judgments and evaluations are made, the parent is
not being offered induction into a teacherly role but is being asked to act as
the agent of the teacher within the home, carrying out teacher set activities
and delivering the products back to the school. The creative engagement of
the parent in setting up and implementing mathematical activities is dependent on them being able to impute, or already having access to, the appropriate evaluation criteria. Both parent and child are put into a position of
powerlessness with regard to the evaluation of their own activity. The only
explicit criteria they are given by which to judge is that the activity should be
enjoyable or fun.

In terms of feedback on the activities, the child is being asked only to
comment on whether the activity was enjoyable or not (58), and the parent
on whether the activity went well or had problems (62). As the basis on
which such judgments are made, and can be made, remains unclear, so the
interpretations of the child's or parent's responses by the teachers remains
open. By this I mean that while children and parents are being asked osten-
sibly to make comments about the activities, their comments may be taken
as an element in the teacher's evaluation of the qualities of the child or
parent themselves.[8] Despite the lack of explicit criteria, the products from
activities are evaluated by the teachers. In meetings for teachers from
IMPACT schools that I have attended there has not been any hesitation to
show, discuss or display what is considered to be good work from home. It is
interesting that in these cases the work, say, for instance, the results of an
activity to build a model boat, while meeting certain criteria relating to the
discourse of primary school mathematics, must be seen to be the work of the
child and not the adult. A parent, interpreting the evaluation criteria as
related to the intricacy and accuracy of the final product, who works with
their child to produce a scale model of the Cutty Sark places themselves
squarely in the zone of negative evaluation. The parent whose child returns
to school with a cork with a toothpick stuck in it is also, however, in jeopardy. The text makes it clear that form of partnership that is being set

up further opens the home to surveillance and scrutiny by the school both in terms of products (12–13–15) and processes (72–73).

This second cluster of observations brings to mind aspects of Bernstein's invisible pedagogy (Bernstein, 1977) and alerts us once again to the possible class basis of the assumptions underlying forms of pedagogic action. There are two sets of acquirers to consider in the case of parental participation projects: the parents and their children. In the case of parents as acquirers, with teachers as transmitters, it can be seen that within the rhetoric of the IMPACT project the hierarchy is implicit. Parents are presented as being partners, peers with teachers. Sequencing rules and criteria are also implicit in that they are not made visible to the parent. Control of what counts as appropriate activities lies in the hands of the teacher; the criteria by which the parent is to evaluate their own and their children's behaviour is implicit and has to be imputed by the parent from communications with the teacher. By way of these factors the parent is encouraged by the school to establish a form of invisible pedagogy within the home. A situation is created where, as above, the child's play can be seen as a legitimate part of her/his mathematical development and the child's everyday activities are colonized by mathematics. Sequencing rules and criteria remain inaccessible to the child as they are unlikely to be accessible in any clear way to the transmitter, the parent. In addition to the effects noted above, at the level of rhetoric, the boundary between work and play is weakened. What parents might have thought of as work (school mathematics) is in fact play (fun). Their play, such as 'family time', playing games with their children, and everyday activities, such as getting the children ready for bed, in fact have potential as opportunities for pedagogic work. As Bernstein has pointed out, and this is borne out by Lareau's empirical work, in working-class families the boundary between work and play is likely to be more firmly drawn than in some fractions of the middle class. Bernstein also suggests that the basis of invisible pedagogy lies in the culture and material conditions of the new middle classes and thus initiatives that revolve around attempts to establish forms of invisible pedagogy in all homes are likely to favour these groups, particularly in the early years of schooling. Interestingly, invisible pedagogies only have limited currency for the educationally ambitious. As formal selection through examination approaches, the demands of new middle-class parents turn to establishment of forms of visible pedagogy in school, with explicit hierarchy, explicit sequencing rules and explicit criteria. Thus, even the successful establishment of the forms and principles of invisible pedagogy within all homes might act to favour particular middle-class groups who have a successful track record in manipulating school practices to their own ends (Cohen, 1981).

Conclusion

This chapter has followed a rather circuitous route. In addressing the question of the social reproductive effects of projects such as IMPACT I have focused initially on the nature of the boundary between home and school in terms of the specific identities that are made available within these sites. Through teacher discourse particular legitimate identities are offered to parents, in relation to which parents are positioned. The constraining effects of this process on both teachers and parents is illustrated with reference to two research studies, not directly related to questions of parental participation, and some evidence that these processes might be at work with the domain of relations between teachers and parents is presented from my own work. All this acts to problematize the setting up of the form of dialogue between parents and teachers that might have the kinds of transformative effects on teacher practice envisaged by the directors of IMPACT in the early stages of the project. It also alerts us to the need to attend to questions of relative power in different contexts when considering relations between home and school. Lareau's study of two US elementary schools has been given as an example of a study that does this and which illuminates some of the mechanisms that might be at work in reproducing social inequalities through practices such as parental involvement in schooling. Finally the possibility that the IMPACT project might be acting in the same differentiating and stratifying manner is explored by looking that one particular type of communication between home and school and the types of statements made.

To set up an effective dialogue between parents and teachers is obviously a complex matter. The IMPACT project has provided, and continues to provide, numerous opportunities for teachers and parents to explore what such a dialogue might look like and how we might move towards more fruitful forms of collaboration. In this light, the kind of critical analysis that I have engaged with here might be seen as not particularly helpful. The arguments elaborated are not, however, intended as destructive critiques, but as indications of the complexity of the area. Above all it is hoped that they help to stop us from making presumptions about the necessary value of what we are trying to do, and prompt us, as practitioners, to continue to ask difficult and awkward questions of our own practice. It is only too easy to become embroiled in what are in essence technical matters, such as how to ensure that more parents return their response sheets or attend 'maths evenings' or do more maths activities at home, while neglecting what the effects of what we are doing and aiming to do might be. At the very least I hope that this chapter has indicated that there may be elements within the practice of teachers that, no matter how worthy our intentions might be, can act to maintain parents in a position of powerlessness in relation to schooling. What's more, some of the attempts that we make, again with the best intentions, to develop a way of giving parents a greater voice in education might act to even more effectively reproduce the very social divisions that we would claim we are trying to counter. The pervasiveness of this division is indicated by Levin's (1987) account of the history of two Toronto free schools. Here, even in a situation where parents set up schools themselves specifically to address their interests and provide a forum for dialogue with teachers, maintaining a voice in the educational domain proved to be impossible. All this serves to indicate that we are in an area in which there are no easy answers and which will stretch the capacity of teachers as reflexive practitioners to the full as we are led towards questioning the nature of the boundary between home and school and thus the very nature of schooling.

Notes

1   There are, of course, exceptions to this rule, for instance the work of Valerie Walkerdine (1988, 1989). It is interesting to note that, however, work such as Walkerdine's might take mathematics education as its focus, but is placed outside what might be considered the field of 'mathematics education'. There are, however, a growing number of mathematics educators (school teachers, lecturers, teacher trainers and researchers within mathematics education departments, and so on) who are adopting critical perspectives and addressing social and political questions within the context of mathematics education. See for example Noss *et al.* (1990) and Dowling and Noss (1990).

2   It is important to note here that these headteachers were talking to a researcher who was known to them as a teacher in same borough. Although they were aware that they were being interviewed as part of a small scale research project, the types of statement made were of the form of that which could be made to someone within the same professional domain. Both the interviewer and the interviewee were primary teachers, albeit with a status differential, and were recognizable to each other as such through both the form and content of the exchange between them. Certain assumptions are made, particular details given, others not given, particular forms of statement acceptable, others not. It is worth considering how different the statements made might be if the conversation were between the headteacher and the parent of a pupil, or a local councillor, or a university based researcher. Similarly consider the kinds of statement that might be made if a parent or councillor or researcher was interviewed by the interviewer.

3   Roberts *et al.* (1977) have shown a similar situation to hold with the mobility orientations of various social groups in Britain. In this study, as in Lareau's, if proclaimed levels of parental aspiration were viewed in relative terms, that is they were measured against the respondents' own starting points, then the relationship between occupational status and ambition disappeared.

4   There is a danger here of adopting too static a model in which subjects are pre-defined with no possibility of escape, change or creativity. The key to avoiding this lies, I believe, in consideration of the multiplicity of specific social identities that can be ascribed to any given individual. We need to consider the manner in which these enter the individual subject, the relationship between them and the manner in which the individual engages in, is constituted by and forms linkages between a number of discourses. See Dowling (1990).

5   This is not to say that in some situations questions of racism and sexism are not high on the agenda of practising teachers. Where they are, however, they can

come to be attacked from, and marginalized by, other discursive positions. Take, for example, Margaret Thatcher's attack on 'anti-racist mathematics — whatever that means' (quoted in *The Guardian*, 3.11.87) and the assertion of the mathematics working party of the National Curriculum Council that parents from ethnic minority groups would not wish their children to do 'multicultural mathematics' as it might be confusing (DES and WO, 1988).

6 Lareau draws on Bourdieu's (1977) notion of cultural capital in her analysis of this situation, though it is questionable whether this notion has sufficient analytic power to address precisely how and why this situation might prevail. In this respect Cohen's (1981) study of the culture of women on a private 'new middle-class' housing estate, and the relation of this to schooling, might be of interest. In her analysis Cohen draws on Bernstein's notion of invisible and visible pedagogy.

7 The booklet is one of a collection built up by Ruth Merttens and I am grateful to Ruth for access to them. This particular booklet was chosen as an illustration because it was thought to be fairly representative of the kinds of material produced by IMPACT schools. There is obviously some variation in the booklets that are produced and, in terms of the concerns of this chapter, these variations in relation to differences in the social composition of the intake of schools would be of great interest.

8 The discussion between teachers drawing up suggestions for a parent and child response sheet mentioned earlier contains a number of references to how one might interpret various responses. For instance, a parent ticking the 'learnt nothing' box on the response sheet was taken as indicating that the parent had not understood what the activity was about rather than indicating that the activity itself might not have been appropriate.

Acknowledgments

This article was written in the splendid isolation of a hotel room in Jakarta, Indonesia. I was thus unable to benefit from the comments of friends and colleagues in London, which would undoubtedly have made this a stronger and more coherent piece of work. I must however, acknowledge, with gratitude, my debt to Paul Dowling, Ruth Merttens and Jeff Vass for many hours of challenging discussion prior to the writing of this piece. Thanks also to Debbie Simmonds of the British Council for the loan of the technology on which I've become so dependent.

References

BERNSTEIN, B. (1977) *Class Codes and Control Volume 3: towards a theory of educational transmissions*, second edition, London, RKP.

BERNSTEIN, B. (1990) *The Structuring of Pedagogic Discourse: class, codes and Control*, volume four, London, RKP.

BOURDIEU, P. (1977) 'Cultural reproduction and social reproduction' in KARABEL, J. and HALSEY, A.H. (Eds) *Power and Ideology in Education*, Oxford, Oxford University Press.

BROWN, A.J. (1990a) 'From notional to national curriculum: the search for a mechanism' in DOWLING, P.C. and NOSS, R. (Eds).

BROWN, A.J. (1990b) 'Schools, homes and mathematical activity: time for critical analysis' in NOSS, R. *et al.* (Eds), *Political Dimensions of Mathematics Education: Action and Critique-Proceedings of the First International Conference*, Department of Mathematics, Statistics and Computing, Institute of Education, University of London.

BROWN, A.J. (1985) 'Primary school variation in an urban education authority: a study and discussion', unpublished MSc thesis, London, Polytechnic of the South Bank.

COHEN, G. (1981) 'Culture and educational achievement', *Harvard Educational Review*, **51**, 2, pp. 270–285.

DEPARTMENT OF EDUCATION AND SCIENCE & WELSH OFFICE (1988) *Mathematics for ages 5 to 16: Proposals of the Secretary of State for Education and Science and the Secretary of State for Wales*, London, HMSO.

DOWLING, P.C. (1990) 'Some notes towards a theoretical model for reproduction, action and critique' in NOSS, R. *et al.* (Eds), *Political Dimensions of Mathematics Education: Action and Critique — Proceedings of the First International Conference*, Department of Mathematics, Statistics and Computing, Institute of Education, University of London.

DOWLING, P.C. and NOSS, R. (Eds) (1990) *Mathematics Versus the National Curriculum*, Lewes, Falmer Press.

DUXBURY, S. (1987) 'Childcare ideologies and resistance: the manipulative strategies of pre-school children' in POLLARD, A. (Ed.) *Children and their Primary Schools: a new perspective*, Lewes, Falmer Press.

FAIRCLOUGH, N. (1989) *Language an Power*, Harrow, Longman.

LAREAU, A. (1987) 'Social class differences in family-school relationships: the importance of cultural capital', *Sociology of Education*, **60**, 1, pp. 73–85.

LEVIN, M.A. (1987) 'Parent-teacher collaboration' in LIVINGSTONE, D.W. *et al.* (Eds) *Critical Pedagogy and Cultural Power*, London, Macmillan.

MENTER, I. (1989) 'Teaching Practice stasis: racism, sexism and school experience in initial teacher education', *British Journal of Sociology of Education*, **10**, 4, pp. 459–473.

MERTTENS, R. and VASS, J. (1987) 'IMPACT: a learning experience', *Primary Teaching Studies*, **2**, 3, pp. 263–267.

NOSS, R. *et al.* (Eds) *Political Dimensions of Mathematics Education: Action and Critique — Proceedings of the First International Conference*, Department of Mathematics, Statistics and Computing, Institute of Education, University of London.

ROBERTS, K. *et al.* (1977) *'The Fragmentary Class Structure'*, London, Heinemann.

SILVERMAN, D. (1983) 'The clinical subject: adolescents in a cleft palate clinic', *Sociology of Health and Illness*, **5**, 3, pp. 253–274.

WALKERDINE, V. (1988) *'The Mastery of Reason'*, London, Routledge.

WALKERDINE, V. (1989) *'Counting Girls Out'* London, Virago.

Chapter 20

Marginal Dialogues, Social Positions and Inequity in Rhetorical Resources

Jeff Vass

Jeff Vass, since 1981, has been developing anthropological forms of enquiry into the issues surrounding teaching, learning, psychological development and communication. His early work concerns communication in special educational settings. He came to the IMPACT project as a researcher in 1985 with a brief to develop ethnographic work in relation to all aspects of the project. He took on co-directorial responsibilities with Ruth Merttens during the development and expansion of IMPACT as a national interventionist project in 1987. In this chapter he turns attention to some broader issues that IMPACT has raised He wants us to consider how it is our culture provides ways for allowing us to formulate ideas about parental involvement. In doing so he draws attention to the manner in which parents and educational professionals and government have to construct forms of talk which are proper to their 'social positions'.

Keeping citizens apart has become the first maxim of modern politics (Rousseau).

Our needs are made of words: they come to us in speech . . . Without a public language to help us find our own words, our needs will dry up in silence. It is words only, the common meanings they bear, which give me the right to speak in the name of strangers at my door. Without a language adequate to this moment we risk losing ourselves in resignation towards the portion of life which has been allotted to us (Michael Ignatieff).

Introduction

In schools, Local Education Authority offices, government departments, staffrooms, parlours and playgrounds people communicate about IMPACT.

Whatever IMPACT is, it becomes redescribed in ways that these settings can handle. We might like to think everyone sees parental involvement from a 'perspective', which suggests that as I move about I will get a different perspective on what parental involvement means from where I now happen to be viewing it, with what 'interests' I now have and so on. This 'perspectival' approach to the phenomenon of differences of opinion about parental involvement is, I feel, naive. It is naive because however much I move about I will not end up with a more detailed picture of the issues of parental involvement in education. What I would miss are the ways in which parental involvement is currently being constructed by the forms and content of the dialogue we are currently having about it. Furthermore it appears that the form and content of the stories we tell about teaching and learning *are already partially constructed* for us by the positions or places we habitually speak from within our culture. In this chapter I want to explore how cultural positions help structure the stories we are able to tell about teaching and learning and how the various participants (politicians, administrators, teachers and parents), through their talk, begin to specify what parental involvement must look like to be acceptable. I leave the reader to judge how and who decides where the definition of 'acceptable' comes from. The future of IMPACT and projects like it depends, I argue, on attending to these questions.

Boundaries

I have experience of participating in dialogue and debate among people who, it might be said, have to address each other across socially constructed boundaries that appear to separate us from each other, for example teachers from parents. While others (e.g. Brown; and Hamilton and Dyne, this volume) discuss the particular place of the teaching profession in constructing 'boundaries' or 'defensive mechanisms', I wish to look at the tragicomic divisiveness that I have been party to in a broader cultural context. I want to suggest that the 'fragmented' quality of our current social life, in which there are numerous examples of 'boundaries' between people, is produced in the course of pursuing our lives in a manner which makes what we do and what we hear intelligible. Furthermore, by rendering what we hear intelligible we find for ourselves positions by which to make ourselves intelligible in ways which stabilize our social worlds.

The world in which we express our opinions, desires and struggle to change our circumstances could be thought of in the following way. We appear to engage in numerous clusters of activities each day as we move in and out of the various 'portions' or 'compartments' into which our reality appears to be structured. While we are able, to some extent, to supply a biographical narrative that 'tells the story' of how we come to be in our current 'situation' in life, we nevertheless feel that our circumstances have not been entirely of our own making (Shotter, 1984; 1988). Furthermore, we may feel, as Ignatieff (1984) expresses it, that the particular 'portions' of the common social world that we do occupy with impunity have, in some sense, been 'allotted' to us. Provided we do not breach the margins of these compartments, there are no recriminations. Provided we 'address' each other according to the accepted etiquettes across the fences between compartments, all remains stable, but we can end up feeling bad. We feel bad because we have ideals or longings which transcend our apparent boundaries, or because we change our job or role and we find we must act in ways which accord with our new position and which contradict the experiences and opinions of our former situation.

I have been present at parent meetings where people have felt very bad indeed. This chapter arises from discussions with parents that have in some way been traumatic. One tearful parent at one such meeting struggled to express a theme which I found to be recurrent in schools where a number of 'choices' were open to parents regarding the future course of their child's education. The choice of leaving your child in a situation where they are happy and enjoying their schooling, or removing them to a setting which you know they will not like, where they may have an unhappy educational experience, but where they will be guaranteed to achieve what the advertisements call 'success', produces a sense of impotence, frustration and bad feeling in connection with a matter which concerns the heart. Well, fine for parents with such choices, some say, but it should be added that for parents whose circumstances do not afford such choices, the frustration and impotence that still loom as the public domain is inflated by advertisers announcing the existence of 'choice' and colouring images of these choices with undebated and unquestioned metaphorical associations with other aspects of our perceived common reality. The structuring of public dialogue in this way lends false credence to the notion that exercising one's civic voice in the public domain does offer opportunities for formulating 'democratic' alternatives to one's current circumstances — by making a choice as consumer.

I discuss, then, the ideas (1) that the inflation of messages in the 'public domain' is all that can be found of any such domain: that currently this situation diverts attention from the 'boundaries' that define us; (2) that socially constructed boundaries help form appropriate educational 'themes' through participants having to demonstrate and affirm their respective positions in the elaboration of those themes; (3) that the administered character of our social order requires participants in formal education processes to take 'calculative' stances in relationships to one another; (4) but that marginality itself, and potentially parent involvement projects such as IMPACT, might offer opportunities for people to formulate ideas about the 'portions allotted to them' and suggest to themselves ways in which they might respond to such circumstances. When it comes to education, we may get a sense of the once-and-for-all-ness of our lives with our children, and of their lives. In brief, the banter that we indulge in to lubricate ways through the myriad compartments provided by our dominant social order in which we have to conduct our business, completely fails us. It falls short in realizing for us, or elaborating, what our passionate longings for ourselves and our children might look like from the point of view of a civic ethos where voicing such desires might actually be expected to lend shape to possible future institutional forms.

Democratic Debate: A Voice Over for Public Discourse Ltd

There is nothing more likely to misfire in a conversational setting (even if staged — and what settings are not, at least partially?) than a debate on education between teachers, parents, industrialists and government. One does not need recourse to Lacanian psychoanalysis to follow the course of this misfiring.[1] As debate proceeds its unity appears to be guaranteed by use of such words as 'education', 'children', 'the needs of the economy', parents, etc. Do debates, therefore, *convert* anybody? They appear as arenas where different interest groups address an issue by 'doing their particular thing' in whatever the vocabulary of the debate happens to be. The boundaries between the groups operate like 'lines of fault', to use a geological metaphor. As a topic arises, e.g. 'the school prospectus', it is lent an attested 'common, public meaning', by simple virtue of the occasion and the definition of the context as a debate. Its public signification renders it an accountable place (a perceived fittedness to the debate and public life) in the development of the public themes of the debate. For example, it is said to 'permit parental choice', 'it contextualizes assessment results', etc. Then the teachers speak. They do so from a within-group situation where the school prospectus becomes accounted as costly in an already over-stretched budget (therefore to the public detriment). The effect is that 'the school prospectus' as a topic for discussion is completely displaced along the line fault that permits a within-group to develop the topic within its internal semantic economy. In effect this minority semantic economy appears to run 'in parallel' to the 'proper' development of the theme. The concerns of this minority are thus 'marginalized'. I will look more closely at this issue later in the chapter where I shall argue that we are not just dealing with 'the way issues are presented'. Rather, I will suggest that the current political and social organization of our lives structures the narrative development of themes we feel we need to discuss in ways which 'sectionalize' us as minority groups. It does this in part by giving shape to new institutions which reproduce constructions of expertise and ignorance and by producing accounts of people in respect of what we currently find 'natural' or 'already given'.

The reappearance of one's contested arguments as the slogans of groups points our attentions to the 'ground' on which we contest views. Billig (1987) puts the idea that participants to arguments share the same 'ground' so to speak by being able to structure argumentation as contradictory viewpoints.

Elsewhere (Vass, 1983, 1985) I have discussed the issue of educationists holding diverse curricular views while nevertheless having to sustain and reproduce the same 'cultural premises' that ground the discourse. We may say at this point that each group is bound to make these contradictory claims and anyway 'that is the name of the game isn't it?' i.e. to use public debate time to reiterate the leitmotif of one's group and hope that this will influence the mathematics of voting. Yes, but what is not available for inspection at such times, and within such debates, is the relative degree of control over what we might term 'rhetorical resources and opportunities'. I refer not just to skill in argumentation, but also to the way in which a governmental position in the argument is able to contextualize the parents' or teachers' positions. In other words while we recognize that any party's contribution to such a debate will appear sloganesque, we may not so readily recognize the rhetorical implications of politicians being able to ground all other contributions as 'partisan' and 'sectarian' while they themselves, in some mysterious way, speak from a common 'naturally engendered' viewpoint which in some sense must speak for all of us.

Before looking at this in problem greater detail, let me now refer to a short example that did arise as a topic of debate, but which was unable to retain a *public sense of place* (*cf.* Shotter, 1986). Its discussion resulted in participants structuring their arguments around within-group or in-house-agendas such that it lost its status as a public theme. The issue of staff appraisal strongly features in the 'concerns' of parents and government. It has been situated neatly, by government, within the theme of the market-place; staff appraisal is 'already' a *good management technique* in running a business. A school is construable as a business and therefore needs adequate staff appraisal. At the time of writing it is clearly repugnant to many that schools should be seen as 'businesses' and to have staff appraisal contextualized in this way. Nevertheless, what possible terms of discourse can this repugnance take and so be aired in public debate? I think the more creative among us can write a novel, produce a film or poem which captures the sentiment we wish to express — but what is the argument? On the other hand those who feel that schools ought to be run like businesses fare better in the debate. The market-place can be indicated as a reality. It is the reality which parents seem to fear that the British education service is not gearing our children — but the market-place was not always the reality, was it? What if I said that families ought to be run like businesses. Is that idea out of the question? Under what conditions does it become reasonable to even suggest it? My suggestion is that to run a family as a business is eminently reasonable already. We have permitted the market-place to be referred to as a natural given (therefore which cannot be changed). However, though I may have great success in supplying as many reasons as you require to support running families as businesses would you be able to tell me why none of them were good reasons? And if you cannot, why not? (*cf.* introduction to Parker and Shotter, 1990).

Social Positionality and 'Themes' for Discussion

The ability to situate particular concerns as 'partisan' concerns is reliant, to some extent, on each participant knowing how to act by knowing how they are themselves situated. Shotter (1989), for example, puts it in the following way:

> ... to qualify for the special, socially autonomous status of citizens, and to be allowed to move freely within all the 'spaces' in their society, human agents must show in their actions, as a special aspect of their perceptual awareness of their surroundings, an awareness of how they are currently 'placed' or 'positioned' in relation to all other agents around them. They must perceive themselves... as surrounded by a morally textured 'landscape' of 'opportunities for action' made differentially available to them according to their location ...

As any group begins to elaborate its concerns in public space, therefore, it must do so in a way which lends credence and reality with how other participants are going to construct the current theme for discussion sensibly as well as demonstrating (in the context of the theme's elaboration) how they are 'positioned in relation to all' the others. Thus parents must allow teachers, or teachers must allow administrators, the 'public semantic resources' in order to develop a theme which is going to do not just that but additionally make references to the positions of the participants (however tacitly this might be achieved). Failure to comply with rules about 'knowing how one is positioned' with respect to the social construction of other participants may render one's own actions as publicly unintelligible. Later, though, I shall discuss how it might be that those in administrative power are able *to use references to their own and other participants' positionality in the actual development of the theme* which renders their concerns as marginal.

When pursuing a particular argument, say as a parent, apparent contradictions may emerge in its semantic structure by virtue of the parents having to respect, at all times, the positional texture of the setting. Thus, while wearing your hat as a parent at a school parent meeting you may well give your vote to a curriculum that attempted to involve you integrally in your child's formal institutional learning. As the employee of a company sited some distance from where you live you may well slightly regret involving yourself in something that, requiring active participation, encroached on something called your 'free time'. At a particular stage in their involvement with IMPACT, some parents have said that they would like to spend 'leisure hours' with their children in the pursuit of more relaxing pastimes than mathematics. In situations such as this, IMPACT work will be marked as 'mathematics', but the same persons are quite capable of referring to IMPACT activities as 'not-mathematics' when they wish to pursue a particular grievance. My purpose is not to point an accusing finger at the fickleness of what we are often pleased to refer to as 'parents'. Readers of Curle (this volume) and Billig *et al.* (1988) may recognize the above situation as one posing contradictory 'dilemmas' for parents. I want to look at some features of our culture which partly give rise to dilemmatic experiences and prevent us from developing a position from which we might resolve them.

In summary, I have depicted ours as a 'post-civilized' culture: one which might be said to consist in of a 'myriad of compartments' (Merttens and Vass, 1990). We all move through a number of these compartments in our daily lives adopting appropriate 'positions' as the situation requires: perhaps deferential to a superior one minute, requiring obedience from another in the next. To be a competent, skilful member of our modern social order is to be able to move deftly through each of the 'portions allotted to us' adopting the positions in them required of us.

Turning our attention, for the moment, to these 'portions' or compart-ments, we might look at how they are locally administered and how people expressing concerns from 'within' them, so to speak, currently develop argu-mentation around the theme of parental involvement.

The Thematic Production of Expertise and Ignorance

It is now quite usual to hear parents discussed as 'kinds of teachers'. Educational and developmental psychology have provided a discursive set-ting in which such an equation could be made. It has been readily adopted in factions of state education provision (Ruth Merttens and I have discussed the historical and psychological background elsewhere; Merttens and Vass, 1990). For now I want to suggest that parents may be ideologically recon-structed as 'teachers' but to render this semantic shift 'accountable', to give parents (as teachers) a place in terms currently ratified by our culture and its social organization there is an ideological cost to be paid.

To grasp the nature of this cost I want to discuss briefly the develop-ment of the response to the introduction of parental involvement activities to schools in England and Wales. I wish to pay particular attention to the production of 'themes' in which to situate how parental involvement has to be discussed. In a research project spanning over three years and having been a participant in the many different contexts in which forms of parental involvement were produced (see Merttens and Vass, 1990; Vass and Merttens, 1987, 1990) I find an article by Murray (1988) to state concisely the ideological position of much of the educational establishment's response to involvement:

> ... parents are not complementary to the educative process. They
> are children's first, probably most important and only continuous
> teacher. We all know how important continuity is in the learning

process and how discontinuous children's experience can be from teacher to teacher and from school to school.

He quotes J. Bennett, the then Secretary of State for Education in the USA, ' "Not all teachers are parents, but all parents are teachers, the indispensible teachers" '. This quotation, however, introduces the following set of statements:

> ... whereas a newly acquired television comes with a detailed instruction book, the new baby enters the household with no such guidance ... there is seldom any planned help or training in parentcraft ... the greatest new investment we can make in education lies in helping parents gain a further understanding of the needs of children ...
>
> When teachers decide to encourage parents to be involved with what is being learned at school and to help their children actively at home it should be seen by both parties against the background of the education of the whole child ... When teachers focus parents' attention, for example, on their children's mathematical development and how it can be extended at home before giving due consideration to their overall education, growth and development, they are forgetting that many have probably had not preparation for parenthood other than biologically.

In producing what he (the author is a county adviser for Primary education) no doubt takes to be a positive response to parental involvement, his argument develops from something we appear to have discovered about parents and which now we can confidently affirm. However in the *formulation* of what such involvement might look like we arrive at a construction of the parents in which their status as the only 'continuous' teachers is brought into alignment with their essentially 'discontinuous' and partial grasp of something called 'the whole child'. Furthermore, their only training is of a biologically derived nature.

I am not iterating the educational establishment's 'stereotypical' view of parents — Murray's comments appear positive it has to be noted. What concerns me is how the development of the rhetorical theme under review can give shape to the production of institutional forms for the 'accommodation' of parental involvement. After all, participation in mathematical work now looks like something 'partial' and undertaken with only what 'biology endows'. The construction of the theme in this way (whatever it might betoken about the construction of parents and children as subjects in educational discourses) invites the development of institutional procedures. These procedures, far from resting on debates about institutions, come to rest on a reassertion of the differentiated distribution of knowledge to which the current expert may refer in moving from some 'outdated view' of parents to the new era of enlightened parental involvement.

In other words, in finding ways to discuss parental involvement and find room for the 'knowledge' parents have in the equation 'Parents = Teachers' a theme is developed in which mathematics as a focus for parental involvement comes to signify discontinuity in the theme of 'the whole child'; then 'parent', as 'continuous presence' in their child's life, becomes *a new focus for institutional attention* because their status takes on a new incompleteness. This institutional attention bears more than a passing resemblance to current social divisions in the construction of ignorance and expertise. For, as Murray concludes he refers to recent developments in the USA where there is 'new major investment by several states in supporting and training parents in parentcraft', and this, he finds, is 'a beginning at the right starting place'. Interestingly, he adds,

> Ironically, the impetus for this in these states in North America is financial. They are concerned that, in the next two or three decades the number of older and retired people will grow while the working population will not. The larger number of retired will be supported by the smaller number of working people and they cannot afford to have anyone not working to capacity.

It was, then, with some disbelief that I read on to see the next statement was, 'For their country's future they have "decided to eliminate illiteracy and innumeracy"'. Thus, a beginning at the 'right starting place' (i.e. parents' deficits in the continuum of knowledge, skills and techniques deemed necessary for 'the whole child') ends up effacing what is described as a matter of some civic urgency. In summary, I would like to ask how it is that the identification of a cultural need (specified as illiteracy and innumeracy) can come to release 'new major investment' by directing institutional procedures toward a new object i.e. parentcraft, the training of parents to be parents. I would also like to note the manner in which the development of an institutional form simultaneously marginalizes the knowledge of one party and claims expertise, via the elaboration of this theme (parents have deficits — they need help — we can help) in the context of 'the way things are', or 'what is natural'. I want, then, to turn to review the character of such reversals and effacements in the construction of themes.

Elocutio and Inventio: The Social Differentiation of Rhetorical Forms

I want now to take a closer look at rhetoric and this issue of the 'development of themes'. So far I have endeavoured to suggest that despite the appearance of our having 'freedom of speech' with which to address issues that concern us in public space, the effects are that simply by entering into parlance we experience an ineffectualness, or impotence, relative to our social positions. This impotence I attribute to an unequal distribution of 'rhetorical resources'. These are not resources to which those who do not have them could simply be 'given access' after some philanthropic campaign. This structuring of resources has to be described as embedded in the 'shapes' and characters of our abiding social institutional forms (by which I mean everything from legal practice to kinship arrangements; *cf.* Giddens, 1978, 1981).

Before I discuss these 'institutional shapes' I want to focus on speaking and persuading. I should say that during the last ten years there has been a growing recognition of the importance of a study of rhetoric in the social sciences as well as in literary activities. The term rhetoric is not being used here in the dismissive sense that Jeremy Bentham voiced, '. . . away with these figures of speech . . . Unhappily, there is no such thing as speaking . . . without such figures' (quoted in Vickers, 1988).[2] He would clearly like to have done away with rhetorical figures of speech in order to speak 'simply the plain truth' (the history of mathematics and logic reflect a desire perhaps to be nonfigural). By Bentham's time rhetoric (the use of figures of speech to persuade) had been structured in a way that different groups of people engaged in different practices employed forms of rhetoric that had come to be characteristic of their group in particular, which I discuss further in what follows.

Perhaps without realizing it, Bentham and other philosophers who employed something called 'logic' were unaware that it had, prior to the twelfth century, been construed as a form of rhetoric: i.e. a persuasive practice rather than something that guaranteed truth in the sense accorded it by nineteenth century science (Volosinov, 1973; Vass, 1982). When political thinkers like Bentham needed to develop new ideas but could not do so with the 'resources' supplied within the disciplines in which they were trained, they turned to a marginal 'non-disciplined' domain of 'everyday activities' where simply speaking 'unhappily' involved the use of 'these figures of speech'. Clearly, 'disciplinary' forms of argument development were being sharply distinguished here from what was to be found in common parlance. The view of rhetoric I discuss in what follows appears more as the language resources which are important to all of us in organizing and constructing the institutional forms in which we live — not rhetoric as verbal disguise to some possible and 'true' description of circumstances.

I have already characterized our common social life as one divided between various zones of activity. I contend that any zone will have its idio-syncratic resources for developing discussion (though not exclusively of course). As I suggested, for Bentham the zone of public discourse was something of a rag bag of 'figures of speech', somehow the 'left-overs' of more professional forms of argument development. So, I want to look briefly at how the history of divisions of labour in rhetorical resources relate to what can be found in this 'common zone' of activity, or 'public domain'.

What had been, and still is, left to the public domain are forms or rhetoric grouped under the classical heading of *elocutio*. Rhetorical figures of speech were classified by their apparent power to do things to hearers. The sorts of things rhetorical figures might do to hearers were, according to Vickers (1988)[3] *movere* (to move), *docere* (to teach), *delectare* (to allure). Teaching in classical times ideally required these effects to be held in balance together with a balance of the forms of elocutio and inventio. Elocutio had been grouped in Roman rhetorical treatises (e.g. Cicero's *De Inventione*) with *inventio, dispositio, memoria* and *pronuntiatio*. Essentially, in my view, they can be considered as practices of composition of themes. Elocutio involves the production of figures of speech, according to Quintillian (quoted in Vickers, p. 43) that the speaker has conceived in his or her mind such that the oratory is 'natural and unaffected' and will 'give the impression of simplicity and reality' and 'appeal to the common feeling of mankind'. Inventio refers to the discovery of 'effective arguments' in the course of dialogue.

While all these practices of composition can be found at large in the everyday communication of all of us all the time, Vickers, Volosinov and others have been interested in the development of the use of rhetorical forms as they, as Vickers puts it (p. 282) have adapted to 'new needs and demands.'[4] For Volosinov, for example, these new needs and demands include the development of specialized institutions which begin to employ practices of composition in professionalized ways. The result, to cut a long story short, is that by the sixteenth century inventio and dispositio 'have been assigned to logic' (Vickers) which itself had undergone professionalization in twelfth century law courts.

Aristotle has already established what a social theorist might refer to as a social division in the types of settings where these practices could be employed, and he also suggests a division of labour in his rhetoric. Vickers (p. 21) summarizes that 'The judge, as a member of a jury in a lawcourt, decides about things that have already happened, which gives the category of forensic oratory. But as a member of a political assembly, what I now identify as a practice of theme composition, changes to one of deliberative oratory.

I wish to pose the thesis that where a particular practice of composition is professionalized, such as dispositio by lawyers, then when used in the public domain by nonprofessionals, one of its effects is to signify the user as a nonprofessional user in the course of the elaboration of the theme. It also signifies a departure from 'accepted' practices of theme development in the public domain, which as I suggested come under the heading of elocutio. I may invent all kinds of 'effective arguments' (inventio) in the course of my gossiping, arguing with friends in what Shotter (1989) refers to as 'unnameable activies, all usually dismissed as a waste of time' and which occur in 'disorderly zones of activity' betwixt and between strongly defined institutional activities. Such methods of composition are denied me in settings of public debate, however. At least I am denied their deployment because they appear in some sense 'unfitted to the circumstances' of public theme development. As I said much earlier, groups such as teachers or parents may present their developed effective arguments and cases — but public taste requires the 'natural' appeal of what currently passes as elocutio.

Elocutio became the dominant public form during the Renaissance as other compositional methods passed into professional disciplines (I am not suggesting any necessary causal relation here). It was described (Vickers, p. 283) as 'the perfect expression of one's ideas' and it connoted 'fine address and practical *savoir-faire* in all pursuits of public and private life'. Elocutio became most closely associated with movere of the, by now, unbalanced pattern of 'effects' that had been described as the goals of rhetoric in classical times. Thus in the public domain we came to expect themes developed in ways that appeal to what we find natural and moving when reiterated to us as listeners in public settings. It may, therefore, come as no surprise to discover that elocutio became rapidly asociated with public ceremonial settings (and what are staged media debates?). Whereas in, say, the law courts we came to expect forms of argument and debate that correspond more to classical dispositio.

An effect of redistributing traditionally available methods for the composition of themes to professionalized institutions meant that in those particular 'sites' those methods developed and became 'restructured' in all kinds of ways. Just as English law develops by an accumulation of 'precedent', so the highly specialized knowledge resources that it makes available to its professionals puts those resources beyond the reach of the person in the street no matter how keen s/he might be on dispositio in private conversation or TV programmes featuring charismatic lawyers.

I am referring here to two phenomena which concern my general argument: first, that somehow 'particular sites' like the legal or teaching professions arose with a strong sense of institutional 'insiderness and outsiderness'; and, second, that within those sites *particular* methods of developing themes became restructured, creating new resources for developing argumentation *within those sites*. I want to deal with the latter problem first.

Somehow the public domain has become a place for experts. While it plays host to many different claims, appeals, concerns, slogans and voices, there are some we find more coherent and 'natural' and all-embracing than others. While it may be considered boring, I suggest that 'economic talk' has become the most obvious and natural public theme — the one to which all other claims must in some sense defer. All other claims on the public ear must be rendered accountable and intelligible by positioning themselves in relation to this economic talk. It is this latter type that is the only kind of talk that we will permit to develop discussion on public themes in any complexity in a public space[5]. We may not understand shares, stock-markets, inflation rates, recession cycles and the like but they somehow seem appropriate topics to be inserted in themes that do concern us. Pressure groups quickly learn how to restructure their concerns to harmonize with economic talk. The market economy in particular deploys homely imagery in discussing the financial abstractions of global capitalism. Televised disputes between economists concerning 'old friends' like inflation and recession appear as if to discuss the latest turn of events concerning characters in a television soap opera. The merits and demerits of chancellors and shadow chancellors and their 'strategies' are discussed as if they were managers picking football or cricket teams.

Those who deal professionally in this domain are able to compose themes and produce alignments of ideas with the peculiar advantage of speaking in the expectation that the introduced idea will appear 'natural' along with the econo-babble (or at least in line with what we all take to be, grudgingly, the ultimate secular judge of human activity). Money, its use, behaviour, scarcity, concentrated over-abundance and ubiquity mark it as peculiar in some way, unlike forms of human exchange that do not consciously involve it. Nevertheless as a signifier for the reality of the market there could be nothing more tangible and ever present minute by minute in our lives. Whatever boundaries we cross, into whatever 'site' we go, money signals the vague but same, common omnipresent horizon of all our immediately palpable transactions. Like Wittgenstein's celebrated idea that our one common language disguises a multiplicity of 'language-games' or contexts with idiosyncratic etiquettes, so money constructs a commonality as rational background to all exchanges and final appeals no matter how they are situated.

This has important repercussions for our grasp of how the 'work of understanding and interpreting' proceeds for participants in public dialogues (and I include here television viewers). What is made available to us, or how do we relate to the kind of discourse I refer to above? No doubt other political figures could have been chosen but Fairclough (1989) develops an in-depth analysis of 'discourses of Thatcherism' through linguistics and semiotics. It will be no surprise, on the contrary I imagine that it would be expected, that the discursive devices of Margaret Thatcher's politics are contrived 'compositions' — and clearly highly successful ones. Fairclough discusses these compositions under the title 'Creativity and struggle in discourse'. Creativity is the operative word here. In 'shifting the ground of British politics' some new alignments in ideas were required and created, but what is particularly interesting in Fairclough's analysis, to which I cannot do justice here, is the manner in which new alignments can become conventions (e.g. schools as businesses) in the context of drawing on previous solutions to the problems presented to her. Here Mrs Thatcher, in argument, draws

> upon combinations of discourse types which have become conventional for her, which do not need to be recreated anew in each

discourse. We may think of these as accumulated 'capital' from all her previous creative restructuring 'work' (Fairclough, 1989).

In following, and making intelligible, Thatcher's current line of argument the listener must, in some sense, be party to the production of new meanings created from 'previous restructuring work'. Not being party to complex economic theorizing, the listener is, however, party to other features of the discourse which he or she has to use to make sense of what is being said. In Fairclough's account he describes her discourse as drawing on the ideas of '"solidarity" of political leaders with "the public"' (something increasingly embedded in public discourse during the twentieth century), and of 'the social identity of a woman political leader' — Mrs Thatcher's ability to refer to herself in discourse as signifying both womanhood and shopkeeper-made-good-through-work. Fairclough looks at many other features of this creativity in discourse. I want to draw attention to those features which allow the development of description and accounts of policies whose complexity would otherwise make them prohibitive in public space.

By concentrating on these features we begin to see the extent to which self-reference to one's own public mythology can be used in the development of one's theme. In public it might act as a device that one's listeners can employ to develop some idea of what is being said, but this surely has consequences for how then another participant to the debate might proceed to engage with the current theme under development.

Contesting the claims of such discourses in public is hazardous. A position in public life with its accompanying 'mythologies' that confer signification to speakers, lends resources, through such means as self-reference to one's own mythological status. Such resources may be denied to the more transient interlocutor in public space. Shotter (1986) has produced an account of how such meanings can arise as 'commonplaces' in our ordinary, everyday practical activities and in communication with one another. In doing so he provides ways of construing not only how 'restructuring work' accumulates and develops but also how the vague and intangible beginnings of our discourses become specified.

The power to compose and develop themes that concern us appears, then, to be differentiated according to what resources have accumulated in numerous sites. The history of the production of the public domain itself as a site with its own peculiar methods for the composition of themes cannot be gone into here. It suffices to note that somewhere between the Renaissance and now the rhetorical 'left-overs' (after the developing professions had taken what they required) elocutio/movere became reconstituted, made effective and proper to some speakers and not to others. This history links, I believe, to the essentially 'administered' character of Western social institutions. Giddens (1978, 1981) outlines the importance of this notion in some detail. I refer to it elsewhere in more detail (Vass, in press) where I consider, in part, the production of home and school as distinctive sites in relation to the kinds of activities that may be said to be properly carried out in them.

My reference to the Renaissance will have alerted the reader to the idea that the construction of our current social order as a multiplicity of distinctive sites began well before the era we identify as marked by industrial capitalism. In itself the division of 'rhetorical labour' to which I have referred cannot account for the actual communicative encounters which we witness and in which we participate. I have argued elsewhere (Vass, 1983, 1985) that the era of industrial capitalism produced its own effects in relation to a social order which was already an administered, class-divided order. I argued this in relation to the development of forms of curriculum for special education and the production of new types of 'special' social identity. With reference to the structuring of rhetorical resources in the public domain the effect of industrial capitalism can be examined in like manner.

I am attempting, here, to get to grips with the situation that public space and resources for the development of themes is made differentially available to us. But also, in some sense, we know about this and develop strategies and means accordingly. While we can make sense of the development of themes in the way Fairclough describes for the Thatcher discourse, as members of the public we routinely disassociate ourselves with what those in power set up. In our joking, gossip and the myriad ways of 'wasting time' Shotter refers to, we produce commentary on the available public meanings and development of themes. When we engage in public debate we do so having formulated our positions from such 'relatively unstructured zones'. In that sense we take a 'calculative' stance with respect to how we structure what we say into public discourse. We speak at 'some distance' from it. It is, in Giddens' analysis, the contribution to our lives of industrial capitalism (not, of course, as a separable 'component') that produces a public space 'denuded of moral meaning' and us as subjects with 'cynicism and a "pragmatic" attitude toward norms'. Thus, there are both negative and positive effects of disassociation from the public domain. As Giddens (1981) says,

> Ideas — or (more accurately) signification — are inherently embroiled in what people DO, in the texture of the practicalities of daily life. Some of the most potent forms of ideological mobilisation do not rest upon shared beliefs (any more than shared normative commitments); rather, they operate in and through the forms in which day-to-day life is organised (p. 68).

Thus, in my account of public space and its resources for the development of themes we can think of ideological mobilization as being independent in some way from what is available to us as 'readers' of publicly developed themes couched in 'shared beliefs'. What typically happens, however, is that when acting in the public domain our talk becomes structured 'irrespective of the actual individuals involved and the particular nuances of their personalities and biographies' (Polan, 1989, p. 302). Polan discusses the political implications of the introduction of national assessment in England and Wales. In doing so, he too notes that 'law cannot be exhaustive in the sense of covering all possible situations, [and that] it still leaves problematic areas of *indeterminacy*.' (Polan, 1989; my emphasis). He goes on to suggest that having one's voice responded to by the granting of legal entitlements has the effect of feeding the requirements of our 'contract society' such that the 'enclaves' within which needs were originally expressed become 'undermined'. As peopleexpress their needs and gain responses to them they end up by formulating and insisting on the 'extension of authoritative legal prescription' (Polan, 1989). In other words, people end up with further bureaucratic constraints which are then placed beyond their ability to manipulate. I am also suggesting, however, that there are good as well as bad effects of our disassociation from public space together with our expression of social needs from within relatively unstructured enclaves. So, while the public domain is increasingly denuded of our moral commitment, through an imposed impotence to act and express ourselves, we do have independent means of formulating ideas about our civic lives.

Addressing Institutional Form in Home/School Dialogue

Resources for debate, inventio (the discovery of effective arguments) the production of new 'figures' for framing discussion can all be found in the sites of relatively unempowered daily activities. Along with Brown (this volume) I concur that 'mechanisms' inserted between the sites of school and home can assume the effect of the more powerful education discourse in providing appropriate 'subject positions' for the less organized forms of address from parents.

Foucault's 'double-edged' sword is realized here as well as in other areas of practice, however. We are left with the problem of being damned if we act and damned if we do not. Without the formulation of our own ideas about what possible shape future institutional forms *might* take there will always be those who will do the shaping on our behalf. The shaping of institutions is a matter of discourse — a matter of the work of language to lend shape to what is as yet a vaguer concoction of feelings and images. If IMPACT (as a version of parental involvement in children's education) were some such mechanism which was in all respects always already formulated then we would have cause to fear. As it is, while providing opportunities for more powerful discourses to structure the activities of participants, in my experience it does offer opportunities for participants to begin to frame questions about the nature of the institutions in which we live. We still have cause to fear. It seems that the area of 'resistance' dialogue in those unstructured zones might be shrinking. We surely have to find ways to address the question of our public lives and find opportunities to come to discuss those boundaries that divide us and that limit our freedom of speech and activity in doing so.

Conclusion

The experience of IMPACT for me has been to make me more conscious of the need to frame questions about public space and the divisions in which it seems to consist. On occasions such as parent meetings in schools questions are asked about institutional determinations and about the foundation philosophies of the curriculum. Parents may be 'fobbed off', teachers may be calculatively manipulated by parents, opportunities for hurt, defence and delusion abound, but so also do opportunities for developing forms of association in which the framing of questions about our common institutional lives can begin to be put. Where else might such questions be put? And if such questions make tentative beginnings in the world, how might we foster their development; and on what might they focus?

Notes

1 It is interesting in this context that Lacan (1977) notes that the greatest fear of the subject is to be misunderstood. The fear, though, is connected to the subject 'misfiring' rather being 'misinterpreted'.
2 Rhetorical studies, in the way I use the term here, have been developing for some time now. Shotter and Billig have been associated with developments in psychology. Rhetorical studies feature in other areas of the social sciences that are concerned with socially constructed realities in discourse.
3 My translations not supplied in Vickers; *Chambers Murray Latin English Dictionary*, 1933, 81.
4 Vickers does not discuss issues of social theoretical concern in his book. He remarks merely that there appear to be shaping conditions in what society takes and develops at any time from rhetorical traditions. Volosinov was concerned with the structuring of dialogue in historical contexts. I am drawing on these accounts to construct a social theoretic account of the structuring of rhetorical traditions such that they provide resources made differentially available to us.
5 Other themes do, of course, figure in public space: such as abortion, gender, equal opportunities and so on. But these latter issues can be constructed *only* as already marginalized issues: as belonging to minority interest groups. Economic issues are more culturally pervasive in that they can, virtually in and of themselves, justify political and civic action *across* all aspects of our lives.

References

BILLIG, M. (1987) *Arguing and Thinking: A Rhetorical Approach to Social Psychology*, Cambridge, Cambridge University Press.

BILLIG, M., CONDOR, S., EDWARDS, D., GANE, M. and MIDDLETON, D. (1988) *Ideological Dilemmas*, London, Sage.

FAIRCLOUGH, N. (1989) *Language and Power*, Harlow, Longman.

GIDDENS, A. (1978) *Central Problems in Social Theory*, London, MacMillan.

GIDDENS, A. (1981) *A Contemporary Critique of Historical Materialism*, London, MacMillan.

IGNATIEFF, M. (1984; 1990) *The Needs of Strangers*, London, Hogarth Press.

LACAN, J. (1977) *The Four Fundamental Concepts of Psychoanalysis* (trans. A. Sheridan), London, Penguin.

MERTTENS, R. and VASS, J. (1990) *Sharing Maths Cultures: IMPACT*, London, Falmer Press.

MURRAY, T. (1988) Parents are not complementary to anything, in 'New Childhood', Somerset, *Journal of the National Association of Primary Education*, Spring, 1988.

PARKER, I. and SHOTTER, J. (Eds) (1990) *Deconstructing Social Psychology*, London, Routledge.

POLAN, A.J. (1989) Emancipation or Surveillance? The Political Implications of New Forms of Educational Assessment, *The Political Quarterly*, **60**, 3, pp. 297–312.

SHOTTER, J. (1984) *Social Accountability and Selfhood*, Oxford, Blackwells.

SHOTTER, J. (1986) A Sense of Place: Vico and the Social Production of Social Identities, *British Journal of Social Psychology*, **25**.

SHOTTER, J. (1989) Rhetoric and the Recovery of Civil Society, *Economy and Society*, **18**, 2, 149–66.

VASS, J. (1982) 'Logic as Discourse: Action and Rationality in Cultural Contexts', postgraduate research seminar paper, February, University College, London.

VASS, J. (1983) 'Cultural Conventions and Instructional Practices in Special Education, unpublished PhD upgrading paper, University College, London.

VASS, J. (1985) 'Personhood and Pedagogy: The Social Production of Special Biographies, paper delivered at departmental seminar, Anthropology, University College, London.

VASS, J. (in press) 'Apprenticeships in the Absence of Masters: authority and guidance in pedagogical communication' in MERTTENS, R., BROWN, A. and VASS, J. (Eds), *Ruling the Margins: Conference Proceedings*, University of North London Press.

VASS, J. and MERTTENS, R. (1987) The Cultural Mediation and Determination of Intuititive Knowledge and Cognitive Development, in EKBERG, K. and MJAAVATN, P. (Eds) *Growing into a Modern World*, Trondheim, Norweign Centre for Child Research, University of Trondheim Press. Vol. 2, Conference Proceedings.

VASS, J. and MERTTENS, R. (1990) 'Sensuous Cognition: The micro-ethnography of children's mathematical practices', paper delivered at Conference on Children of Europe, Goteborg, Sweden.

VICKERS, B. (1988) *In Defence of Rhetoric*, Oxford, Clarendon.

VOLOSINOV, V. (1973) *Marxism and the Philosphy of Language* (trans. L. MATEJKA and I.R. TITUNIK) Cambridge, MA, Harvard University Press.

Chapter 21

Family Math in Toronto

Peter Saarimaki

Peter Saarimaki is one of the founders of the Family Math Program in Toronto, Canada. This program, while sharing many of the basic aims of IMPACT, has important differences both in its history and in its mode of practice. Peter describes how the programme was set up, its background in 'EQUALS', another program designed to raise achievement in mathematics, and the practices and routines which came to characterize 'Family Math' in Toronto schools. Having visited IMPACT in England, Peter is in a position to be able to draw out the links and explore the differences between these two initiatives in parental partnership.

Introduction

Virtually everyone connected with schools agrees that it is important for parents to be involved in their children's education. Twenty-five years of research supports, this view (1988) and yet parental involvement remains more a part of the rhetoric of schools than of their reality. This chapter describes one project designed to increase parental involvement in schools through mathematics, and how it was adapted by a Canadian educational authority in Toronto, Ontario. Family Math, its name and its focus, differs from IMPACT in its training and in its home/school link. While IMPACT makes a direct connection between the curriculum in the classroom and the activities at home, Family Math provides activities that give parents and children a general understanding of the philosophy of math education. Thus the activities are not designed to fit back into the student's classroom, but rather to make parents aware of the value of an activity-based approach, the use of manipulatives, the role of problem solving (especially in open-ended investigations), and the impact of talk, especially when everyday language is used.

Family Math out of EQUALS

In 1977 a program began in California trying to address the issue of how we can encourage *all* students to continue with maths when it becomes optional. The program attempted to encourage interest not by just collecting a lot of activities but by promoting a way of thinking about equity, mathematics, learning processes and the people in education. EQUALS originated at the Lawrence Hall of Science in the University of California at Berkeley, California.

Equity issues were related to the special difficulties of female and minority students, and were dealt with by trying to build positive experiences and attitudes and trying to get students to take as much school math as possible to increase their future options. The mathematics thinking revolved around the parts of math that relate to the whole by, for example, using multiplication in other areas, such as computing statistical answers or using number-line rectangles to illustrate factors, products, square numbers, division and other relationships. Mathematics was also portrayed as:

— linked to careers;
— having a content balance that went beyond arithmetic;
— active (including use of manipulatives, diagrams, calculators and computers, and many other problem-solving strategies and tools);
— powerful (by teaching for understanding).

In considering the learning processes it was realized that the following factors were of great importance: learning how to think is more important than fast answers; we all need experiences solving open-ended problems; group work allows us to talk maths and clarify ideas; and supportive risk-taking opportunities are necessary. The people in education centre around the student and all play an important role in shaping students' futures. The main adults include teachers, parents, administrators and other educators (Fraser, 1989).[1]

EQUALS, the parent project, gave rise to a daughter, Family Math, in 1981. Realizing that many parents would like to help their children in maths, but just don't know how to begin, Family Math attempts to answer the following questions:

— How can I help my child with math at home?
— What role will math play in my child's future schooling and work?
— Is it possible to have fun with math?

A Family Math course is run, rather than taught, by one or more adults, including teachers, parents and community workers. It gives parents, together with their children, opportunities to develop their problem-solving skills and to understand mathematical concepts in areas that reinforce and supplement the school math program. It also provides a setting and a role model for families to enjoy doing maths together (Stenmark, Thompson and Cossey, 1986).

Family Math Arrives in Toronto

In the winter of 1987, two program (curriculum) consultants with the Board of Education for Toronto participated in a one week training program on Family Math at Berkeley. They returned to set up, with other consultants in the mathematics department, the first Toronto-based training program. To help start the program, one of the originators of Family Math was invited up from California to lead the Toronto team.

Since the start in June 1988, we have run two training sessions each school year, one in the autumn (usually early November) and a second in spring (usually in April). Each time we work with teams from eleven schools, each made up of three teachers, three parents and one administrator, with variations due to local school arrangements. Very often the teams were accompanied by their school community adviser (a board employee who liaises between the parent community and the educational community, with connections to the local schools trustee). To release the teachers on the teams for the two days, budget was approved centrally for supply teachers. The actual allocation of supply teachers is handled by one of eleven areas overseen by a school superintendent. Thus it was easiest to suggest each superintendent nominate one school at a time according to their priorities.

The training sessions run for two consecutive days, handout materials are provided along with lunches and a copy of the book *Family Math* Stenmark (*et al.*, 1986) for each team member. At the training sessions, there are some discussions about the philosophy of Family Math and some time for plannng the local school program, but the majority of the time is spent on hands-on activities, using manipulatives, working as groups on open-ended problems, discovering new ideas, talking about maths . . . and having fun!

Family Math Comes to Life

Once a school team received their training, then the real fun could begin. The teams went back to their schools and started to plan for their Family Math classes. In most cases the in-school team would be expanded to include, at least on an advisory level, the local curriculum consultant (math when available, but also science and early childhood consultants were involved), the school-community adviser and someone from the administration. They grappled with many questions and a local plan evolved. Some examples may help illustrate this process.

School Purple (a fictitious school) decided to run a series of six weekly evenings for families in the junior division (students in grades 4 to 6, roughly ages 9 to 11). Since the gym was usually booked by local community groups and therefore not available, and since the team had three teachers and three parents, they decided for most of the activities to divide the families into three smaller groups and meet in classrooms. This arrangement limited the maximum number of participants to twelve to fifteen families per group or about forty-five families maximum in total. The instructors allocated themselves so that each pair was made up of a teacher and a parent. To keep the formalities low key, the opening night introductions would be held with everyone gathering in the library for juice and cookies and having the principal deliver some words of welcome. Her instructions were to keep it simple, emphasize the chance to talk about math and showcase the parent-teacher partnerships.

School Green on the other hand had access to the gym and felt there was a large number of families interested in coming, so they worked as one large team and offered four fortnightly evenings for anyone who wished to come from the primary division (grades 1–3, ages 6–8). In fact, out of a population of about 200 pupils, more than 120 families signed up. The local math consultant was enlisted to run the evenings by starting the activities with an overhead projector, and then the team went from table to table to encourage, ask questions and generally support the investigations.

At School Purple, since the enrolment was limited, each student in the junior division took home an invitation to their parents. The team used a computer program to print up the cards which said 'You're invited to join me for a series of evenings on Family Math', and was signed by the student. The personal approach worked very well and the course was full the next morning, as the children bounded up the stairs to hand in their parents' acceptances to the classroom teacher.

School Green sent home a general notice through the principal's weekly newsletter. At both schools, the local home and school association, or parent–teacher group, arranged for refreshments to be set up and served (their expense) and for babysitting for younger brothers and sisters. In most cases the babysitters were paid out of funds provided by the school-community adviser. The evenings were usually only for one to two hours and started at times varying from 6:30 to 8:00 depending on the ages of the children, the other groups running programs (e.g. the local Guide troop might also use the facilities before or after Family Math) and the proximity to hockey play-offs (some things are best not interfered with).

Family Math Activities

When parents think about helping their children with schooling, reading comes to mind quite easily; they can read to them, look at picture books, go to the library ... all fun and enjoyable activities. What about helping with math? All most parents can think of is to use flash cards to help their children learn the multiplication tables, or insist they do their homework *before* going out to play.

Family Math provides parents with activities to help their children with maths at home. We encourage families to go away from the classes and continue doing these activities so children see that their parents value the subject and these problem-solving approaches to it. These experiences will help children to persist when the going gets tough or when mathematics becomes an optional course at school.

When parents think back to the math they learned in elementary school, they generally remember addition, subtraction, multiplication, division, fractions, decimals, percentages and maybe some measurement and some shapes. Today's curriculum also includes topics such as informal geometry, probability and statistics, recognizing patterns and relationships, logical thinking, estimation, and the appropriate use of calculators and computers in all areas of mathematics.

Family Math activities are problem-solving in nature, requiring thought as opposed to answers that are based on memorizing. They represent a wide range of topics in mathematics, from the standard strands of arithmetic, measurement and geometry to areas such as probability and statistics, spatial visualization, patterns, estimation, calculators and careers. The link to careers and the future is introduced through role models and career-based activities. These activities ensure that the reason for studying mathematics is clear.

The activities in Family Math are presented in a supportive, collaborative, cooperative environment to make math more comfortable while at the same time providing a solid foundation for risk-taking because participants feel do not threatened. The content is incorporated into models of teaching styles and learning styles, and the discussions afterwards reflect more on the process than the product to encourage parents to recognize the open-endedness of so much of mathematics. If children and parents continue to feel that mathematics is based on 'one-way-one-solution', then we will continue to have maths anxiety and math phobia. On the other hand, as we come to see the 'funnel of knowledge' opening up, rather than converging, as we see the various paths leading to solutions from a starting point, as we see the rich variety of ways that others view problems . . . then we will see our children (and adults) developing into 'self-directed, self-motivated problem solvers, aware of both the processes and uses of learning and deriving a sense of self-worth and confidence from a variety of accomplishments (Ministry of Education, 1980, p. 2). This is an image of the learner worthy of emulation.

What Do Parents Say?

Each school in running Family Math programs — and they all eventually ran it more than once for different age groups and/or different topics — adapted the materials to its own locale. One example is the game 'Hurkle' (Stenmark *et al.*, 1986, p. 198). Hurkle is a small, fuzzy creature who likes to hide but participants can find clues to his location on a coordinate grid with compass directions. The leader knows the hiding spot and responds to coordinate guesses with responses such as 'Hurkle is north-east of your guess'.

One school made the grid to be a stylized map of their neighbourhood, with the school at the centre of course and all the local streets and favourite haunts labelled. Guesses as coordinates referred to a number of streets over and up, or to actual street corners for younger children, but responses were still in terms of compass directions. Children enjoyed being the leader and choosing their favourite corner to hide Hurkle. Some even started using half-blocks, which opened up the game and challenged the participants.

After being subjected to these evenings of fun and frivolity, after children measured their parents' heads (and vice versa), after parents had to fit all the pieces in the box, after families voted on some heady question with spoons of water, after cutting out shapes and trying to stay in shape mathematically, after all that and more, what did people have to say about Family Math?

Why wasn't maths this much fun when I went to school?

The hands-on activities were great. Math games that we can do at home will benefit our other children as well.

With all our lives and schedules so hectic, my time with my children is usually confined to driving them somewhere. It was really nice to have 'the excuse' to sit down and talk with my child for these evenings.

I think I learned as much as my child . . . about maths, about school, even about my child.

Several schools have built on the good connections by Family Math newsletters. They tend to be combinations of reports on current programs plus more activities that can be done at home. Sometimes they are also able to include responses after activities have been tried out at home.

There have been other fall-outs or developments from the Family Math programs. One area revolves around videos. So far four schools have produced short videos (fifteen to twenty minutes) illustrating how Family Math was run at their school. One benefit has been the increased awareness of the role of mathematics by other parents in the school when it is shown at a parents' night. The videos have also been shown to interested parents from other schools and general community members at local mall displays. This is all good public relations for education in general because, by example, it shows what the new philosophy of learning centres around.

Because of the vital role that parents play in organizing and running these evenings, the schools also get very good coverage in the press, both local and in the larger city newspaper. The print media seems eager to write up success stories about parent-teacher cooperative efforts.

The mathematics department of the board also responded to the interest in on-going activities to be done by parents and children at home by producing a document which formatted activities to be sent home on a monthly basis. The activities are usually related to a theme for the month. On one side of the paper is calendar with a little question; e.g., 'How many ways can you make seven?' or 'Predict how many days will have rain this month, and then keep a record for the month'. The document for teachers also included some references to books to read which were related to the monthly themes. These encouraged a multicultural and multiracial approach.

Calendar Math also includes references to books to read related to the themes that also encourage a multicultural and multiracial approach. We have made use of traditional games and activities to reflect this approach (e.g. the dreide game, a traditional Hanukkah game, or rock-paper-scissor for the Chinese New Year).

The Future

Where do we go from here? Locally, in Toronto, we continue to offer Family Math training to eleven more schools twice a year. We are also planning to run a training session for grade 7–8 schools (ages 12–14). At some of our recent training sessions we have had school teams from other boards hoping to encourage the other boards to offer it themselves to their schools.

Other jurisdictions in Canada are starting to implement Family Math programs as the word spreads. We have heard of initiatives beyond metropolitan Toronto in such diverse locations as London, Ontario, Vancouver, British Columbia, and even in the North-West Territories.

When we realize that the best way to learn about something is to do it and to talk with others, I'm reminded of Michael Marland's comment in *Language Across the Curriculum* (1977) that

> The way of making ideas truly one's own, is to be able to think them through. And the best way to do this for most people is to talk them through.

This talking is not merely a way of conveying existing ideas to others: it is also a way by which we explore ideas, clarify them, and make them our own.

Note

1   For further information on EQUALS write directly to EQUALS, Lawrence Hall of Science, University of California, Berkeley, CA, 94720, USA.

References

FRASER, S. (1989) *SPACES*, Berkeley, California, Dale Seymour Publications.

MARLAND, M. (1977) *Language Across the Curriculum*, Oxford, Heinemann Educational books.

MINISTRY OF EDUCATION (1980) 'Family Math's Offspring', *Issues and Directions*, Ontario, Canada.

SAARIMAKI, P. (1988) Parents and Schools, *The Harvard Educational Letter*, **4**, 6, Nov/Dec.

STENMARK, J.K., THOMPSON, V. and COSSEY, R. (1986) *Family Math*, London, Addison-Wesley.

Chapter 22

Including Parents:
The Dynamics of Resistance

Dorothy Hamilton and Deryck Dyne

Dorothy Hamilton, in addition to her work in therapy, was one of the support teachers most involved in the implementation of PACT (the shared reading initiative) in ILEA in the 1980s. Here, Dorothy and Deryck argue that it is possible to look at the behaviour patterns of teachers, headteachers and educationalists in relation to parental involvement in reading and/or maths through the eyes of a therapist. Setting up a Kleinian perspective, they describe the types of resistance encountered and explain the dynamics involved. The use of this sustained metaphor enables the exploration of many of the rationalizations frequently produced to account for reluctance or failure to implement such initiatives. We also have much to learn about ourselves through the use of this type of analysis.

Educators differ widely in their responses to the radical proposal that parents and teachers should work in partnership over children's learning. While many have welcomed the idea, and done their best to put it into practice, others have ignored or downright rejected it. In this chapter we look at these positions from psychodynamic perspectives, and try to show that the first indicates a state of fundamental health, while the second is frequently based, pathologically, on inhibition and defence. Conscious of the dangers of applying theory in the absence of the client, and still more dubiously to a profession of hundreds of thousands, this chapter nonetheless attempts to diagnose the causes of the resistance underpinning the second position, and by implication to suggest suitable treatment.

Central to psychodynamics is the proposition that much is going on besides that which can be observed, even by the subject. If we take as a basic definition of the psyche that with which human beings mediate between stimulus and response, psychodynamics states that much of that mediation, though certainly intentional, is quite unconscious. We should stress therefore that what we say need not indicate any conscious intention, or indeed understanding, on the part of the educators we discuss.

Starting with the first position then, and bearing in mind that health is rarely as interesting as pathology, we run through a perspective or two fairly rapidly, our main purpose being to establish what we see as healthy in order to look more clearly at what is not. Of what does the position consist? Characteristically, it is a readiness to recognize outstanding research like that from Coventry in the early 80s, and to put together, or accept, a rationale as to why that research should show results so far ahead of anything education has tried to do without benefit of parent involvement. It also includes the will to put the idea into practice, in different forms according to the circumstances of different schools and neighbourhoods, to accept and ride the difficulties, and to enjoy the results. The attitude is characteristic mostly of headteachers and teachers 'at the chalk face'. In the new conditions they create, parents and teachers talk to each other, and discover increased understanding and mutual respect; parents and children work together, and discover shared enjoyment and a deepening of family bonds. Everyone discovers the pleasure of shared achievement, as the children learn more, and more eagerly. Frequently the proponents publish their work, or try to spread it in other ways, feeling that it is too good to keep to themselves.

We choose two psychodynamic languages to describe this position. In the language of Humanistic depth psychology, the proponents possess a self-concept which enables risk-taking on the basis of *objective knowledge* of the problem and of the partial solutions advocated by researchers and pioneers; this combines with a *subjective knowledge* of their own capacities, and the ability to imagine the reality of the endeavour by empathically identifying with its many parts. *Empathic knowledge* is an attempt to overcome the difference, the gap, between what I choose to perceive and what is actually going on 'out there'. Rogers (1974) calls this gap *incongruency*, and it is a sort of measure of our vulnerability. Where there is a high level of *congruency* — a low sense of vulnerability — to take up the idea will excite the proponents' sense of self-esteem and of belonging; they will rejoice in the manifestations of what they regard as desirable growth in all partners, the extension of possibilities made possible by invention. When, as is inevitable, they get it wrong, they will examine the nature of the wrongness and try to improve their strategies.

The language of the Humanists is sometimes dismissed as tending toward the Utopian; they may sound omnipotent, even saviouristic. Nevertheless, this language allows a way to express a basic faith in ourselves, our pupils and our pupils' parents, and the belief that things can somehow be done better than they are if only we can see how. Similarly, though rather more esoterically, the language of the Kleinian psychoanalysts expresses a like psychological state — with implications that have much relevance for parent-teacher cooperation.

The Kleinians speak of the '*depressive position*', which in educational terms might be expressed as achieving a balance between despair (emptiness) at the gap between what is desirable and what is actually achieved, and gratitude (fullness) derived from the moments when we get it right — when the children give us back what we have sent out to them. To 'teach' is to be always aware of the reality of this gap (and, potentially, the pleasure of bridging it), since the activity of teaching has no real meaning — is even non-existent — unless somebody has actually *learned* as a result of it. In the depressive position, we abandon omnipotence ('can I help them to learn?'), yet know ourselves not impotent, that if we try appropriately we can be potent, 'good enough'.

The Kleinians would see the joining of teachers and parents as a non-envious adult agreement to avoid reinforcing, by externally-imposed divisions, the internal *splitting* between 'all-good' and 'all-bad' which precedes the achievement of the depressive position, and to which the inner life of the infant is subject. They would recognize that the child's emotional learning base has been continuously built through *introjected* (digested, made mine) experiences of communication with the parent from the earliest moments of life, and see that educators have somehow to join with this learning base, in order to 're-pair' and so reinforce the child's capacity to learn.

As Klein shows, it is part of a child's business to try to split the parents so that it can have the relationship with each under its own control. There can be few parents who, in showing affection for each other, have not had their child try to get between them, or have not had a child run from one to the other to get different rulings on the same appeal. The traditional apartheid of home and school builds upon the child's existing ambivalence; home and school each become the opportunity for a split super-ego function, to be played against the other: you 'ought' to do it this/that way. To some degree, this is both inevitable and healthy, but if the split is too complete, reality begins to outdo fantasy, and the child finds the split more real than is wanted.

In a healthy family, the child is allowed to split and defeat the parents sometimes, but never to lose the sense that the parents' bond together is fundamentally undamaged by its destructive wishes, and creates a safe territory in which to live and feel included. Similarly, children need the teacher-parent bond also to exist to include them. Where it does not, and where a child cannot find the inner resources to bridge the gap between the two worlds, impaired capacity to learn may be the least of the damage inflicted. In extreme cases, the split allows alienation and later truanting; such a child falls between two defeated authorities, loses the sense of being a member of either grouping, and drifts toward a subculture of loneliness and delinquency.

There is an urgent need to replace the traditional pair of diadic relationships — child–parent, child–teacher — by the triadic relationship: child–parent–teacher. Then the prototype Oedipal situation outlined above can move toward resolution, rather than artifical perpetuation. It is such joining, or *reparation*, that provides the emotional basis for learning.

The Kleinian language, necessarily condensed here, may sound technical and convoluted — no doubt meaningless to some. Were we to expand on its meanings, however, we should only end up with the fundamental propositions that good comes from good experiences, integration from experiences of integration, growth from experiences of growth. Health comes to much the same thing in any language. It is where things go wrong that an unfamiliar language can sometimes be useful, by highlighting and analyzing in its own dimension, and perhaps pointing new ways to resolution.

This brings us to the second position, the proponents of which set forth a range of well-tuned arguments. Teachers point out that no parent can possibly be expected to grasp the technical intricacies of, say, teaching reading, gained by themselves so painstakingly through years of training and developing expertise in the classroom. Psychologists expound the confusions that arise in children's minds when exposed to different learning strategies. Headteachers bemoan the parental apathy which prevents their setting up the full and free dialogue in which they would otherwise be so ready to engage. Academics agree the research looks promising, but are working on another area of dazzling importance to education which (though it cannot actually be shown to enhance children's ability to learn) demands their undivided attention. Inspectors and advisers are concerned above all to preserve the *professionalism* of the profession, and administrators will certainly consider this very important question once further evaluation has taken place, the present set of projects is completed, the schools have been suitably prepared for such a major undertaking, and — of course — the necessary finance becomes available.

These positions are not necessarily frivolous — each obviously connects with reality at certain points — but each is a fragment, a *part-object* in Kleinian terms, presented by specialists from their own (split-off) perspectives. Those who look too narrowly through specialist spectacles see what the spectacles allow; they easily attribute meaning to highly selective patterns, in a self-validating and comforting circle. It is the technique of politicians everywhere to present an argument that avoids the main thrust of the situation, and, from a marginal premise, put forward an omnipotent case.

So for all their apparent rationality, the arguments are not rational — since they oppose, or bypass, what manifestly works and is born out by research and by experience. They are defensive *rationalizations*, springing from a hidden emotional base. As the Guinness advertisement has it: 'I haven't tried it because I don't like it'. These arguments are redolent of the dynamics of *resistance*. Resistance to what, then?

Resistance is a reaction to a threat. Where the threat is known and understood, defence against it can be appropriate; we can carry umbrellas, and take out insurance. Where it is known about from report — mugging, say — we can avoid certain places at certain times, travel with friends, and alert the police. Where the threat is not known but imagined, however, and report indicates no threat but on the contrary much gain, resistance becomes a defence against something else altogether and we are now in the world of the *paranoid*. Then, like Thurber's aunt, genuinely believing our fears to be rational, we shall put bulbs into light sockets to prevent the electricity draining away, throw shoes down the hall to keep the burglars out, and stay away from the party to avoid having to be seen and laughed at for enjoying ourselves.

Where is the threat in parent–teacher collaboration? Let us consider the premises: for the benefit of the child principally, and with the promise of spin-offs for the adults, teachers and parents are asked to work together to promote *learning itself*, hitherto the province of the teacher's supposed expertise. Clearly such cooperation will require a breakdown of traditional role relationships. In place of the schizoid splitting of roles, we are to complement and reinforce one another. Parents cease to be strangers who do or do not turn up to parents' evenings to be persuaded that their child is awkward, or to the PTA to help raise funds. They become co-workers, part of the process. The teacher no longer operates in a closed system in which he or she is the only authority, is no longer defended by the split and by parents' deferential attitudes, often based fearfully on their own schoolday experiences. By using the parents' concern for the child, and the child's closely dependent relationship with the parent, as tools within the learning process, and by then recognizing that success above traditional norms must be attributed to the involvement of the parent, success can no longer be seen simply as a function of the child's ability and motivation and the teacher's skill. In these circumstances, the expertise of the teacher, like electricity, may be felt to be draining away; the parents become burglars out to steal professionalism, and those same parents may even, as they come to understand better, *smile* at the antics of the teachers.

Loss, invasion and embarrassment — suppose they variously comprise a threat to educators' identities as specialists in a profession. If we look at why many teachers enter training, it is at least arguable, and certainly once true for the authors of this chapter, that being in the presence of children confers adulthood on otherwise insecure persons. Suppose the resistance is at base a rationalization of *anxiety* — the anxiety of annihilation of the known, and especially of the known identity of myself, with the concomitant loss of potency and of control.

Freud understood this problem a long time ago. Central to his thinking is the idea of a stimulus which we fear will so overwhelm us that it must be warded off. Above all, my sense of myself must be protected. This protection is achieved by what Freud called *defences*, not themselves necessarily pathological, any more than a bread knife is necessarily a lethal weapon; the question is of its use. The misusers of defences erect plausible arguments which 'stand to reason'. They shelter behind *denial*, the outer perimeter of defence, which in its most perfect form makes it as if the event never happened, and uses the immense forces of *repression* to keep the memory or idea from ever becoming conscious. It is still possible to find schools that have never heard of the huge benefits of involving parents.

Defence can take a wonderful variety of forms. Parent involvement, as yet unadopted by the educationists and therefore still perhaps only a fashion, can be viewed as through the eyes of middle-aged parents meeting another excitement from their adolescent children, and kindly but firmly dismissed: parent involvement, yes, an interesting idea — not suitable mind you for conditions in our particular establishment — doesn't it rely on certain age-groups ... social class ... reading materials ...? — and further carefully-selected misinformation. And when we do see it taken up by those know-all guilt-creating educationists out there, those dissatisfied invaders who, instead of loving what we do already, have brought *another* baby into the world, with which we are required to join, we must resist, as adolescents to parents, and treat the new with the distance it deserves. So we take it up after a fashion, but show that it fails 'here', employing a kind of *reaction formation*, in which, though we do not want to share the world with the new baby, we know that hurting it gets no brownie points from mummy and daddy; 'love' the brat, and show concern when you must, but ignore and attack it when you safely can. Thus, either way, the school applauds with lip-service, but avoids the need to get its hands dirty.

Some teachers like to tell horror stories about parents who can definitely be shown to have pushed their children too hard. The stories themselves may be perfectly true, and the teachers' deeply-felt indignation justified, so far as it goes, but — exaggerated and hysterically *displaced* — this criticism becomes pathological when the evidence of malefaction by a few parents is considered sufficient to call into question the value of the whole idea for everybody. The assumption is suddenly that *all* parents will overburden their children. How can we explain so illegitimate an inference, unless we look below the surface of ordinary reasoning? It seems fair to guess that the teacher, frightened and angry about doing this dangerous parent bit, is displacing fear and anger about his or her own failings onto parents, via the device of *projection*. Similar processes can be used around competence. Competent equals good, incompetent bad. Such *splitting* is often used to justify the use of untrusted parent talent to help out with the perennial problem of the slow-learner goats, while keeping them well away from the school's sheep.

Educators sometimes suggest that the success of the research results is based, like so many other educational experiments, on the 'Hawthorne Effect', and cannot therefore be expected to last. In this, they are perhaps employing *dissociation* to shield themselves from recalling the actual meaning of the effect, in which the subjects believe themselves to be special, cared about, and involved in something important, and therefore do better. Since parents can largely to be relied on to care a great deal about their children's welfare and progress, they might fairly be thought to produce a sort of built-in Hawthorne Effect, and indeed the lasting successes traced by the research results support this idea.

Perhaps most damaging though is the major and widespread tactic, involving most of the defences at once, in which schools appear actually to embrace parent involvement, and then put into practice a facsimile purporting to be the real thing. 'Yes, our parents did hear their children read, or help them with maths — but it was a flash in the pan; they've fallen off now, they just didn't have the staying power'. On closer examination, it transpires that those parents have been asked to perform identical operations month after month, often with stupefying 'reading-scheme' books, required to fill in cards with vacuous comments when they have nothing new to say, and starved of any possibilities of development or of real communication with the teachers. This is a travesty of educational principles which in only the most backward of our schools would be applied to the pupils: but is quite often thought good enough for parents. In reality, it masks an attempt at *obsessional control*, marked by the technique of *witholding*, with highly predictable results. Freud traces such a need to control to the *anal stage* — a point at which much of our profession may not unfancifully be thought to be fixated.

Let us change tone for a moment. In trying to explain educators' negative reactions, we have tried to show some of the supposed threats against which they attempt to defend themselves, but the many and various forms of resistance and indeed sabotage are not reactions specific only to parent involvement; they are evidence of a much wider set of problems about identity, competence and power. It is only fair to note that educators have learned to be cautious of the manic element in the profession. One of the features of education for some decades has been the development of yet one more liberating scheme, usually abandoned after the first flush of enthusiasm because the children did not respond. Equipment and work-sheets spawned by such schemes languish reproachfully in many unfrequented recesses of our schools. Here is a process that constitutes a three to four year *manic depressive* cycle of urgent hope, disappointment and then cynicism. Part of the unconscious social function of the conservatives is to stand against those who charge, filled with energetic enlightenment, towards to momentary realization of their latest inflation. Fanatical hope also denies reality. Neither depressed conservatives nor manic progressives have a monopoly of the truth.

Of course we know that a school is not necessarily bad because it does not involve parents. We have visited many, and seen congenially messy rooms buzzing with happy children producing good work. These schools have much invested in what they are doing, and may not see how to integrate parents' help without at least temporary losses which in prospect may seem unacceptable. They have thought carefully, worked seriously, and have a system that does what they planned it to. Many such schools seek to defend themselves against the threatened lively muddle which might become chaos, producing a state of vulnerability and possible loss of the school's control. Yet their arguments are not quite good enough. A glance at the research findings will show us that schools *ought* to involve parents. The findings are startling, and outshine anything comparable; children's learning races ahead where parents are involved. Those findings are given strong support by the concept of healthy learning outlined earlier, suggesting reasons why progress without the involvement of parents will be achieved *despite* their absence, and is unlikely to be of the same quality. The extraordinary way in which the research results have been largely mislaid by the educational world should alert us; their persistent bypassing by planners, advisers and administrators suggest a case of *suppression* (not necessarily conscious) rather than mere carelessness.

It is easy for psychodynamicists to believe in parent–teacher collaboration, because it expresses many of the basic tenets of our profession, but in describing resistance to it, we stand in danger of producing yet another form of teacher-bashing, adding our own epithet of 'pathology' to the familiar politics of condemnation, or those of urgent exhortation as a means of getting a bigger return to investment. We seem to be demanding a taxonomy of teachers by psychodynamics, in which those who are 'healthy' will adopt parent involvement and make it work, those manically hot for the revolution will adopt it, fail and pick up a new saviourism, and those fearful for their own identities will hold back and watch developments, suppress the existence of the idea, or ensure that it cannot work.

The truth is, not so much that our diagnosis is wrong, as that it must be applied far more widely than to those unfortunates who attempt to teach our children in a social climate in which the schizoid and the paranoid are endemic. We treat our schools and teachers much as we treat the children. They are the objects of much concern, much interfered with, much required of, and much attacked when they fail to live up to our wishes, yet we keep them largely split off, ignored and unsupported. In this context, the current heroic political notions of parental choice and parent governors are baubles on a tree attacked by acid rain.

Alice Miller's (1987) work has some useful contributions to make here. Miller focuses on the child's experience in trying to deal with pressures and abuses consciously and unconsciously put onto it by the parents. These pressures and abuses are evidence of a lack of trust, care and respect from the elders, and evoke many and varied 'dramas' — methods of making sense of the experiences, and surviving. They leave permanent and more or less disabling modes of relating to the world. We believe that Miller's mode of descriptive analysis of the predicament forced upon children is equally applicable to the world of education, in which schools (and colleges) generally, and many teachers individually, are also treated without appropriate trust, care and respect, and are therefore pressured and abused. It is hardly surprising that they enact their own dramas of sadness, confusion and despair — and resist.

So it is not simply that teachers need to take up the idea. Parents and everybody else need to as well, so that the context in which education is practised can move toward that healthy capacity to join what signifies the 'depressive position'. In those few areas where community education is genuinely practised, resistance to working in partnership with parents is rare. Conversely, in a paranoid-schizoid context, teachers' sincere attempts to make the idea work are rendered almost impossible by the climate and conditions. Parent–teacher cooperation poses us with the requirement that we all, teachers, parents, educationalists and psychologists of all kinds, confront the complexity of child growth collaboratively rather than competitively.

One of the supremely important elements both of meeting the demands of the market place and of being an effective teacher is that of relevant invention. In our present climate, the hedging of schools and LEAs by the requirement to be cost-effective within an increasingly prescribed system is that energy is diverted from invention into survival. In psychoanalytical terms, this produces the kinds of fears that encourage the defensive and the obsessional. It restricts the personal excitements, initiatives and responsibilities of teachers and schools, and so attacks the bases of self-esteem and of voluntary belonging. We face the ascendance of the technologies of instruction and the diminishment of what, however at times it has been inflated and saviouristic, has been seen as education. Parent–teacher cooperation, we believe, has the capacity to restore the context of this wider concept of education, quite apart from the fact that it does, actually, improve standards.

References

MILLER, A. (1987) *The Drama of Being a Child*, London, Virago.

ROGERS, C. (1974) *On Becoming a Person*, London, Constable.

WIDLAKE, P. and McLEOD, F. (1984) *Raising Standards: Parental Involvement Programmes and the Language Performance of Children*, Coventry, Community Education Development Centre.

List of Contributors

Richard Border, Primary Adviser, Oxfordshire.
Tim Brighouse, Professor of Education, Keele University.
David Bristow, Inspector for Mathematics, Warwickshire.
Andrew Brown, Lecturer in Education, University of London.
Linda Calvert, Teacher, Humberside.
Kerry Carrie, Teacher, Oxfordshire.
Deborah Curle, Researcher, IMPACT.
Deryck Dyne, Psychotherapist, Institute of Psychotherapy, London.
Dorothy Hamilton, exPACT co-ordinator, Psychotherapist, London.
Sylvia Harrison, Parent, Oxfordshire
Martin Hughes, Reader in Education, Exeter University.
Sue Hunter, Parent, Humberside.
Ian Lewis, Senior Curriculum Officer, Gwent.
Ruth Merttens, Director of IMPACT, University of North London.
Alwyn Morgan, School and Community Officer, Humberside.
Tricia Nash, Researcher, University of Exeter.
David Owen, Adviser for Mathematics, Devon.
Peter Saarimaki, Director, Family Math Programme, Toronto.
John Smith, Lecturer in Maths Education, University of North London.
Lin Taylor, Lecturer in Maths Education, University of North London.
Gary Thomas, Lecturer, Oxford Brooks University.
Paul Tremere, IMPACT co-ordinator, Humberside.
Chris Tye, Teacher, Barnet.
Jeff Vass, Director of IMPACT, University of North London.
Felicity Wikeley, Researcher, University of Exeter.

Index